"Meherwan Irani has set the bar impossibly high for himself by titling his first book the *No. 1 Best Indian Cookbook in the World,* but true to form he may have understated the reality. From street food to truck stops and from villages to palaces, Irani has written the most impactful book on Indian cookery since the first books from Madhur Jaffrey set the world on a collision course with deliciousness. If you love Indian food, Irani decodes the entire canon for the home cook without oversimplifying or diluting the most delicious of global cuisines."

—**Andrew Zimmern,** chef

"Meherwan Irani has strong opinions that will piss off approximately 60 percent of the Indian diaspora—and that's exactly why this book matters. He's given us permission to cook his delicious, loud, truly accessible food—the Chai Pani way. There's a new number one cookbook on my shelf."

—**Matt Rodbard,** co-author of *Koreatown* and *Koreaworld*

"Chef Meherwan Irani's book is more than a cookbook—it is a journey of flavor, memory, and migration. Through vibrant Indian recipes and heartfelt stories, Chef Meherwan celebrates heritage while reimagining tradition in a new world. Each dish reflects the spirit of home, resilience, and the power of food to connect cultures and generations."

—**Vikas Khanna,** chef and restaurateur

No. 1 BEST INDIAN COOKBOOK IN THE WORLD

जय महाराष्ट्र
जय गंगा माँ भेल पुरी सेंटर
पाणीपुरी
शेवपुरी
चटणीपुरी
दहीपुरी
मसालापुरी
जय गंगा माँ भेल पुरी सेंटर

No. 1 Best INDIAN COOKBOOK in the World

At-Home Recipes from the Streets, Truck Stops, Villages, and Palaces of India

MEHERWAN IRANI
with Jamie Feldmar

Photography by
Tim Robison and Poras Chaudhary

Art, Design, and Additional Photography
by Mikey Files

TEN SPEED PRESS
California | New York

CHAAT

SANDWICHES & ROLLS

CAFES, CANTEENS & CHINESE FOOD

SIGRI (GRILL)

GHAR KA KHANA (HOME COOKING)

BIG TICKET

DESSERTS & SWEET MEATS

DRINKS

PANTRY

PLEASE ALLOW ME TO INTRODUCE MYSELF

Hello, friends! My name is Meherwan Irani, and I'm here to tell you that Indian street food is the best food on the planet.

It's an audacious claim.

But check out the people in line for my restaurants, Chai Pani and Botiwalla. It's *all* of the people. The adventurous foodies, the comfort food conformists, the "I don't like okra" crowd, aunts, brothers, kids, grandparents—the entire freaking family tree. On any given day, a banker in a suit is perched next to a graduate student with a backpack, next to a plumber in overalls, next to an Indian auntie in a cardigan.

They are your neighbors and mine: people who've heard about this restaurant that makes Indian food that is exciting and approachable. What brings them all together is the craving for delicious flavors; the desire for warm, hospitable service; and the pleasure of dining in an over-the-top-styled space that both surprises and delights. We give them all of that and more, gladly—because along the way, we're quietly ushering them into the cult of the greatest cuisine known to mankind.

With its mind-blasting combinations of colors, flavors, and textures, Indian street food has some of the best bites you can put in your mouth. And I'm not just talking about kathi rolls and samosas (though kathi rolls and samosas are both delicious and have their places in this book; see pages 78 and 119). There's a whole universe of Indian street food out there, from the crunchy-soft-spicy-cool world of chaats to the constellation of hearty homestyle cooking at roadside dhabas (truck stops) to the seemingly limitless sandwich iterations Indians have invented. Not all Indian food is street food, but all Indian street food, taken together, represents the best of what Indian food has to offer.

This is why I'm such a vocal proponent of the stuff. I see street food as a gateway to the whole, wide, glorious world of Indian cuisine. I believe that once Americans get a taste of a golden-crisp vada pav, or a crunchy-sweet-sour bhel puri, they'll go all in.

According to the food media, Indian food has been teetering on the brink of its breakout moment for about a decade now. I call bullshit on that. Between the explosion of award-winning Indian restaurants across the country, Oprah's inclusion of my Indian spice blends as one of her favorite things, and the fact that Chai Pani won the James Beard Award for Outstanding Restaurant in 2022, the truth is: We're already here. I just want to democratize it.

This all means the timing is near perfect for a cookbook that brings Indian street food home. This book is for both hungry fans who are ready to embrace the Indian food revolution and anyone who doesn't yet know what they're missing. Learning to make Indian street food at home is a blast—and it's really, truly, not that hard. If my mom could come visit me in South Carolina when I was a broke-ass grad student thirty years ago and find 90 percent of what she needed to cook the foods of my youth at the Piggly Wiggly, you can, too.

A whole lot of people out there are dying to eat this stuff, and I feed many of them every day. But those who can't make it to a Chai Pani or a Botiwalla—and those who have and want to recreate the magic at home—need someone friendly to show them the way. That someone is, much to my own surprise, me!

My entire culinary career has been built around translating Indian food to appeal to American eaters. I grew up eating across this particular East-West divide, with my mother cooking for Westerners at our bed-and-breakfast in India, and it's part of why Chai Pani and Botiwalla have been so successful. Not to toot my own horn, but I've found I'm eminently qualified to help Americans figure out how to do this stuff at home—it's literally how I've eaten and cooked my entire life.

I'm all too aware that cooking Indian food at home can seem intimidating to people who aren't used to it. It truly is not as complicated as you may think. I won't call for many specialty ingredients—instead, it'll be lots of ginger, garlic, onions, chillies, vegetables, meats, and yogurt. The only slightly complicated ingredients might be spices and spice blends, though many of these are becoming increasingly common in even the most mainstream grocery stores (and for any that aren't, I conveniently happen to run Spicewalla, a direct-to-consumer spice company). That said, I'll offer plenty of hacks, including substitutions for anything that isn't easily accessible—true to the spirit and beauty of Indian street food, which is about cooking with what you have on hand and *not* about rushing out to buy a bunch of stuff you don't really need.

In addition to the recipes, I'm also throwing in a handful of asides on Indian street food and culture—the great debate over rice versus roti, the time-honored tradition of auntie holdbacks (those little home-cook hacks your aunties never want to reveal), and so on.

When you set foot in any of my restaurants, you feel like you're at a party—an easy, casual, fun, friendly, colorful, supremely delicious party that you had no idea would be such a good time until you showed up. That's how I want this book to feel, too.

Though this isn't a Chai Pani or Botiwalla cookbook, many dishes from my restaurants are the foundation for recipes you'll see here. And because it's a book, it can and will go beyond my restaurants, diving into all the mind-blowing, wide-ranging, sticky-sweet-spicy-fragrant-crispy-chewy-hearty-refreshing glory of Indian street food. There are chaats and kebabs, of course, but also hearty stews cooked at roadside cantinas for long-distance truckers, sweet-and-sour Chinese-Indian stir-fries, Parsi-style omelets that somehow look and taste like the Southwest scramble of your dreams, and more—so much more!

BEGINNINGS

I never thought I would write an Indian street food cookbook—or any cookbook, for that matter. I didn't even start cooking professionally until I was pushing forty, following a midlife crisis. But after doing this for a while, I've realized I'm probably one of the Indian chefs best suited right now to help Americans figure out how to make Indian street food at home (though maybe not for the reasons you might think—e.g., I never went to culinary school).

Obviously, I am Indian, but I had kind of a funny childhood. I was born in London to a Hindu mother and a Parsi father (see opposite), both of whom followed a spiritual leader named Meher Baba. This was in the sixties, when it was trendy for Westerners to find themselves a guru and travel to India in search of spiritual enlightenment (see: The Beatles).

All those hippies needed to eat, so my paternal grandparents opened a bed-and-breakfast in Ahmednagar, home to Meher Baba's ashram. We

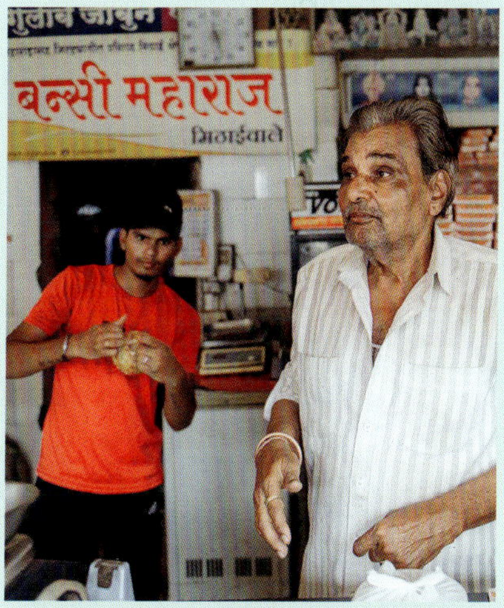
बन्सी महाराज
मिठाईवाले

Prince
MH.01.BT.3252

moved there from England when I was four, and my mom developed a talent for cooking Indian food that Westerners liked. Her food was bright and simple, with lots of vegetables and fresh herbs and a light touch on the spices.

My mom was a great cook, but like all Indian kids, I loved visiting our town's (often-completely-over-the-top) street hawkers, who lured customers in with eye-popping hand-painted signs and the intoxicating smell of hot fried dough. When Mom wasn't looking, my brother and I would sneak out to get our fix of buttery-hot pav bhaji and magically featherweight fried pakoras.

Given that I grew up surrounded by a merry gang of Western freaks, I decided to go to America as soon as I could. When I finished college in India, I started looking for MBA programs in the States, winding up at the University of South Carolina. I got a part-time job waiting tables, proceeded to fall madly in love with my boss's daughter, Molly, and quickly decided to drop out of business school and move to California with her. I was young and in love—who needed an MBA?

In California, I got a job as a luxury car salesman. I've always liked people, and can be pretty persuasive, so I was good at it—and thus had money to spend on my favorite hobby: eating. One day, a buddy took me to an Indian grocery store called Viks Chaat & Market in Berkeley. It was in the warehouse district, in a room in this little cinderblock building with a window into the kitchen where a stern auntie mixed up bhel puri and dosa batter.

I hadn't seen this stuff since I was a kid. Most of the Indian restaurants I'd come across since moving to the States served gloppy butter chicken and saag paneer, not street food. Even if Viks' versions weren't always on a par with those of the street vendors of my childhood, it was a revelation to even *see* some of these foods again, let alone taste them. I'd bring my white friends to this unassuming box of a building to try chaat and samosas. Of course, they absolutely loved it, exclaiming, *"Whoa, THIS is Indian food?!"*

In those moments, I realized there was a huge business opportunity alongside the cultural longing I felt: I desperately wanted my well-meaning American

buddies to see that the food of my people went well beyond naan and tandoori chicken. Indian street food was clearly a gateway drug, if someone would just package and sell it the right way.

For years, my mind had been a nonstop generator of entrepreneurial ideas. The idea of opening a restaurant kept coming back to me, but I had a mortgage and a kid in private school; I also had a good stable job (or so I thought). So when the Great Recession hit, Molly was the one to point out to me that this was really an opportunity to take that big jump. I could write a business plan, use my mom's recipes, hire good people—and just maybe make this thing work.

It took a few years for me to realize that *I* could be the person to bring Indian street food to the masses. Molly and I had a daughter, and we moved to Asheville, North Carolina, in 2005. I stopped selling fancy cars and started selling fancy houses, which was great while it lasted. But when the market crashed in 2009, I realized I needed a new plan.

I wrote the entire menu in one frantic night—bhel puri, aloo tikki, pakoras, my mom's okra fries. Molly convinced me to add a salad ("white girls love salad" was her pitch) and a few other items that would round out the menu and help ease Asheville diners into this whole new cuisine.

The name I chose is a triple entendre. *Chai pani* literally means "tea and water," and it's what we say in India when we're going out for a quick bite of chaat or something small and snacky from a street vendor. It also denotes hospitality: If you ever visit an Indian household, you'll be offered a plate with some cookies or crunchy snacks, a cup of chai, and water to drink. And finally, *chai pani* is a small bribe—more like a tip, really—that's a commonplace part of day-to-day errands in India. I felt it was ideal—just familiar enough, cheeky enough, and catchy enough to work.

I hired a small crew of novice cooks, none of whom had ever made Indian food, and called in my mom to come teach us every auntie hack she'd ever known (see page 56). On the day we opened, in 2009, there was a line down the block. We were wildly underprepared. My mom was working the line. Since we couldn't afford a modern payment system, we had a fifty-dollar cash register from Office Depot that I'd half-assedly wired to a printer in the kitchen. Paper was flying everywhere, and food took an hour to come out. It was chaos.

A year in, with our shit slightly more together, we got our first major write-up—in *The New York Times.* After that, the phone never stopped ringing with people calling us to make reservations (which we don't take). I found the whole thing thrilling, hilarious, and slightly surreal, but I also saw it as a sign we were onto something.

We found a space in Atlanta to open a second Chai Pani in 2013, and the minute we announced we were opening, it was a big deal. The second Chai Pani had three times as many seats as the one in Asheville, and we did three times the business right out of the gate. Then, in 2015, we got a call from a developer working on a ginormous food hall in downtown Atlanta called Ponce City Market. They wanted a whole new concept, and I came up with Botiwalla, which is an homage to India's Irani cafes.

If my idea of Chai Pani was to help introduce more people to Indian street food, I saw Botiwalla as a way to really blow down the gates. I wanted to transcend ethnicity—and get as many butts in those seats as possible. If I got this right, I thought, Americans would be ordering an Indian wrap as casually as they do a taco, pizza, or burger. We kept the menu simple and approachable—lamb burgers, chicken tikka rolls, masala smashed potatoes.

It worked.

Botiwalla opened in the Ponce City Market in 2016. It was immediately slammed (this time we were prepared). It was such a hit that we opened a second Botiwalla in Charlotte, North Carolina, a few years later, then one in Asheville, and, right now, as I write this very sentence, we're finalizing a deal to open fifteen more Botiwallas over the next five years in other cities, including Boston, Chicago, and Washington, D.C.

In 2018, I took an unexpected detour into the spice trade. I was starting to gain a reputation in the chef community as a spice whisperer specializing in custom blends. An offhand conversation with my primary restaurant supplier turned into an opportunity to form a spice company that would source a variety of global spices for professional chefs and restaurant kitchens. Spicewalla may have started as a wholesale spice supplier for restaurants, but when home cooks found out about our custom blends and wanted in, we started selling retail, too. A few months later, Oprah anointed Spicewalla as one of her "favorite things," and the brand (obviously) completely exploded. (We're now carried in almost 2,000 stores across the country.)

In 2022, after I'd been nominated for the Beard Foundation's Best Chef Southeast four times, the original Chai Pani in Asheville won the award for Outstanding Restaurant. It was huge for our team. Never in my wildest dreams did I think it would happen, but apparently the Beard Foundation fell for the story of the little Indian restaurant that could. To us, it was proof that we really have built something that's changed the face of Indian food in America.

This recognition led to my writing this cookbook. I want to get even more Americans psyched about cooking and eating Indian food, of course. And I want them to be able to use street food—the most delicious, fun, and approachable kind of Indian food that exists—as their entry point. My East-meets-West upbringing and nontraditional journey to becoming a chef—as well as the smashing success of my restaurants—puts me in a unique position to help make that happen. Also, since not everyone can visit my restaurants, getting this stuff down on paper means that anyone, anywhere, will be better able to experience what Indian street food has to offer.

I grew up with an Indian mother who excelled at making our cuisine accessible and delicious without dumbing it down or sacrificing any component of our identity or heritage. And my food has never been about recreating traditional Indian cuisine in America. Cooking this way builds trust between the two cultures within which I've spent my whole life, and my ultimate mission is to make more people fall in love with this food. Come along with me as I distill my years of hard-earned, self taught knowledge into the number one best cookbook for the greatest cuisine in the world.

zomato

HOW TO COOK FROM THIS BOOK

Cooking Indian food can feel intimidating to the uninitiated, so before we dive in, let's take a moment to get you in the right mindset with these three tenets:

1. Indian food is all about creating layers of flavor and texture.
2. Improvisation is encouraged.
3. There's no such thing as three square meals a day.

Let's break these down, shall we?

LAYERS (AND LAYERS) OF FLAVOR AND TEXTURE

One thing Indian cooks have totally figured out is how to create a layering effect with flavor. We're like painters who start with a base and build on it with contrasting flavors and textures. The combinations and layers might at first seem confusing, or like *too much,* but somehow they work. I'm not saying we just dump a bunch of ingredients into a pot all at once. As with other cuisines, there are sequences that have been refined over many generations.

In this book, I'm trying to strip away a lot of the mystery surrounding the core sequences in Indian cooking while staying true to (and teaching you about) the essentials. I really want the dish you cook to taste as good as the one you ate in my restaurant, or on the streets of India.

EMBRACING JUGAAD

Jugaad is an attitude that inspires so much that's brilliant in modern India. The word doesn't have an exact translation, but it's basically the Hindi/Urdu/Punjabi word for "MacGyvering shit to make it work, using only what you have immediately on hand." Jugaad is like a hack, a clever and resourceful work-around to an everyday obstacle. Street vendors in India are typically masters of jugaad. Have a blender but no electricity? Take the rear tire off a bike, jerry-rig the chain to a motor, and pedal furiously to generate enough electricity to fire up a smoothie's worth of blender power. Need a vessel for deep-frying puri? Why not repurpose an old steel drum, which conveniently converts into a rolling cart when it's empty? I bring all this up to say: In order to get the most out of this book, you must adopt a jugaad mindset. Don't be afraid to go off script—that's the whole spirit of street food, and of this book. So, yes, we're spending this section talking about my specific ways of doing things. *However,* absolutely do not let the lack of a certain ingredient or piece of equipment prevent you from cooking something that calls to you. The most important message of this whole book is "Feel comfortable working with what you've got." Don't let minor obstacles get in your way; instead, get creative, using what you have on hand to develop your own workaround. You may just find you like it better that way. It's an approach that has worked really well for me. I'm not classically trained; everything I've ever done in the kitchen has involved trial and error. I'm not afraid to make a mistake, because I find that in order to know what you like, you have to cook a lot of things you don't like. **In fact, it's making mistakes—not following these recipes exactly—that will make you a better cook.**

HEY! WHAT'S FOR DINNER (Lunch, Midnight Snack, Morning After . . .)?

Because this food is rooted in places, occasions, and times of day, this book is not organized by mealtime. Street food is food to feed the masses, wherever they are when they want or need to eat. It's attuned to the rhythms and cycles of busy streets and alleys, religious festivals, and truck stops. So the best way to use this book at home is to read the chapter intros: These can help you decide what aspect of the greatest Indian cuisine in the world you want to dive into today, tomorrow, or next week, and plan accordingly.

People sometimes get hung up on ingredients and/or techniques in a way that reduces their flexibility in the kitchen. I find it far more useful to think in terms of building blocks of flavor, chiefly—as Samin Nosrat succinctly put it—heat, acid, fat, and salt, but also umami and the deep flavor notes of a slowly reduced masala. Feel free to choose or find ingredients that match those building blocks. For example, if you understand what acidity does in a dish, you can substitute a lime for a lemon, or vinegar for yogurt, and so on. Once you start thinking in terms of these flavor fundamentals, you can let your jugaad flag fly, improvising and substituting in myriad ways to use what you have with brilliant results.

HEAT

This is probably the aspect of Indian food that's most misunderstood. Let me start by saying, emphatically, that the chilli pepper is not native to India. If we reflect for a minute, we realize we already know this, but still, let me repeat: The chilli pepper is *not native to India.* It was brought from the Americas by Portuguese traders in the sixteenth century, during the height of the spice race between Spain and Portugal.

For thousands of years before Europeans brought new spices to India, Indian food was not spicy-hot. We used many flavorful spices, and the hottest we used was black pepper. (Europeans called chillies "chilli peppers" to indicate that these American fruits were spicy-hot like black peppercorns.)

The recipes in this book aren't going to blow your tongue off with heat. For me, the heat from chillies is meant to be used as judiciously as the sourness of limes. Nobody brags about how mouth-puckering their dish is, or advertises that they make the sourest dishes. So it's crazy to me that somehow, one of the hallmarks of how much a Westerner likes Indian cuisine is how much heat they can handle. In my cooking, when I do call for heat, I'm looking at three very specific chillies:

TYPES OF CHILLIES

1.

With fresh green chillies, such as serrano or Thai, I'm looking for the vegetal taste of a green pepper plus some heat. The amounts I call for in the recipes are a general guideline—you can always adjust to your preference. Note that Thai chillies, though smaller in size, are roughly twice as spicy as serrano chillies.

2.

Dried Kashmiri chillies, used ground or whole, are bright, balanced, and fruity, and they deliver what I call an intuitive heat—their heat is proportional to the amount you put in, so a pinch of powder is a pinch of heat. Ground dried Kashmiri chilli has a deep coral-red color that's responsible for the vibrant shade of tandoori chicken and other classic Indian dishes. Cayenne is an acceptable (though hotter) backup, albeit in the way that a Honda can stand in for a Rolls-Royce. If you buy a bag of whole dried Kashmiri chillies, they'll last for years (and you can grind them yourself). Or buy Kashmiri chilli powder from Spicewalla or any South Asian grocer. If you only stock up on one type of dried chilli, let it be Kashmiri.

3.

Dried byadgi chillies are distinct from Kashmiri chillies (above). Small and slender, they're one of the most common chillies in India, with a mild heat, deep red color, and slightly funky aroma. We don't sell them at Spicewalla, but if you're so inclined, go to your e-commerce shop of choice and grab a bag (it will last forever).

All this being said, if you choose to ignore all of the above, whatever dried red chilli your local grocer carries—usually in a plastic bag near the herbs and spices—will, in the spirit of jugaad, work just fine. (I might stay away from some Mexican chillies like chipotle, ancho, and guajillo because their flavor may skew too smoky for these recipes. But if by happy accident you make an Indo-Mex dish that tastes fantastic, please DM me immediately and I will induct you into the jugaad hall of fame.)

ACID

In Indian cooking, a handful of acidic ingredients add sourness or tartness to dishes—or serve to balance flavors. Some of these are fresh (like lime), some fermented (chiefly pickles, or our beloved yogurt). And if you've ever wondered about the real trick to nailing restaurant-quality Indian food at home, I have one word for you: tamarind. (Opposite I have a few more words about tamarind that will help you get the most out of it.) Here's how we acid-trip in India.

Limes

The most common source of acid in India is a freshly squeezed lime. We use it while cooking, as a finishing touch; to neutralize the smell of turmeric and garlic on our fingers; and to cleanse our palates between bites. We save the rind to help scrub pots and pans. (Are you getting a sense of how the lime reigns supreme in Indian kitchens?) Of the limes common in the US, Key limes are most reminiscent of the smaller, sweeter limes I grew up with, but regular Persian limes will work just fine anywhere limes are called for in this book.

Pickles

In India, pickling is rarely done in vinegar; instead, small acidic fruits (including berries) and vegetables are pickled in a distinctive blend of oil, lime, and spices. We rarely cook with our pickles; instead, we use them as condiments to balance the acidity of a meal.

Tamarind

This sweet-and-sour fruit is indigenous to tropical Africa but has been part of the Indian diet for so long that most Indians claim it as our own. It supplies some of the defining taste characteristics in chaat and other Indian foods. It's impossible to imagine bhel puri, or samosa chaat, or pani puri (I could go on) without the zing of tamarind.

Tamarind is commercially available in three forms: a dried block of pulp, a wet (or soft) block of pulp, and a more highly processed paste.

- Dried tamarind often has fibers, and sometimes seeds, still in it. It comes in bricks that are hard to break apart, and it needs to be soaked in lots of hot water before the pulp is loose enough to cook with (and you'll still have to contend with the seeds and fibers unless you strain them out).

- My preferred form, "wet" tamarind pulp, can be used to make tamarind paste. Like dried tamarind pulp, it comes in block form, but it's softer and, often, seedless. A block is cheap and lasts more or less forever when it's stored in a cool, dry place. Here's how to use it to make 1 cup of tamarind paste:

  Break off a 1-ounce chunk of tamarind from the wet block (the chunk will be about 1 inch per side). Submerge it in 1½ cups of very hot water for about 10 minutes to soften it. Mash it with a fork while it's in the water to help break it up and facilitate the soaking process. Let the mashed tamarind sit for about 10 minutes, then set a fine-mesh sieve over a bowl and pour the tamarind and water out into the sieve. Squeeze out as much water as you can, then transfer the paste to an airtight container; it will keep in the refrigerator for several weeks. We call for it in the Shrimp Patia recipe on page 197, among others.

- Commercially made concentrated tamarind paste, typically sold in a jar, can, or plastic bottle, is my least favorite option. While convenient, it often contains preservatives and other additives that can give it a chemical flavor. Subpar tamarind paste is often the culprit in a disappointing meal at an Indian restaurant (which is why we use the wet blocks to make paste in our kitchens). If this is all you have or you don't want to deal with rehydrating the pulp, go forth: Just know it will probably lack the depth of flavor you'll get from using pulp.

Yogurt

India's beloved yogurt is another essential source of acid. We use it in cooking, and also as a condiment, whether in the form of raita or just served as plain or sweetened yogurt. At home in India, we made yogurt daily, in a small clay pot, with a little of the previous day's yogurt as a starter. Once a necessary way for preserving leftover milk before the age of refrigeration, freshly made yogurt is a constant in millions of Indian kitchens. Seeing it for sale as a distinct product in grocery stores here—often filled with fruits and syrups and all kinds of far-fetched add-ins—just about blew my mind.

In India, yogurt is prized for its cooling properties (it's often paired with spicy-hot foods); its digestive benefits, especially as part of a heavy meal; its meat-tenderizing action when used as a marinade; and its thickening properties.

In this book, I call for thicker strained yogurt, like Greek yogurt or skyr, for cooked dishes or marinades, and regular plain yogurt for condiments. All yogurt should be full fat. It's not crazy to have both kinds of yogurt in your fridge; unless you stick a dirty finger in there, they'll last for a long time. If you see a little liquid separating and floating on top, just pour it out or stir it back in—your yogurt is perfectly fine.

FAT

At the risk of having a billion Indians rake me over the chula on social media, I'm going to categorize the oils of India by region. As with any generalization, there will be crossovers, exceptions, and deviations, and a bunch of people who just have to be right all the time, so bear with me. In eastern and northern India, where I grew up, I ate foods cooked in mustard oil. In central India and Gujarat, almost all the cooking at home uses groundnut (aka peanut) oil. In a handful of states, such as Andhra and Tamil Nadu, sesame oil is a thing. In southern India, coconut oil is not just used in cooking but is slathered all over the body and hair.

All of that said, when I cook at home I almost exclusively use grapeseed oil (a neutral oil with a high smoke point), and I tend to use canola oil for deep-frying. You'll see these preferences reflected in the recipes in this book.

But wait—what about ghee? Contrary to popular belief, most Indian food is *not* cooked with ghee. Ghee is a luxury fat made by slowly cooking butter to separate the solids out to yield a deliciously nutty, caramelized butter that adds major richness to everything it touches. Ghee shows up only a few times in this book, mostly in the Big Ticket chapter, and it's more a flex—to help you feel good about the work you put in—than a necessity. Making ghee isn't terribly complicated, but honestly, store-bought is fine. If you use it a lot, ghee can be kept at room temperature; if it's going to take you a year to get through a small jar, keep it in the fridge.

SALT

When I was growing up in India, there was never just one type of salt. Depending on what part of the country you were in, you used rock salt, sea salt, or volcanic salt. There was never salt on the table—it was expected that the cook would perfectly season each dish (and guests dare not either complain or adjust the salt to their personal preference).

None of those things apply in America: I now use kosher salt exclusively. If you've read many other cookbooks, you may be aware of the battle between Morton and Diamond for kosher salt supremacy. What's important to know is that they are not interchangeable, as their grains have different structures, which means the same measure of each yields different results. For the sake of consistency, pick one and make it your life partner. I'm a Diamond man, and all of the recipes in this book were tested accordingly.

Almost all of my recipes will instruct you to salt at specific points. Here's why: I want you to taste as you go, so you're learning not just what a finished dish tastes like, but what certain components of the dish taste like. Salt brings the flavor of other ingredients forward on the tongue. Without salt, I can't tell if my tomato sauce is sweet enough or if my coconut curry has enough acidity. I think salting as you go is a great habit for all types of cuisines, and while I haven't looked for scientific proof of this, I find that salt works in a sense like a spice in that incorporating it throughout the cooking process gets it into a dish's DNA more than just adding it at the end ever could.

SWEET

The savory recipes in this book use little to no refined sugar, with a couple of exceptions—chai and sweet yogurt sauce. However, I do use jaggery in a number of recipes, where it's an important enough flavor component that you should go out of your way to find it. Jaggery is one of the most basic forms of sugar: It's sugarcane juice that has been boiled until it's reduced to a hard block of musky earthy-brown sweetener with a flavor unlike any other sugar on the planet. It can be bought in small chunks or in larger blocks; whatever form you acquire, store it in an airtight container where it can't get damp. Look for jaggery that's a deep brown in color, not a pale blond—darker jaggery has been cooked longer and has more of the earthy caramelized flavor that makes it unique.

The only real way to break jaggery up into manageable chunks is to smash it: At home, I usually wrap a chunk in a kitchen towel and bash it into powder with a heavy pan. At our restaurants, we go through so much jaggery that we melt ten-pound blocks into jaggery syrup and store it in the fridge. In the recipes in this book, powdered jaggery is usually melted into a sauce or other liquid. You can follow my lead and smash it to a powder, or acquire powdered jaggery from a South Asian grocer. Either way works.

UMAMI

Of the five basic tastes (sweet, sour, bitter, salt, and umami), umami is the most difficult to describe, its essence seeming to vary from culture to culture, captured in the meatiness of soy sauce or roasted mushrooms, or the funk of fish sauce or stinky cheese. India's umami-rich foods tend to be less processed, and since so many Indians are vegetarian, the meatiness that comes with certain types of umami is less common.

Here are a few of the most common sources of umami in Indian cuisine—and make no mistake, these umami bombs light up the palate in a way that even inveterate meat eaters find addictive.

- **Black rock salt** adds a sulfuric perfume that's both heady and verging on overpowering. It's an ingredient in nearly all masalas, including chaat masala, which gives street food its characteristic zing and funk. (Chaat masala is called for frequently in this book, and as I note elsewhere, store-bought versions are fine.)
- While Americans may toss them, **cilantro stems** are valued for adding body and flavor to many Indian dishes. Their flavor when fried, along with the holy trinity of onions, chillies, and ginger-garlic paste, creates a base layer of herbaceousness for many sauces and gravies in this book.
- **Hing** (aka asafetida, aka God's armpit) is—well, I won't lie: This stuff on its own smells awful. But a little pinch of it adds incredible umami and an almost meat broth–like flavor to South Indian curries. Hing is the resin of the asafetida plant, which is collected, formed into sticky blocks, dried, powdered, and finally sold under a few brand names that almost every Indian is familiar with, the most popular being L.G. Many core Indian ingredients have secondary or tertiary benefits beyond basic nourishment, and hing is known as a great digestive. It's added to lentil dishes like dals and sambars not only for the flavor it brings but also because it helps people digest legumes. I've started using it more and more in lentil-free situations (steak rub, anyone?) because I love the flavor, and because I think it works wonderfully in a surprising variety of dishes.
- **Mustard oil** can taste acrid and bitter, but when it's tempered to its smoking point, it adds a lovely pungency to everything from grilled meats to vegetable stews.
- Ah, **curry leaf:** the herb somewhat responsible for the curry confusion of the world. To my mind, it's unique as a flavoring agent, though if you can't find it, don't let that stop you from making any of the recipes that call for it. There's nothing herbaceous about it, but it adds umami, sending taste buds into overdrive. Curry leaves have a nifty ability to balance out all the other (sweet, salty, sour, bitter) flavors in a dish. For more, see page 23.

MASALA

And finally, if there's one thing I want to convince you to try as a cook, it's this: Break away from the European mirepoix technique of sweating onions, carrots, and celery to form the flavor base of a dish. Instead, embrace the Indian masala technique of extracting every drop of water from onions, green chillies, and garlic-ginger paste to create a flavor base bursting with sweetness and spice.

This masala holy trinity (plus other, recipe-specific spices) is how the gateway dishes to Indian cuisine for many Americans get their incredible depth of flavor (I'm looking at you, chicken tikka masala, saag paneer, and vindaloo). A bonus: Cooking onions, chillies, and ginger-garlic paste into a heady blend with the color and consistency of rich marmalade will teach you the number one skill of any accomplished chef: patience.

HOW TO SHOP LIKE AN INDIAN COOK

If you were to open my fridge or pantry, there's little indication other than a handful of spices that I'm an Indian chef and I cook Indian food. Even the spices could easily be used for Southwestern or Mexican cuisine. My point is this: All around the world, people are cooking with many of the same ingredients, including onions, ginger, garlic, cilantro, tomatoes, potatoes, greens, rice, dairy—you get the idea. In my opinion, the greatest differentiators among cuisines are the ratios in which these ingredients are combined and the techniques with which they are cooked. That said, I'm going to just give you a quick rundown on how I stock my kitchen so you'll be able to make pretty much everything in this book.

GINGER AND ALLIUMS

I always, always, always have on hand several whole bulbs of **garlic** and a palm-size hunk of **ginger** root. Ginger is one of the few instances where I will implore you to look for organic (preferably a piece with lots of fingers rather than a single large root with no fingers); organic has a far better flavor and aroma. You can use whatever **onions** you have; my preference is for smallish red ones, which have a sharper flavor and remind me of the Indian red onions I grew up with, which are like a cross between shallot and red onion.

FRESH HERBS

Mint and cilantro are the two herbs I call for most commonly. **Mint** is easier to grow than mold on cheese. It's a weed. You have to try really hard to kill it, and having a steady supply of fresh mint is very handy—for the recipes in this book and for all kinds of cooking. If you can't or don't want to grow it, a few sprigs of mint kept in a glass of water somewhere near a window will last for weeks.

Cilantro is fussier. It's essential to these recipes, but it's harder to grow and it turns slimy quickly, whether you refrigerate it, stick it in water, or store it in the vacuum of deep space. I don't have any real advice here, and I'm sorry. But I will note that it's okay to use almost all of the stems in a bunch in almost all of these recipes; just trim off and discard the last 2 inches of stem.

Not many of these recipes call for **curry leaves,** but for the ones that do, fresh curry leaves are literally a chef's kiss. As in, you should always kiss anyone who brings you fresh curry leaves. Curry plants are surprisingly easy to grow, and they're quite hardy (I've tried to kill mine three or four times, and not only has it refused to die, but in a big, curry-scented FU, it's bushier than ever). If being a curry leaf farmer is not in your immediate plans, many Asian grocery stores sell frozen packets of curry leaves; as a last resort, dried curry leaves can easily be found online.

DARK, LEAFY GREENS

Growing up in '80s India, I don't think I'd ever seen a head of romaine lettuce (or arugula or butter lettuce or the other fussy, delicate members of the spring-mix club) until I came to America at age twenty. But when I got to the South and encountered **collards, mustard greens,** and **kale,** I felt instantly comfortable: Those are the kind of greens I grew up with in India. Dark, leafy greens should be a staple in your fridge. They last for weeks, and they are way more versatile than salad greens. I always have various dark greens in my fridge and three or four bags of spinach in my freezer: Thus armed, you can take on many of the dishes in this book.

NANDINI
नंदिनी
नंदिनी
नंदिनी
STAR

FROZEN VEGETABLES

I am a passionate advocate for prechopped frozen vegetables. You're far more likely to actually incorporate vegetables into your cooking if you have a freezer stocked with cauliflower, carrots, peas, corn, and the almighty spinach. Blanching and flash-freezing is an excellent way to preserve the color, texture, and nutrition of most vegetables. So as seductive as that TikTok reel is where the bro chef throws a bunch of fresh vegetables onto the counter and, through the miracle of high-speed scrubbing, converts it into a pile of perfectly diced mise en place, it's unnecessary. Let the magic of industry do it all for you, and reap the benefits of being able to whip up a delicious, nutritious meal at the drop of a hat.

TOMATOES

If you are a discerning produce gourmand, you will probably notice that many of my recipes, especially those involving a masala base, call for canned crushed tomatoes, not fresh. *Hold up,* you may say. *Are you telling me that cooks across India are cooking with canned crushed tomatoes?* No: They are using vine-ripened tomatoes, bought at a roadside vegetable stand and then pureed in a blender or crushed by hand and strained to get a base with which to start cooking.

You are free to follow their lead. But look: Why make your life harder than it needs to be? The Italians figured it out: vine-ripened crushed pomodoros in a can, and if that's good enough for them, it's more than good enough for me. These are my tomatoes of choice, and my recommendation, for all my sauces; just (this should go without saying, but I have to say it) make sure you choose unseasoned, unsalted tomatoes that don't contain any basil or oregano. You'll sometimes notice the addition of citric acid, which is fine. When I do use fresh tomatoes—which is more often than not in my chaat recipes—I like Roma tomatoes, which are firm enough to hold up to being tossed, drizzled, and chaat-ified.

TUBERS AND ROOT VEGETABLES

Potatoes are truly the backbone of Indian cuisine—they are endlessly versatile and they last forever, to the point where a bag full of them stored in a cool, dark place should be the first line on a prepper's insurance policy. Second in line is the carrot, followed by turnips, radishes, and pretty much anything else that has hairlike strands when it comes out of the ground. All these vegetables are brilliant additions to your pantry that keep for a long time and should always be there.

DAIRY

There's only one recipe in this book that calls for milk, and yet I go through half a gallon a week, all in the service of chai (see page 265). (Well, that's not completely true. The other time I go through a lot of milk is when I'm making paneer; see page 274.) For both recipes, you want the real deal: whole milk, preferably non-homogenized, so you have to shake the shit out of the bottle to reincorporate the cream. And if you happen to live somewhere where your local milk purveyor doesn't give a flying F about USDA regulations, get unpasteurized. (If you find such a purveyor, DM me, but otherwise make sure to keep them secret.)

In India, milk arrived every day, not bottled, not pasteurized, but poured straight from the large metal canister into which it had been pumped straight from the cows' udders. We boiled it, let it cool, skimmed the cream off the top, used what we could during the day, and then stirred in some of the day's yogurt as a starter for tomorrow's batch. I'm not expecting anybody reading this to try that today, but I still look for really fresh, non-homogenized milk, preferably from a local farm, in grocery stores. This isn't just my nostalgia—you will actually make better chai, better paneer, and better yogurt with non-homogenized milk. (If you're curious to know more, there's a great chapter on milk science in Harold McGee's book *On Food and Cooking.*)

FLOURS

In India, we don't have a generic word for "flour," because everything that could be called a flour has its own name (besan is chickpea flour, atta is whole wheat flour, and so on). In contrast to the West, with its literally all-purpose flour, we have a handful of specific flours used in specific ways.

Besan

I'm still not sure why the Western world has largely ignored besan, or chickpea flour, but the street vendors of India certainly haven't. Pakoras, bhajis, and vadas are delightful golden nuggets fried in a batter made with seasoned chickpea flour. Besan is naturally gluten-free and doesn't absorb a lot of oil, and with the addition of various amounts of baking soda, it makes batters that range from spongy to shatteringly crisp when fried.

In American grocery stores, garbanzo bean flour is also labeled as chickpea flour. Garbanzo bean flour works fine, but true besan is made from small split brown chickpeas, or gram, which are not the same as garbanzo beans. (In India gram is also known as "channa dal.") Garbanzo bean flour is coarse and fluffy, while besan is finer and smoother in texture. You can easily find besan online or at any Indian grocer, and a bag keeps for well over a year when stored in a cool, dry place.

Atta

Indian whole wheat flour is known as *atta.* It's coarser and nuttier than American versions, and it's the traditional go-to for making everyday breads like rotis and parathas. Atta is ground from a wheat varietal with a higher protein content than Western whole wheat flour or all-purpose flour. (A brief aside: My maternal grandparents grew it, along with rice, as a rotational crop.) Chakki atta is stone-ground and absorbs more water, making softer, more pliable breads.

LENTILS (DAL)

Rice and dal are the building blocks of the Indian diet for good reason: Together they form a complete protein profile, which is especially important in a nation packed with vegetarians. There's a dizzying

7 x 10
MFGD BY :
(INCLUSIVE OF ALL TAXES)

array of lentils and other pulses in Indian cuisine, but for this book, we'll focus on just two: masoor dal, or red lentils, and toor dal, or yellow lentils.

Red Lentils (Masoor Dal)

These easy-to-find mild-flavored lentils cook very quickly, which is ideal if you're trying to whip up dal in a hurry. They absorb other flavors well and don't need any pre-soaking.

Yellow Lentils (Toor Dal)

Hearty yellow lentils tend to stay chunkier than red lentils when cooked and have a nuttier flavor. They take longer to cook, and it's helpful to presoak them in water for a few hours.

FRIED CHICKPEA NOODLES (SEV)

Sev is noodles made of besan (chickpea flour) and fried to a crackling crunchiness; it's used as a chaat garnish or as a snack in its own right. We make our own sev at Chai Pani using a fine noodle extruder, but there are many high-quality brands, such as Haldiram's. Sev is typically seasoned with spices such as turmeric, hing, and red chilli. In its thicker form, it's also a component of the crunchy Gujarati snack mix called farsan. Thin, fine sev is sometimes sold as "nylon" sev, and it's my preferred garnish for the chaat in this book, for that all-important crunch factor. (The thicker versions are most often used in dried snack mixes.)

CORN POHA

Commonly seen in the chaat recipes, corn poha are little kernels of flattened dried corn, which puff up in a hot pan with a few tablespoons of oil and then turn crispy: They're like the best possible version of cornflakes. Fried poha is available, too (and plain cornflakes will do in a pinch), though it's definitely more fun to make your own.

AGED BASMATI RICE

There's rice, and then there's *rice,* and then there's aged basmati rice. Aging basmati helps develop the rice's aroma, gives it a delightfully nutty flavor, and helps make it fluffier and less sticky when cooked. Look for basmati rice that's been grown in the foothills of the Himalayas and aged a minimum of six months, though ideally longer. The terroir of this region gives basmati its distinctive, intoxicating, earthy scent. (And no, Texmati won't cut it.) Fun fact: Aging also gives basmati rice its distinctive long grain—the longer you age the rice, the longer the grains will get. I like Daawat brand, which is aged for over two years, though Royal (aged six months) is a widely available and acceptable substitute.

MAGGI HOT AND SWEET TOMATO CHILLI SAUCE (MAGGI KETCHUP)

This condiment—basically tomato paste plus red chilli puree—is the glue that holds together everything from a Mumbai toastie (see page 81) to streetside noodles. Personally, I see absolutely no need to own a bottle of ketchup if you have a convenient supply of Maggi ketchup (confusingly, this is not the Maggi product called "Rich Tomato Ketchup" but the one called "Hot and Sweet Tomato Chilli Sauce"). Sweet, spicy, and tangy, it's everything ketchup wants to be but doesn't have the balls to reach for. If you're in a pinch, substitute regular ketchup with some sriracha stirred in.

A MOMENT FOR SOUTH AMERICA

The chilli is not the only culinary necessity the Portuguese brought from South America to Asia and beyond. They also transported the starchy, fluffy, delicious, endlessly versatile, hearty, belly-filling, multipurpose tuber known as the potato, transforming continents and cultures. And the tomato hitched the same ride! Together, the potato and the tomato had a huge impact on Indian food (more than the chilli), becoming pillars of our cuisines—including our street food.

THE INEVITABLE PAGE ABOUT SPICES

You might think that a book about Indian cuisine is going to have reams of pages about spices, but here's the deal: you get 3 pages. And this is largely because Jamie, my co-author, is sitting across from me and giving me the stink-eye. But people—my good people—most cookbooks don't go on at you about how tomatoes or garlic or basil work. They're just ingredients. You buy good-quality ingredients, use them according to instructions, and end up with a dish that tastes good. That's all spices are—ingredients. It's not important, as some would have you believe, to have an expert-level understanding of spices to make good food. But since Jamie insists, and since I happen to own a somewhat well-regarded spice company, here are a few high-level guidelines for using spices.

The first guideline is that the way a spice smells and the way it tastes are often two completely different things. For example, cardamom has a beautiful, grassy, floral, exotic scent. But pop a pod into your mouth, and it's bitter and soapy. So it's important to understand that sometimes we use spices such as clove, cinnamon, and cardamom for the scent of the spice, which is a product of the naturally occurring oils within it. Sometimes we use spices with no scent but a distinct and important flavor—think of mustard seeds, which don't smell like much on their own but add a ton of flavor when bloomed in oil. And sometimes, we use a spice such as black peppercorns for both its scent and its flavor.

Next, when possible, if the spice exists in a whole (seed or pod) form (for example, cumin, coriander, cinnamon, clove, nutmeg) and a powdered or ground form, buy the whole form. Like coffee beans, once you grind spices, they start losing potency and flavor. So it's better to grind them fresh in small doses as necessary.

Toasting a whole spice before grinding agitates the oil and flavor molecules, making the spices more aromatic. I think of it as activating the flavor locked inside. To toast whole spices, place them in a small skillet and set over medium-high heat for 2 to 3 minutes, until you can smell the spices. Turn off the heat and immediately remove the spices from the pan so they don't burn. Once they have cooled, grind them into a coarse powder in a dedicated coffee grinder (see page 35). I hate spices that have been ground into talcum-powder consistency—they're hard to pinch up with your fingers, and they burn quickly. The point of grinding spices is to crush them up just enough to release their flavor, so you don't need to obliterate them.

Whole and ground spices should be added to a dish at different times. Whole spices will usually come in earlier, around the time we've made our masala trinity of onion, garlic, and chilli; as they fry in the oil, they imbue it—and by extension, the entire dish—with their flavor. Powdered spices come in later, because they'll burn if you add them too early. It's really important to understand that all spices—whole or powdered—must be cooked in oil for at least a few seconds to unlock their flavor. If you add spices during the braising, stewing, or simmering stage, they (unlike herbs) just sit there on top of the liquid and don't actually add flavor to the dish. So remember to fry your spices in oil—early if whole, later if powdered—*before* adding wet ingredients like tomatoes, coconut milk, or stock.

A related technique is tadka, which allows you to get that delicious spice-filled flavor into a dish (often something liquid-y, like dal or broth) but doesn't begin with heating oil. Tadka, which is also known as vaghar or chonk, is the act of blooming spices or other aromatics in hot oil, then pouring the whole sizzling mess directly into a dish's liquid, where it can infuse everything with its flavor. We call for this technique a handful of times throughout the book, notably in My Grandma's Dal (page 199) and Vada Pav (page 73).

LAXMI
Sneha

One last thing: Store your spices like your coffee—in an opaque container out of the light and away from the heat. It drives me crazy that spices in grocery stores are sold in clear plastic or glass, especially because people at home often store them near their range or oven. Spices lose their flavor and potency over time, and the oils in certain spices can go rancid when exposed to light and heat. Spicewalla spices are sold in tins for this very reason.

ESSENTIAL INDIAN SPICES

People seem to have this idea that Indian food involves an endless number of spices, when in reality, the dozen or so spices and spice blends outlined below will get you 90 percent of the way there. Conveniently, Spicewalla sells everything here, blends included, except for one (dhana jeera).

Turmeric

Obvi, we're talking about turmeric powder. Turmeric is a root that looks a little like ginger, and if you want to get really fancy, there's a bunch of YouTube instructions for how to buy fresh turmeric, dry it, and make your own powder, which would probably be incredible. I've never done that, but since this is one of the most adulterated spices in the world (just after saffron), it's not the worst idea. That said, if you choose to buy powder, as I do, look for a dark marigold-orange color—turmeric should be neither too reddish nor sunflower yellow.

Cumin

Cumin is one of the world's most popular spices (beloved equally in Indian, Latin American, and Middle Eastern cuisines), and possibly the single-most-called-for ingredient in this book. Most cumin seeds on the market are a gray-brown color, but high-quality cumin will be more yellowish-brown. As explained above, there really is no need to buy powdered cumin if you keep a good supply of seeds to grind yourself.

Roasted Cumin Powder

This is different from regular cumin powder, which we also call for a lot. When ground, roasted cumin releases one of the most exciting smells of all Indian spices—a gorgeous, nutty, earthy, heady scent; it's used as a finishing spice. Making roasted cumin powder is as simple as it sounds—toast cumin seeds in a dry pan over medium heat until they darken and become aromatic, 2 to 3 minutes; let cool, then grind in a spice grinder or mortar and pestle. Store in an airtight container away from light and heat for up to six months, when it'll start to lose some of its aroma and potency. It's also available in shops and online (it's sometimes labeled "toasted cumin powder").

Make sure you differentiate between unroasted cumin powder (used in cooking), and roasted (used as a finishing spice). Sprinkle it on top of anything that needs a pop of nutty flavor at the end. Most chaats, dals, rice dishes, and anything topped with yogurt or raita benefits from a sprinkle of roasted cumin powder on top.

Cinnamon Sticks

In Western grocery stores, you'll find reddish-brown cinnamon sticks with tightly curled bark in a long, thin cylinder—that's cassia. In Indian grocery stores, you'll find lighter brown, brittle, paper-thin bark in both tightly rolled sticks and flat pieces. That's Ceylon, and it's what most Indian cooks use; it tends to be sweeter (and so is less of a shock to the palate if you bite into a piece in a biryani). If you're using cassia cinnamon, just break up the sticks into two or three pieces and, since they stay hard, take them out of the dish when you're done cooking.

Green Cardamom

When using whole pods (which I recommend), I smash them once to split them open, allowing the flavor from the seeds to infuse the dish. Some green cardamom has pods that are a beautiful grassy hue, and it's downhill from there. There are various grades of green cardamom, from jumbo large (which I recommend) to grind quality. You probably won't find a wide variety in a typical grocery store, so this is one of the few times when tracking down a source of large green pods is worth it. Don't buy too many pods at one time—they will yellow and lose their potency over about 8 to 12 months.

Why not just use seeds or powder, which you can easily buy? Because the pod is like this magic flavor protector, keeping the seeds inside fresher for longer. Cardamom is truly one of the spices that is more about the scent than the taste, so I almost exclusively use pods.

Black Pepper

Buy black peppercorns whole and grind them yourself (are you picking up on a trend yet?). Look for peppercorns from Tellicherry or Malabar. (Cambodia has some fantastic black peppercorns, too, but since this is an Indian cookbook, we're keeping it local.)

Coriander

The problem with store-bought coriander powder (other than the obvious fact that it will be less potent than home-ground) is that it's ground too finely. I like my spice powders to be coarse, not fine like talcum, but coriander in particular should be coarsely ground. Toasting it before you grind it (see page 30) helps release its grassy notes into the oil, which is all the more reason to buy seeds whole. The most common type of coriander at the grocery store is labeled "Moroccan" (and is, inexplicably, grown in Canada); the seeds are small and yellowish-brown. These are shit, and you shouldn't buy them. Indian coriander is greenish-yellow and the seeds are much larger; one whiff from a jar and you'll understand why they're the real deal.

Brown Mustard Seeds

Throughout this book, we'll be using a lot of mustard seeds, so I need to point out that we're talking exclusively about brown mustard seeds (which are, fittingly, dark brown). Mustard as a condiment doesn't really exist in India; ergo, the yellow mustard seed is functionally useless. One of the primary ways Indian cooks incorporate mustard flavor into our cooking is by popping the seeds in hot oil to release their mustard-y flavor, which then infuses the entire dish. (In recipes that use this technique, I'll explain how to do it.)

Dhana Jeera

Dhana jeera is a simple, quintessential spice mix that's equal parts toasted cumin powder and toasted coriander powder. The two spices are used together so frequently that Indian spice merchants just went ahead and made them into their own new spice, as we are wont to do. Spicewalla doesn't sell dhana jeera, but you can easily make your own or buy it online or at any Indian grocer.

SPICE BLENDS

In addition to the spices mentioned above, Indian cooks often turn to a handful of premade blends, or masalas. Just about every household and shop in India has its own version, so there are no hard and fast rules.

In this book, the spice blends you'll see called for most often are chaat, garam, and tandoori masalas. You can buy them all premade—and, in fact, because they contain so many ingredients, I recommend buying chaat and tandoori masalas (look for MDH, Everest, or, of course, Spicewalla brands). I do provide a recipe for garam masala on page 277.

Blends fall under a few categories: finishing blends, which are added to a dish at the end as a garnish, and tend to be pungent and aromatic (e.g., chaat masala and garam masala); cooking blends, which can be used to flavor the Indian holy trinity of onions, garlic, and chilli (e.g., sambar masala or goda masala); and marinating blends, used for meat (e.g., tandoori).

There is another spice blend worth mentioning that's a little different from the masalas above. When Indians cook meat, we tend to season almost any cut with salt, turmeric powder, and ground red chilli—regardless of other spices or masalas also used. The salt seasons and helps tenderize the meat (particularly important for goat); the turmeric adds flavor and has an antibacterial effect; and the ground chilli adds a base layer of heat so you don't end up with a dish where the curry tastes spicy but the protein is bland. We don't really have a name for this meat rub, but we do tell you to use it in nearly every recipe in the Sigri (Grill) chapter (page 164), so it's worth mentioning here.

HOW TO ORGANIZE YOURSELF TO BANG OUT THESE RECIPES WITH MINIMAL TIME AND EFFORT

A lot of chefs and cookbooks blather on about mise en place (having everything in place before you start cooking). This makes prep seem like such a big fuss that some people get turned off. My take: Being organized in the kitchen means setting myself up for the least amount of extra work and cleanup. Those are important factors in my deciding whether I'm going to get up and cook something or eat cereal for dinner.

My goal is to provide you with recipes that require minimal prep, equipment, and cleanup. Think about it: A street vendor has no storage space and maybe a three-by-three-foot surface area on which to prep, cook, and serve, and everything has to be packed up and carted off every day, usually on the back of a bicycle. Street vendors are fastidiously organized for speed and economy of movement. When there's a line of hungry office workers on a twenty-minute break, they don't have time for the samosa guy to misplace his tongs.

Here's how to be like the samosa guy:

- **Clear your sink and your kitchen counter.** If you're starting off with a sink full of dirty dishes or a counter cluttered with unopened mail, it's going to take you more time and energy to get started and will also lead to a somewhat flustered and haphazard cooking experience, as you scramble around looking for cooking tools or counter space. Get yourself clean and clear, then proceed.

- **Pre-wash and trim any vegetables you'll use.** Pre-open any cans, bottles, or tins of spices. Pull out and have handy your measuring cups and spoons. Get the tools out for whatever you need to cut, grate, pulverize, puree, etc. Having ingredients and implements out and ready to go before you start cooking is a tremendous timesaver and helps the whole process flow smoothly, with no panicked pauses as you try desperately to remember where the Microplane is.

- **Pick a ladle and stick to it.** Grab the one ladle with which you can finish the entire dish from beginning to end—stirring, scraping, scooping, serving. More efficient, fewer dirty dishes.

- **Get out the trash can or compost bin.** Drag it over to right next to where you'll be and open the lid so you can dump in scraps and waste as you go. If there's no room for the bin, put a large metal bowl on the counter into which all your scraps can go, so that you can contain and dump them all at once.

- **Rinse and wipe off everything as you go.** Doing this, instead of throwing everything into the sink for later, has turned out to be the most helpful habit I've formed. If you're organized, there's plenty of time to clean a spatula or knife when you're done with it. Those 5 to 10 seconds of rinsing and putting each clean tool on the drying rack will save you a collective 15 to 20 minutes of cleanup later. Also, if you need to use the spatula again, the one you rinsed is right there next to you. How convenient.

- **Finish components early.** Some of these dishes have multiple components that require some prep work. If, for example, something needs to be pureed or blended—like a chutney or a masala—think of it as a condiment that you want ready *before* you actually start the cooking process. The more components you can have finished before you turn on the heat, the quicker the dish will come together.

For a head start on making future cooking from this book a lot easier, go ahead and knock out Ginger-Garlic Paste (page 276), Tamarind Chutney (page 271), Green Chutney (page 270), Sweet Yogurt Sauce (page 273), Raita (page 274), and Garam Masala (page 277). Each one takes maybe 5 to 7 minutes, and they all keep well, so they'll be ready whenever you are.

AN ASIDE ABOUT ASIDES

Sprinkled throughout this book are a series of short pieces on topics that fascinate me about Indian food. I'm dropping them in like little Easter eggs where I think they'll add depth or context to a recipe or technique. I fully expect to generate millions of irate comments from Indians around the world with these. Don't bother contacting me to contest anything—I will have changed my name and gotten a fake passport by the time you see this.

My perspective is that this stuff is complicated. The history of why people eat what they do and the way they do is an ever-shifting tapestry that weaves together region, religion, migration, history, climate change, and the entire kitchen sink that is the human condition. I like thinking and talking about why things are the way they are—not trying to prove a point or telling anybody how they should do something. I just feel that exploring these kinds of questions leads to a deeper appreciation of the food we eat.

CHAAT

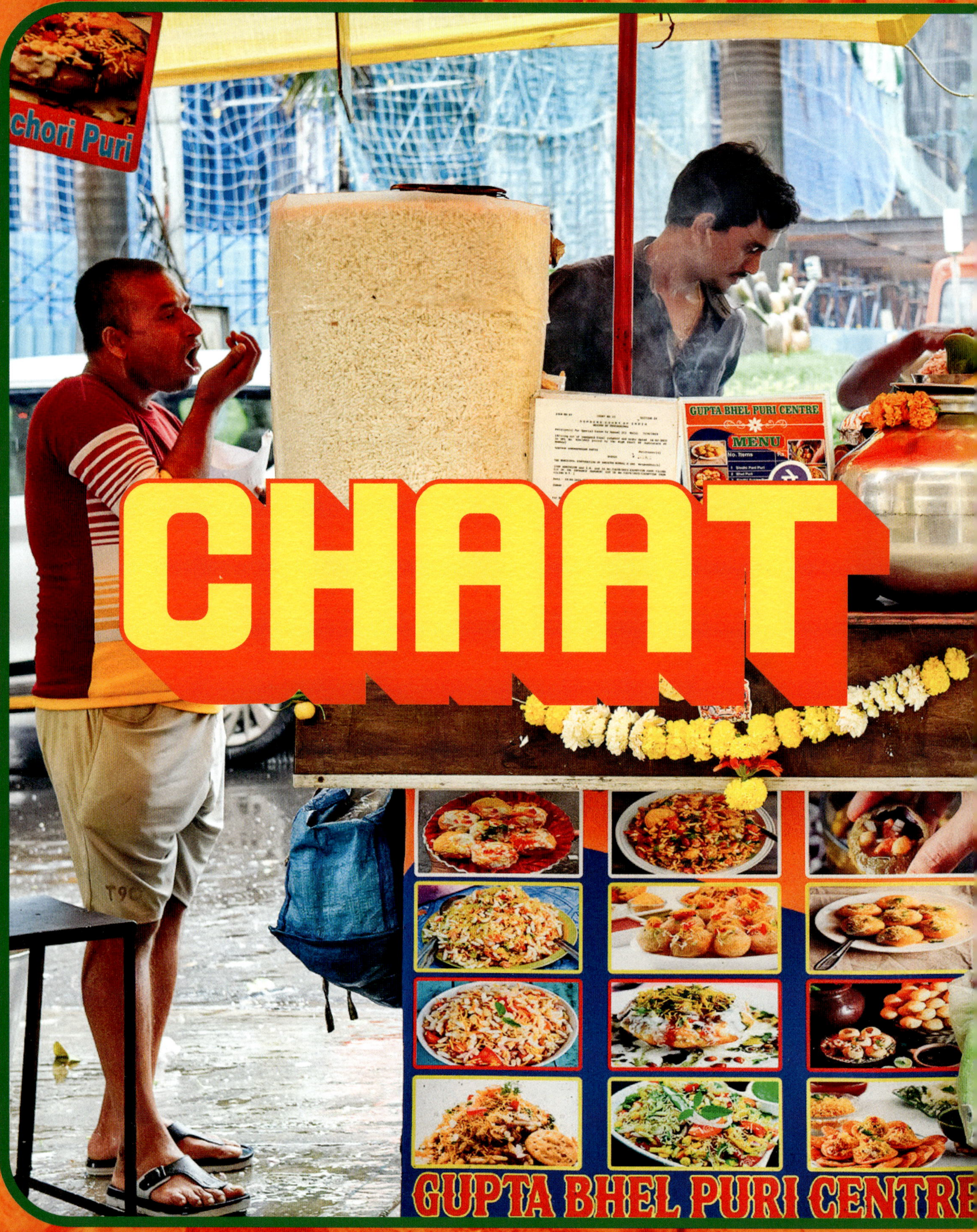
chori Puri
GUPTA BHEL PURI CENTRE
MENU
GUPTA BHEL PURI CENTRE

चाट

CHAAT is the cornerstone of Chai Pani, and it's the heart of Indian street food. No other category of food captures the chaos, noise, paradoxes, and color of India quite like chaat. That said, it's really important not to confuse all Indian street food with chaat. Chaat is a genre of Indian street food—arguably its Bollywood star.

Invented in India's big cities during the industrialization boom, chaat is itself a melting pot in which lots of things that don't make sense together get nestled up to delicious effect. It's the quintessential "whole is greater than the sum of its parts" type of food. The word means "to lick"—as in, your fingers. But I think the true essence of chaat is that lip-smacking sensation you get when heat, acidity, pepperiness, and sweetness are all balanced perfectly to form perfection in your mouth.

That way-better-than-the-sum-of-the-parts sensation comes largely courtesy of chaat masala, aka the taste of the streets. The geniuses who thought to combine sulfurous black rock salt with mouth-puckering green mango powder, roasted cumin, and tiny amounts of lots of counterbalancing spices should be given a Nobel Prize for the culinary arts. Chaat masala is the scintillating through-line of this book, and the smell and the taste of it permeates almost all the dishes at Chai Pani, with good reason.

Most chaats should be eaten immediately after they're assembled. Chaat's ephemeral nature—including the sensation of eating something made right in front of you—is a big part of its delight and mystique as a food group. Chaat can't be prepared ahead, stored, or standardized. Every bite is just distinct enough to keep you coming back for more, chasing that flavor high that exists only for that moment.

There's an entire galaxy of chaats, and we're not going to be able to cover them all here. However, we are going to attempt to break a few of my all-time favorites into two buckets:

1. Salad-y chaats. In these chaats, small bits of crispy crunchy things like puffed rice, cornflakes, and/or crispy chickpea noodles are tossed together, much like a salad but with mouthwatering chutneys.

2. Fried crispy chaats. If it's cooked in oil and it crunches, it will be here. Feel free to mix and match recipes from this chapter, maybe serving a half-dozen or so of your faves along with one Big Ticket dish (pages 219 to 243) for a truly banging party.

SALAD-Y, CRUNCHY THINGS

BHEL PURI

Serves 2 to 4

Arguably the most quintessential of all chaats—and definitely one of the chaat holy trinity (bhel puri, pani puri, and sev potato dahi puri)—bhel puri, aka Rice Krispie salad, makes absolutely no sense while you're watching it being made, and then you take your first bite. It's essentially puffed rice tossed with other crunchy, tasty things (like Chex Mix), made more magical with finely diced red onion, cilantro, and a dressing of green and tamarind chutneys, then eaten with a spoon.

Because bhel puri and its brethren have both wet and crunchy components, they must be eaten moments after assembly, on the spot—you cannot take it to go, you cannot even walk to find a seat. If you're not standing and shoving this into your mouth as quickly as it's handed to you, it's not even worth eating.

The far-flung provenances of the ingredients in bhel puri are a remarkable example of how dishes reflect the influence of migration and the inventiveness and adaptability of street vendors. The wheat puris are North Indian, the puffed rice is very South Indian, and the sev is totally a Gujarati thing (as is the tamarind chutney). These regional ingredients combine to make a snack that is infinitely more delicious than the sum of its parts.

- 1 medium Yukon Gold potato, boiled in salted water, peeled, and cut into ½-inch cubes (optional)
- 1½ cups mamra (see Notes)
- ¼ cup finely diced red onion
- ¼ cup finely chopped cilantro leaves
- 2 tablespoons Tamarind Chutney (page 271)
- 2 tablespoons Green Chutney (page 270)
- 1 cup coarsely broken papdis (see Notes)
- ¼ cup sev (see page 29)
- ¼ teaspoon chaat masala (see page 33)

In a large bowl, combine the potato (if using), mamra, onion, and cilantro. Add the tamarind and green chutneys, and mix well with a spoon, being careful not to smash the puffed rice or potato too much. Add the broken papdis and gently fold to combine.

Serve in small bowls, topped with sev and a fine dusting of chaat masala. Eat immediately for maximum crunch.

Notes: *As far as I know, puffed rice, or mamra / murmura, is only ever used in bhel. It's almost exactly the same as Rice Krispies from the breakfast cereal aisle, just toasted longer to give it more of a snap, crackle, and pop. It's available in most Indian grocery stores and online. In a pinch, unsweetened puffed rice works just fine: Toast it in a 350°F oven for 5 to 7 minutes to perfect the crunch and make it slightly nuttier.*

Papdis are round wheat discs about the size of hockey pucks—a sort of Ritz cracker equivalent. You'll find them in Indian groceries. You don't have to cook them, though throwing them in the toaster oven for a minute or two before serving them can bring out their crunch.

CORN BHEL

Serves 4

Bhel is essentially a salad made of things you wouldn't normally put in a salad. When I first came to the US, I instantly recognized that the variety of ingredients in any grocery store—available under one roof year-round through the magic of global transportation—could lead to some bhel flights of fancy. Here, roasted charred corn niblets are bhel-ified with the usual suspects: diced red onion, cilantro, mint, and corn poha (or corn flakes—yes, you can use Kellogg's), dressed with a cumin-lime vinaigrette inspired by Oprah.

4 ears of corn, husks intact

1 medium English cucumber, peeled, seeded, and diced

1 medium red onion, diced

3 Roma tomatoes, diced

½ cup coarsely chopped cilantro leaves

4 thinly sliced mint leaves

2 cups fried corn poha (see page 29) or corn flakes

¼ cup Cumin-Lime Dressing (page 270)

Preheat the oven to 500°F. Place the corn ears on a sheet pan and roast until the kernels look lightly browned when the husks are peeled away, about 40 minutes.

Remove the corn from the oven and, when it has cooled enough to handle, remove and discard the husks and silk. Standing each cob upright, use a chef's knife to cut the kernels off of the cobs and transfer to a medium mixing bowl. (You should have about 3 cups of kernels.) Discard the cobs (I save these to make corn stock later, if that's your thing). Add the cucumber, onion, tomato, cilantro, mint, and poha to the bowl and stir to combine.

Drizzle with the dressing, toss to evenly coat, and serve immediately. (Leftovers don't hold up well.)

BHEL PURI
PG. 42
GREEN MANGO CHAAT
PG. 46

CORN BHEL
PG. 43
SPDP
PG. 47

GREEN MANGO CHAAT

Serves 2 to 4

Pretty much anything that you shove into your mouth and then have to lick off of your fingers afterward is fair game to be called chaat. Here, crunchy, tangy, juicy green mango comes along for the chaat party, too.

1 cup finely diced green mango or green apple

¼ cup finely diced red onion

¼ cup finely chopped cilantro leaves

2 tablespoons golden raisins

2 tablespoons roasted unsalted peanuts

2 tablespoons Tamarind Chutney (page 271)

2 tablespoons Green Chutney (page 270)

1 cup fried corn poha (see page 29) or corn flakes

4 or 5 fried curry leaves (optional; see Note)

In a large bowl, combine the mango, onion, cilantro, raisins, and peanuts. Add the tamarind and green chutneys and mix well with a spoon. Add the corn poha and gently fold to combine.

Just before serving, top with the curry leaves. Eat immediately.

Note: *To fry curry leaves, heat about 2 tablespoons neutral oil in a small sauté pan until shimmering. Add the curry leaves—they'll crackle, pop, and blister, darkening within a minute. Promptly remove with a slotted spoon to a paper towel–lined plate. Unfortunately, fried curry leaves don't store well, so fry to order.*

SEV POTATO DAHI PURI (SPDP)

Serves 2 to 4

SPDP! The bite that delights! The supersized caviar of the chaat world! Delicate yet exploding with contrasting textures and flavors, it captures the chaos and wonderment of the streets of India like no other dish.

Like bhel puri, SPDP must be served quickly, because the second the chutney hits the puri, it gets soggy and starts to fall apart. It must also be eaten in one go; this might seem like too much, but I assure you that the instant you bite down, the SPDP reduces to almost nothing but an explosion of flavors. It truly is a party in your mouth, and should be experienced the way God intended: quickly and gloriously.

- 12 fried puris (see Note)
- ¼ cup roughly mashed boiled Yukon Gold potato (from about 1 medium potato, peeled and boiled in salted water)
- ¼ cup finely minced red onion
- ¼ cup finely chopped cilantro leaves
- ½ cup Sweet Yogurt Sauce (page 273)
- ¼ cup Tamarind Chutney (page 271)
- ¼ cup Green Chutney (page 270)
- ¼ cup sev (see page 29)
- ½ teaspoon roasted cumin powder (see page 32)

Using your fingernail or the tip of a knife, poke a small (½ inch or so) opening in the top of each puri so that you can fill it. (You might break a few, but the puris don't need to be perfect, and you'll get the hang of this step very quickly once you figure out how much pressure it takes to create an opening without crushing the whole puri.)

Once all of the puris have holes poked, it's time to move quickly. Arrange the puris on the plate you want to serve them on. One by one, gently push about 1 teaspoon mashed potato into each puri. If a hole isn't big enough, chip away at the edges so you can get the potato inside. With your fingers, place a healthy teaspoon-size pinch each of onion and cilantro on top of the potatoes. (A small spoon can also be helpful with this.)

To finish, pour in approximately 1 teaspoon each of sweet yogurt sauce, tamarind chutney, and green chutney. Drizzle another teaspoon or so of the sweet yogurt sauce on top of the puri—it's okay if it's overflowing. Garnish with a healthy sprinkle of sev and more onion and cilantro, and dust with roasted cumin powder. Serve immediately and eat in one bite.

Note: ***Puris are little flat wheat discs that puff up when fried. Pre-fried versions are sold as pani puris; they look like little hollow golf balls. While convenient, pani puris are delicate and break easily, so proceed with caution. I recommend toasting pani puris in a toaster oven at 350°F for about 5 minutes before carrying on with the recipe.***

Unpuffed puris are less fragile, but they do require you to deep fry them in 4 to 5 inches neutral oil for a few minutes until they puff up into said golden-brown hollow ball. Although it's an additional step, the nice thing about buying unfried puris is that a small bag will have over 100 puris that will last forever, so you can always fry up some fresh puris if you keep them on hand.

A. KRISHNAMURTHI
Meherbaan
K. RAVI SHANKAR

FAMOUS DESI SALAD *(AKA WHITE GIRL SALAD)*

Serves 4

When I was planning my second restaurant, Botiwalla, I was eager to lean completely into my passion for marinated and grilled meats. This was going to be my no-compromise, no-holds-barred homage to kebabs, tikkas, tandoor—all kinds of delectable meat morsels sizzling over an open flame. In this vision, the only role for a vegetable was as a garnish.

I was quickly shoulder-checked by the force of nature that is my wife and business partner, Molly, whose impeccable intuition (thankfully) balances out my hyperfocus. She unequivocally stated that if I didn't have some type of salad on the menu, I'd be alienating a lot of people—primarily white women—who would see no reason to come to my temple of meat.

I knew she was right, but I wasn't happy about it. So in a desperate attempt to maintain some shred of my vision's integrity, I persuaded Molly that cabbage was a salad green and, to prove it, came up with this recipe. From a practical home cook's standpoint, it's genius, since a head of cabbage lasts much longer than a head of lettuce. I hate having to go to the grocery store when I have a whim to cook something, so a salad made from cabbage, carrots, and green onions—all things that keep well in the fridge—is a great back-pocket option.

This salad has since become one of our all-time bestsellers at both Botiwalla and Chai Pani—among white girls and desis alike. It's best made and served on the same day, though it can be kept (albeit in a decreasingly crunchy state) overnight in the refrigerator.

3 cups finely shredded green cabbage (about ½ head)

3 cups finely shredded purple cabbage (about ½ head)

1 cup thinly sliced carrots (about 2 large carrots)

¼ cup coarsely chopped cilantro leaves and stems

1 cup Cumin-Lime Dressing (page 270)

Kosher salt

½ cup sev (see page 29)

½ cup Masala Roasted Cashews (page 270)

⅓ cup thinly sliced green onion (2 or 3 green onions)

1 tablespoon sesame seeds

In a large salad bowl, combine the green and purple cabbage, carrots, cilantro, dressing, and a pinch of salt; mix well to evenly distribute the dressing. Sprinkle with the sev, cashews, green onion, and sesame seeds. Serve immediately.

VEGGIE PAKORAS WITH SWEET YOGURT SAUCE

Serves 4 to 6

It seems like every culture has a fritter—batter-and-fry is a universal culinary language. India has mastered the art of frying, and the pakora is one of the finest fritters in the world. Almost always made with chickpea flour that's been flavored perfectly with a pinch of savory spices, pakoras are gluten-free, crunchy, and never greasy. People chow down entire classes of vegetables they swear they would never eat when those veggies are stuffed into a pakora. This recipe calls for kale, as at Chai Pani, but you can use almost any vegetable you have on hand. It also makes a little more pakora masala than you'll need; it will keep—just sprinkle the extra on grilled or roasted meats or vegetables.

PAKORA MASALA

1 teaspoon cumin powder

½ teaspoon turmeric powder

1 teaspoon ground Kashmiri or other red chilli (see page 18)

½ teaspoon ajwain or caraway seed powder

1 tablespoon kosher salt, plus more as needed

PAKOTA BATTER

1 cup besan (chickpea flour)

1 fresh Thai or serrano chilli (depending on your heat tolerance), finely chopped

1 small bunch cilantro, finely chopped (about ⅔ cup)

2 cups neutral oil, for frying

2 quarts thinly sliced vegetables, such as kale, brussels sprouts, red onion, bell pepper, or potatoes

¼ cup Sweet Yogurt Sauce (page 273), for serving

To make the pakora masala, combine all the ingredients in a small bowl and set aside.

To make the pakora batter, in a large bowl, combine 2 teaspoons of the pakora masala with the besan, chilli, and cilantro and stir together. Pour in about 1 cup of warm water a little at a time, stirring constantly, just until the mixture is the consistency of pancake batter. Cover the bowl with plastic wrap or a clean kitchen towel and set aside. (You can make the batter up to two days in advance and keep it in the fridge until ready to use, just bring the batter to room temp before frying.)

Preheat the oven to 200°F. Set a wire rack in a sheet pan lined with paper towels; place the prepared pan near the stove.

To fry the pakoras, in a large heavy pot over high heat, heat the oil until it reaches 325°F on a deep-fry thermometer.

Scoop handfuls of sliced veggies into the pakora batter and immediately (but carefully!) drop the batter-coated blobs into the hot oil, working in batches to keep the pakoras separate. Fry until golden brown, 3 to 5 minutes, turning each pakora with a slotted spoon every minute or so to cook evenly. Remove the pakoras from the oil with metal tongs or the slotted spoon and place on the paper towel–lined rack. Immediately sprinkle each pakora with a hefty pinch of salt, and slide this first batch of pakoras into the oven to keep warm.

Before you fry the next batch, fish out any stray batter droppings so they don't burn and discolor the oil. Bring the oil back up to 325°F, then scoop, coat, and fry more pakoras in batches until you are out of vegetables or batter.

Serve pakoras hot with sweet yogurt sauce on the side. Pakoras are best eaten the day they're made.

KINGFISHER
PREMIUM
LAGER
FIGHTER

MASALA SMASHED POTATOES

Serves 4

I'm not the first person to smash a potato, but I haven't seen anything quite like it in India. While Indians do have fried potato chaat, they tend to douse it with sweet yogurt sauce and chutney like they do with many fried potato–esque creations.

This dish to me is an elevated French fry. It's all about texture. When done right, every bite has crunchy, craggy bits of potato, plus soft starchy bits, too. (This is part of why it's important to use fingerling potatoes here—for all the little craggy corners.) And this is one of the few dishes where chaat masala gets to shine, instead of competing with a bunch of chutneys and condiments.

2 pounds fingerling potatoes (about 20)

5 tablespoons kosher salt, plus more for seasoning

About 2 quarts canola or other neutral oil, for deep-frying

2 teaspoons freshly squeezed lime juice

1 teaspoon chaat masala (see page 33)

¼ cup coarsely chopped cilantro

Maggi ketchup or regular ketchup mixed with sriracha, for serving

In a large pot, combine the potatoes, 5 tablespoons of salt, and 1 gallon of water; cover and bring to a boil over high heat. Once the water is boiling, take off the lid, lower the heat to a simmer, and cook until the potatoes are fork-tender, about 10 minutes. It's important to not overcook the potatoes—they should be soft enough to smash, but they should hold their shape even when smashed. Drain the potatoes, spread them out on a sheet pan, and set aside to cool to room temperature. (They can be stored in the refrigerator at this point for smashing and frying later, just bring them to room temperature before using.)

Spread plastic wrap on the counter, lay out the potatoes, and smash them with the base of your palm until you feel the edges split and they are flattened but not falling apart (the plastic wrap keeps them from sticking to your work surface). The idea is to force most of the inner part of the potato out of the skin, so you get as many crunchy, crispy fried edges as possible.

In a large heavy-bottomed pan over medium-high heat, bring about 1 inch of the oil to 330°F to 340°F. Set a paper towel–lined plate, or a wire rack set over a sheet pan, next to the stove. Add the potatoes to the oil, working in batches to avoid overcrowding. For ideal crunch-to-starch ratio, cook until dark golden brown on both sides, flipping once, about 5 minutes total. Remove the potatoes from the oil with a slotted spoon and place on the prepared plate or rack. Season lightly with salt. Repeat with the remaining potatoes, bringing the oil back to temperature between batches.

Once all the potatoes are fried, put them in a large bowl and add the lime juice, chaat masala, and cilantro; toss to combine. Serve with Maggi ketchup or regular ketchup with a hit of sriracha. Leftovers keep, tightly covered, for up to 5 days in the refrigerator. Reheat them in a toaster oven or air fryer for best results.

AUNTIE HOLDBACKS

Commercial Indian cookbooks are a fairly recent phenomenon. While Madhur Jaffrey was busy helping introduce and popularize Indian cuisine in America, in India, cookbooks were, ironically, still a novelty and not something that anybody in my family owned. Families had recipes, of course, which were handed down from mother to daughter—or from father to son on the streets. This way of passing down recipes created a black market economy of legendary tips and secrets that I affectionately call "auntie holdbacks."

A holdback is this: If one auntie asks another for a recipe, some seemingly minor but actually totally key step will be intentionally omitted to ensure that the upstart auntie recipe will never be as good as the OG recipe. Even when I was getting recipes from my own mother, she would—with no malicious intent—leave out a fairly critical piece of information (that I would later discover and confront her with). She'd invariably wave it off as a minor detail that didn't seem important enough to include. This all convinced me there was some sort of culinary Darwinism at work.

My promise to you, dear reader, is that I am not holding anything back in this book. If anything, I may overemphasize certain aspects of a key technique or ingredient. Throughout, there are a few hacks that I overtly refer to—like the Dunghar technique on page 229—and, for the most part, I've extracted and provided every last ounce of auntie and uncle holdback information so you can reap the maximum benefit of these deeply buried family secrets.

GREEN BANANA CUTLETS

Makes about 6 cutlets; serves 3 to 5

Parsis love what we call cutlets (pronounced cut-less*) so much so that the word has become a term of endearment—for example, a mother might call her child "my little cutlet" while pinching their cheek.*

A cutlet (the edible kind) is basically seasoned, minced filling—either protein or starch—formed into a patty, panko'd, and pan-fried. This is a throwback homestyle recipe; it's typically made with plantains, but I use unripe bananas—I've found they're actually tastier and, because they're less starchy, they make for a lighter croquette. I boil and mash green bananas, mix them with mashed potatoes, form them gently into cutlets, and pan-fry them. (I have also made cutlets with mushy, overripe bananas; they are also delicious, but this is the OG technique.) These are a great snack with chai.

The potato-banana mash can be made in advance and held in the refrigerator for up to 3 days before you form and fry the cutlets. In fact, even if you're serving cutlets for two, make the whole batch so you can have cutlets for a few days. Make sure to bring the mash back to room temperature before frying.

2 medium Yukon Gold potatoes, peeled and cut into large chunks

3 green bananas, peeled and cut into large chunks

Kosher salt

½ teaspoon cumin seed

½ teaspoon coriander seed

1 cup diced red onion (about 1 medium onion)

2 teaspoons minced fresh ginger (about a 1-inch knob)

2 teaspoons minced garlic (1 to 2 cloves)

1 tablespoon finely chopped cilantro leaves

1 finely chopped fresh Thai or serrano chilli (depending on your heat tolerance)

2 tablespoons freshly squeezed lime juice

⅔ cup all-purpose flour

⅔ cup panko

2 large eggs

1 cup vegetable oil

Maggi ketchup, for serving (optional)

In a large pot, combine the potatoes, bananas, a pinch of salt, and 1 gallon of water; cover and bring to a boil over high heat. Once the water is boiling, uncover the pot, lower the heat to a simmer, and cook until a fork or knife pierces the potato easily, 15 to 20 minutes. Drain the potatoes and bananas well, and let them cool enough to handle.

Smash the potatoes and bananas together with a potato masher until they form a somewhat smooth paste (a few lumps are okay).

In a small dry pan over medium heat, toast the cumin and coriander seeds until they're fragrant and start to darken slightly, about 1 minute. Slide them out of the pan to cool, then crush them with a mortar and pestle or grind them in a coffee grinder dedicated to spices.

Add the crushed cumin and coriander to the bowl with the mashed potatoes and bananas, along with the onion, ginger, garlic, cilantro, chilli, lime juice, and ½ teaspoon salt. Stir to combine, working the mixture into a soft dough (don't overwork it). Taste and add salt as needed.

Put the flour on one plate and the panko on another and beat the eggs in a shallow bowl. To form the cutlets, divide the dough by hand into balls larger than golf balls but smaller than tennis balls, ⅓ to ½ cup of dough each. Press the balls gently between your palms to flatten them into discs (cutlets) about ½ inch thick.

Dust each cutlet well with flour, coat it in beaten egg, then turn it in the panko, making sure it's well coated. Set the cutlets on a plate as you finish them.

Heat the oil in a large heavy-bottomed pan (cast iron works great here) over medium-high heat, and fry the cutlets in batches, turning once, until they're brown and crispy, 2 to 3 minutes per side. The cutlet ingredients are mostly cooked already, so you're really just getting a nice crust on the outside.

Sprinkle with salt and serve immediately, with Maggi ketchup on the side if you like. Cutlets are best served hot and fresh but are still tasty if you hold them for a few hours, though leftovers don't keep overnight.

PALAK PAKORA CHAAT

Serves 4 to 6

Now that you've mastered the art of the pakora (see page 50), let's chaat-ify it! Palak is spinach (you could also use another dark leafy green, like collards), and it can easily be transformed into chaat with a few lashings of chutney, sweet yogurt sauce, and sev. This may sound like a familiar formula if you've been making some of the other chaats in this chapter, but remember: This particular combination of flavors is just a jumping-off point for exploring chaat.

Don't have time to make chutneys? Just squeeze some fresh lime juice over the pakoras. No sev? Try a handful of roasted peanuts or diced cucumbers or tomatoes, and there you go. The basic idea of a chaat is adding texture, freshness, and herbaceousness, and once you get the hang of that tangy-sweet-salty, compulsively snackable flavor profile, you can't be stopped.

PAKORA BATTER

1 cup besan (chickpea flour)

2 teaspoons Pakora Masala (page 50)

1 finely chopped fresh Thai or serrano chilli (depending on your heat tolerance)

1 small bunch cilantro (leaves and stems), finely chopped

1 cup warm water

3 cups vegetable oil

2 to 3 loosely packed cups whole-leaf spinach, stemmed, washed and dried, and cut into strips

Kosher salt

TO SERVE

¼ cup Tamarind Chutney (page 271)

¼ cup Green Chutney (page 270)

¼ cup Sweet Yogurt Sauce (page 273)

½ teaspoon roasted cumin powder (see page 32)

¼ cup sev (see page 29)

To make the pakora batter, combine the besan, pakora masala, green chilli, and cilantro in a large bowl. Pouring slowly and stirring steadily, add the warm water a little at a time until the mixture is the consistency of pancake batter (you may not need all of the water). Set aside.

Preheat the oven to 200°F to keep the fried pakoras warm.

In a large heavy-bottomed pot, heat the oil over high heat until it reaches 325°F. Place a paper towel–lined plate, or a wire rack set over a sheet pan, next to the stove.

Grab handful-size portions of the spinach and dip into the pakora batter to coat. Carefully drop each batter-coated handful into the hot oil; work in batches so you don't crowd the pakoras. Fry the pakoras until they're golden brown, 3 to 5 minutes, turning with a slotted spoon every minute or so to cook evenly.

Remove the pakoras from the oil with metal tongs or the slotted spoon and place on the prepared plate or rack. Sprinkle each pakora with a pinch of kosher salt while it's still hot and slide the pakoras in the oven to keep warm. Fish out any stray batter droppings from the oil so they don't burn and discolor the oil, and bring the oil back up to 325°F before frying the next batch.

To serve, arrange the pakoras on a platter in a single layer. Drizzle tamarind chutney, green chutney, and sweet yogurt sauce over each pakora, sprinkle with roasted cumin powder, and finish with a healthy sprinkling of sev. Serve immediately.

OKRA FRIES

Serves 4 to 6

Let me get this out of the way right up top: Yes, you have to cut this okra by hand. You're probably staring at a pound of okra right now, wondering how you're supposed to cut these knobby, wobbly things without taking a finger off. And you're right to be concerned. Cutting hundreds of bushels of okra a week is a rite of passage at Chai Pani—something we subject new hires to so they get their knife skills up to speed.

Here's our technique: First off, go slowly until you're proficient. With the fingers of one hand, firmly hold the okra pod lengthwise and carefully slice a thick sliver along one side to create a flat surface. Turn the okra onto this new flat side to make it stable, then cut it into thin lengthwise strips. (You don't have to cut the ends off.) Godspeed.

The end result of this recipe is quite possibly the greatest food alchemy I've ever experienced—the transformation of a much-reviled vegetable into something hot, crispy, salty-spicy, and completely addictive. The okra fries at Chai Pani are one of our all-time bestsellers, and we probably sell more okra as an institution than any other restaurant in the US.

1 pound okra pods

2 quarts canola or other neutral oil, for frying

1 teaspoon kosher salt, plus more to taste

1 teaspoon chaat masala (see page 33)

Juice of 1 lime

Using the technique described at left, thinly slice each okra pod lengthwise, cutting it into thin strips about the width of shoestring fries.

In a large heavy-bottomed pot with high sides, heat the oil over medium-high heat until it reaches 350°F. Preheat the oven to 200°F to keep the fries warm before serving, and set a paper towel–lined plate, or a wire rack set over a sheet pan, next to the stove.

Working in batches to avoid overcrowding, add the okra to the oil and cook for 2 to 3 minutes, until the fries are evenly light brown and crispy. Use a skimmer or tongs to gently turn the fries to ensure even cooking.

As they finish cooking, transfer the okra to the prepared plate or rack and hold in the oven until all the fries are done, for up to 30 minutes before serving.

Bring the oil back to temperature between batches—this is one of those recipes where an oil thermometer is definitely helpful. There will be some okra seeds floating around in the oil between batches, too—try to scoop these out before you fry the next round, but there's no need to be super fussy about it.

Once you're ready to serve, pull the hot okra out of the oven and, in a large bowl, toss it with the salt, chaat masala, and half the lime juice. Taste, and add more salt and lime juice to your liking. Okra fries are best served immediately.

PASS PASS
NEW

FENNEL-CRUSTED EGGPLANT FRITTERS

Serves 6 to 8

Eggplant, like okra, is often reviled for its spongy texture and bitter flavor. One of the reasons this is the no. 1 best Indian cookbook in the world is because it teaches you to take challenging flavors and textures and transform them into something you can't get enough of. The Okra Fries on page 64 are one example. This is another.

Soaking the eggplant in milk is crucial here—this simple step tempers the vegetable's bitterness and gives it a delightfully creamy taste, which contrasts well with the seasoned crunch on the outside. I also recommend using table salt in the dredge instead of coarser kosher salt; it incorporates better. When making these (or the Masala Smashed Potatoes on page 54, or the pakoras on page 50, for that matter), I like to work in batches and serve them up as soon as they're fried—that's when they are the most blindingly delicious. People are usually congregating in the kitchen anyway, and this is a great snack to make fresh and hand out while folks are milling about with pre-dinner drinks.

2 pounds Italian eggplant
2 cups whole milk
1 tablespoon fennel seed
1 tablespoon cumin seed
1 cup besan (chickpea flour)
1 teaspoon ground red chilli, such as Kashmiri (see page 18)
1 teaspoon turmeric powder
1 teaspoon table salt
2 quarts canola or other neutral oil, for frying
Kosher salt, to finish

Halve the eggplants lengthwise and slice into ¼-inch half-moons. If your eggplant is particularly wide, you may need to cut it into thirds first. Place the slices in a large bowl, add the milk, and let soak for 30 minutes.

While the eggplant soaks, prepare the dredge. In a small skillet over medium-high heat, toast the fennel and cumin seeds until they're popping and aromatic, 30 to 60 seconds. Allow the seeds to cool and then coarsely grind them in that dedicated coffee grinder we talked about on page 35.

In a large bowl, combine the ground fennel and cumin, the besan, ground chilli, turmeric, and table salt. Use your fingers or a (very dry!) whisk to ensure the ingredients are well incorporated.

Set a wire rack over a sheet pan lined with paper towels. Remove 5 to 10 slices of eggplant from the milk and pat dry on paper towels. Coat the eggplant slices evenly with the dredge and transfer them to the rack. Repeat until all of the eggplant slices are dredged. (I like to keep a paper towel on the side of the dredge bowl to continually dry my fingers between batches so the dredge doesn't get clumpy as I work.)

In a large heavy-bottomed pot over medium-high heat, bring the oil to 325°F, using an oil thermometer to check the temperature. The oil should not come more than halfway up the side of your pot to help minimize splattering.

Working in batches to avoid overcrowding, slide 5 to 10 fritters into the oil, carefully and slowly, by placing the bottom inch of the fritters into the oil then letting them gently fall into the oil away from you. Cook until golden brown, 3 to 5 minutes, flipping if needed. Transfer the fritters to the rack set over the sheet pan.

Sprinkle the fritters with kosher salt while they're still hot and serve right away and as-is, no dipping sauce or chutney required. The eggplant is so creamy inside that you won't need any additional sauce. Be careful on that first bite, as the fritter innards will be very hot.

DAHI VADA

Makes 20 to 25 vadas; serves 4 to 6

Dahi vada literally translates to "yogurt and fritter." Keeping with the best chaat traditions, it's a perfect example of repurposing some foundational components of the genre—sweet yogurt sauce, chutney, and vadas—into myriad combinations. In this book I've tried my best to select recipes in which, though some components are similar, the end result is very distinctive; this recipe is a perfect example.

Dahi vada are popular in Delhi and North India, where they're also known as "dahi bhalla," a Punjabi word for vada. Traditionally the vada are soaked in salted water as soon as they come out of the fryer; then the water is squeezed out and the vada are dressed with yogurt and chutneys, making for a cold, spongy, savory bread pudding–type texture that Indians love and many Westerners find peculiar. I personally prefer to skip the soaking, to retain the crispy, crunchy textures I've always associated with chaat. (You will need to soak the dal for 4 to 6 hours before cooking, so plan ahead.)

VADA

1 cup split urad dal (see Note)

1 teaspoon cumin seed

Pinch of hing (optional)

1 teaspoon coarsely chopped fresh Thai or serrano chilli (depending on your heat tolerance)

1 teaspoon coarsely chopped fresh ginger (about a ½-inch knob)

½ teaspoon kosher salt

¼ to ½ cup chilled water, as needed

1 tablespoon coarsely chopped golden raisins

1 tablespoon coarsely chopped cashews

3 to 4 quarts canola or other neutral oil, for frying

Nonstick cooking spray

TO SERVE

1 cup Sweet Yogurt Sauce (page 273)

¼ cup Green Chutney (page 270)

¼ cup Tamarind Chutney (page 271)

Roasted cumin powder

Ground red chilli, such as Kashmiri (see page 18)

Place the urad dal in a large heavy-bottomed pot and wash it three or four times with cold water, mixing the dal lightly with your hand while rinsing. Drain the water completely after each rinse, until the water runs clear.

Cover the dal with 2 to 3 inches of water and soak at room temperature for 4 to 6 hours. After soaking, pour off excess water from the dal (you don't have to get it all out, just whatever's on top).

Place the dal and any residual soaking water in a blender. Add the cumin, hing (if using), green chilli, ginger, and salt. Pulse a few times until you have the beginnings of a very coarse batter. Add ¼ cup of the chilled water and blend for about a minute, scraping down the sides of the blender with a rubber spatula halfway through. Add more chilled water about 1 tablespoon at a time, until you have a thick, fluffy batter. Be judicious—don't let the batter get too thin: It should resemble creamy, fluffy mashed potatoes. Transfer the batter to a bowl and whisk it for 30 to 45 seconds to aerate it. Gently fold in the raisins and cashews.

Add the oil to a 6- to 8-quart pot suitable for frying and heat to 325°F (use an oil thermometer; you'll definitely have to check the temperature). Set a paper towel–lined plate beside the stove.

To test whether the batter is the right consistency, dribble a bit into the hot oil. It should rise immediately. If it sinks, whisk another teaspoon of water into the batter to thin it out.

Spray a large spoon or ice cream scoop with nonstick cooking spray and scoop golf ball–size balls of batter into the hot oil. Work in batches to avoid overcrowding the pan. The vada should float to the surface pretty quickly—if they don't, your oil probably isn't hot enough. Fry until golden brown on both sides, turning once, 2 to 3 minutes total.

Place the vada on the lined plate. Press on one; it should have a slight spongy give, like a donut hole.

The traditional way to serve vada is to portion 3 to 5 of them on a small plate. Douse with 3 to 4 tablespoons of sweet yogurt sauce. Drizzle at least 1 tablespoon each of the green and tamarind chutneys on top, and sprinkle with roasted cumin powder and ground red chilli. Take a test bite and adjust the amounts of yogurt and chutneys accordingly—you do you. Dahi vada are, perhaps unsurprisingly, best eaten hot and fresh.

Note: ***Somewhat confusingly, husked split black lentils actually appear white in the bag. Appearances aside, look for lentils labeled "urad dal" or "black lentils." Be aware that many South Asian grocers also sell non-husked urad dal, which is black in appearance; make sure you are buying the husked version.***

SANDWICHES & ROLLS

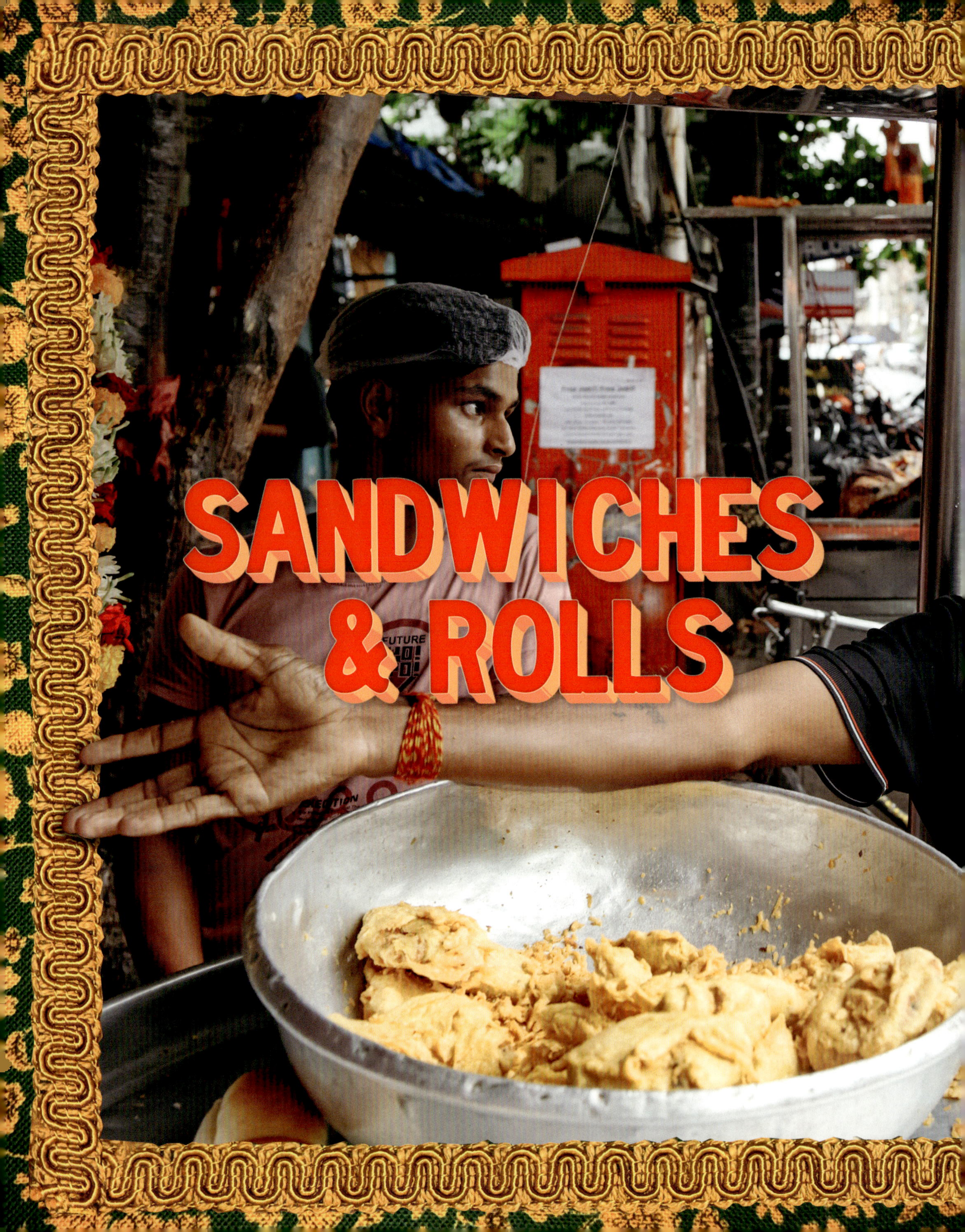

सैंडविच और रोल्स

Most of the recipes in this chapter owe their origins to the industrialization of India. As the workday stretched out for factory workers and the luxury of sit-down meals evaporated, street hawkers—with their never-ending ingenuity—figured out ways to convert all kinds of foods into something you could easily hold and eat. Sandwich bread is a relatively recent import to India, so the street food in this chapter is in a newer and constantly evolving category.

And oh, what a category it is! Here you'll find vada pav, the greatest version of carb-on-carb snack to exist on this earth, along with the mighty Botiwalla lamb burger and the Indian version of an egg sandwich, which will replace your bacon-egg-and-cheese forevermore. This is also where the beloved kathi rolls find their home, and, in a nod to my Anglified Parsi grandmother Viloo, little British-style finger sandwiches on soft, squishy white bread.

In true keeping with the ethos of the street vendor, I will encourage—nay *insist*—that you store-buy your naan, pav (essentially Hawaiian rolls), or bread, instead of trying to figure out how to make it yourself. Street vendors aren't making their breads, and neither should you. Instead, focus, as they do, on assembling the most delicious combination of ingredients that you can possibly put between two slices.

VADA PAV, THE GOAT

Makes 6 sandwiches

This is, without question, the greatest sandwich of all time. Who would have guessed that a starch-on-starch sandwich could capture the imagination of a billion-plus Indians? It's hard to describe exactly why the vada pav works so well, but I'll try. The magic of batter, hot oil, and chutneys transforms ordinary potatoes and bread into a creamy-crunchy, spicy-sweet ultimately soothing bite that practically forces you to come back for more.

Whoever invented it deserves a Medal of Honor because if there's one dish that powers the everyday workforce in the metropolis of Mumbai, it is the vada pav. This dish is so much a part of the DNA of Indian street food that even McDonald's in India had to adapt it, in the form of a McAloo Tikki.

Vada pav is almost certainly Maharashtrian in origin, and was likely invented in Mumbai. It's almost always enjoyed on the street, served piping hot by your favorite among the legions of vada pav hawkers. The best of them are mini celebrities, with countless TikToks dedicated to their mastery of the craft.

At Chai Pani, I've noticed that many Indians—and Mumbaikars in particular—order the vada pav, and the vada pav alone, as a litmus test to see if it's worth ordering anything else. It's quite hilarious to see a server deliver a single vada pav to six stone-faced Indians. Inevitably, they start adding on.

It is the Chai Pani recipe I present to you now, and while it's adjusted for home cooks, there's only so much adjusting I can do: You will need to deep-fry the vada in canola oil. It's impossible to completely avoid deep-frying if you're cooking Indian street food, so just make peace with it. If you don't have both a deep enough pot for deep-frying and a deep-fry (oil) thermometer, skip this dish and others of a similar nature. But trust me: The benefits are worth the investment in both.

2 pounds Yukon Gold potatoes, peeled

3 to 4 quarts canola or other neutral oil, for frying

PAKORA BATTER

1 cup besan (chickpea flour)

1 teaspoon turmeric powder

¾ teaspoon ground red chilli, such as Kashmiri (see page 18)

½ teaspoon cumin powder

¼ teaspoon ajwain (optional)

Pinch of kosher salt

1 tablespoon finely chopped cilantro

1 teaspoon coarsely chopped Thai or serrano chilli

½ cup warm water

TADKA

3 tablespoons neutral oil, such as grapeseed

1 teaspoon mustard seed

¼ teaspoon hing (optional)

4 to 5 fresh or dried curry leaves (optional)

1 teaspoon coarsely chopped Thai or serrano chilli (depending on your heat tolerance)

1 tablespoon Ginger-Garlic Paste (page 276)

1½ teaspoons turmeric powder

Kosher salt

¼ teaspoon chaat masala (see page 33)

1 teaspoon freshly squeezed lime juice (optional)

1 to 2 tablespoons coarsely chopped cilantro (optional)

TO SERVE

Unsalted butter, for griddling

6 pav or Hawaiian sweet rolls

½ cup Mint Chutney (page 272)

¼ cup Tamarind Chutney (page 271)

¼ cup Dry Garlic Chutney (page 273)

Bring a large pot of water to a boil. Add the potatoes and cook until they're fork-tender, about 20 minutes; drain. Return the potatoes to the pot and let them sit uncovered for 5 minutes to steam dry. With a potato masher or the back of a spoon, roughly mash the potatoes; you want a slightly chunky texture.

To make the pakora batter, in a large bowl combine the besan, turmeric, ground chilli, cumin, ajwain (if using), salt, finely chopped cilantro, and green chilli and stir to combine. Pouring slowly, whisk in the warm water, just until the mixture resembles thick pancake batter. Taste and adjust the salt if necessary. Set aside.

To make the tadka, heat the 3 tablespoons of the neutral oil in a small sauté pan over high heat until it's shimmering. Add the mustard seeds and, when they wiggle and pop, turn the heat down to medium to avoid burning. (Make sure the oil is hot enough that the mustard seeds actually start to pop—otherwise they're not flavoring the oil!)

Add the hing (if using), curry leaves (if using), and chilli to the oil. The curry leaves will splatter when they hit the oil, so be careful! Add the

Continued

TOPOGRAPHY-FIRST CUISINE

Most people who are into food have an intuitive understanding that cuisine is regional, and that it develops in accordance with what grows where, and with who created and perfected the region's dishes and cooking styles. I love that in Italy, for example, so much attention is paid to specific foods produced in specific regions—foods that define entire communities and give a sense of pride and tradition to the cuisine. Yet for some reason, in the West, Indian food tends to be seen as a monolith—which is patently ridiculous when you consider how massive India is and how ancient our culinary traditions are.

For those who haven't spent time in the subcontinent, it may be hard to understand just how our geography and topography has dictated the cuisine. India rises from sea-level tropics to the highest mountain range in the world, like, really fast. One land formation, the Deccan Plateau, rises from sea level to 2,000 feet in one sheer cliff—there's nothing gradual about this ascent. The glacial melt from the Himalayas feeds some of the greatest rivers in the world, the Ganges and the Yamuna, and on top of all that, we're a peninsula, surrounded by open sea that separates us from (and connects us to) Africa and Southeast Asia.

We're also hemmed in by the Great Thar desert to the northwest, so topography has dictated not just what grows where but also which immigrants—and invaders—have historically been able to make it here to influence different parts of the country. Ancient trade routes between Mesopotamia and the Indus Valley brought influences from the north millennia ago and, of course, there's the impact of colonizing and of colonial trade beginning in the seventeenth century, as ships from Europe arrived in the south and west of our subcontinent. All this has shaped Indian cuisine in dramatic ways over many hundreds of years.

One of my all-time-favorite street dishes, vada pav (see page 73), demonstrates the complexity of the culinary influences on our cuisine. Vada pav collapses multiple regional specialties into one dish, and it could only have been created in a city like Mumbai. Let's break it down:

- *The pav, or bread, came via Portuguese traders through the only ports they had access to, Goa and Mumbai on India's west coast. Because of the topography of the region, bound by mountains and sea, pav stayed pretty much right where it landed, in what I like to call the "pav belt."*
- *The potato in the sandwich was also brought by Europeans, introduced to South India by Portuguese and Dutch traders in the seventeenth century. But the tubers grow well in the central plains of Maharashtra and Madhya Pradesh, and they continue to dominate the cuisine there.*
- *Tamarind came from East Africa through Gujarat, and became a prominent feature in Gujarati snacks before making its way to Mumbai and onto the vada pav.*
- *The chickpeas in the batter came to Gujarat from the Mediterranean basin and, like the pav, pretty much stayed there. Why? That's where they grow best.*
- *And finally, the peanuts and red chillies in the dry garlic chutney, introduced from different parts of the world, grow best in the arid climate of the Deccan Plateau, and so have since become essential components of Deccan cuisine.*

That all of the above combine into sandwich form to make a quintessential regional dish shows the ingenuity of Indian cooks learning over centuries to layer ingredients and adapt techniques in order to perfect this one dish.

A TOPOGRAPHICAL HISTORY OF VADA PAV

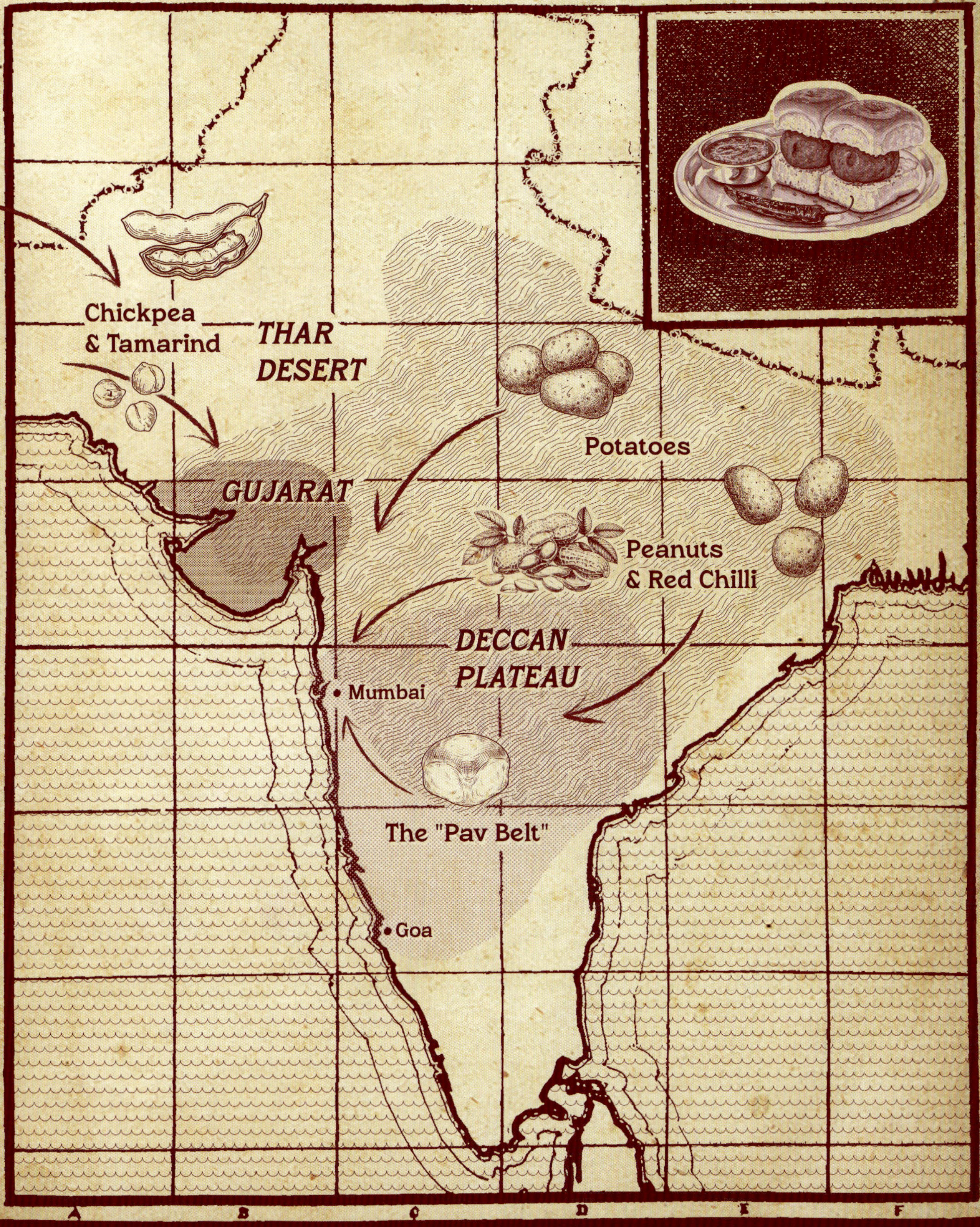

KATHI ROLLS

Makes 4 rolls

The kathi roll has a murky provenance. While most agree that the word kathi *refers to a stick or skewer upon which chunks of chicken, lamb, or beef are cooked over a grill, the modern-day kathi roll is usually more burrito-like, filled with either shredded or chopped meat. If grilled chunks are what you're after, direct your attention to the tikka roll recipe on page 184. This kathi roll is more of a shredded meat situation, and doesn't require the use of a grill.*

The other major distinction between a kathi roll and a tikka roll is that kathi rolls involve a masala omelet that is adhered to the paratha you wrap the meat in. It's one of those things that sounds weird on a menu, but one bite and you realize that the eggs add an unctuous mouthfeel and magical umami flavor, so much so that you don't even need any another condiment or chutney. (There is one possible exception to what I just said. A drizzle of the green chutney on page 270 will give you the complete Indian street food experience, but even without it, the kathi roll is complete and delicious.)

One last note: We have a recipe for parathas on page 215, because they are a fun, simple rainy-day project to serve alongside chai. But for this kathi roll, frozen store-bought parathas are better. They come par-cooked and hold up better to the double cooking this recipe requires—and you don't even have to defrost them. I like Kawan brand parathas, which are readily available in the freezer section of Indian groceries and online.

1 pound boneless, skinless chicken thighs

2 tablespoons Ginger-Garlic Paste (page 276)

Kosher salt

3 teaspoons tandoori masala (see page 33)

Neutral oil, such as grapeseed

1 teaspoon distilled white vinegar

1 lime, halved, plus more for serving

3 large eggs, beaten

⅔ cup very thinly sliced white onion (from 1 small onion)

1 to 2 fresh Thai chillies or 2 to 3 serrano chillies (depending on your heat tolerance), finely chopped

¼ cup finely chopped cilantro, plus more for garnish

1 teaspoon chaat masala (see page 33)

4 frozen parathas

In a medium bowl, combine the chicken thighs, ginger-garlic paste, 1 teaspoon salt, 2 teaspoons of the tandoori masala, 1 teaspoon oil, the white vinegar, and the juice of half the lime. Toss the chicken with the marinade to coat evenly. Marinate in the refrigerator for at least 1 hour and up to 4 hours.

Heat the oven to 500°F. If your oven has a convection setting, use it. (And if you have a countertop oven, it's perfect for this small amount of chicken—and it tends to get hotter faster.) Place the chicken on a sheet pan lined with parchment paper, making sure each piece has at least 1 inch of space around it. Bake for 15 minutes or until the chicken has reached an internal temperature of 165°F and is lightly charred around the edges. Remove from the oven and set aside.

In a small bowl, whisk together the eggs, a pinch of salt, and the remaining 1 teaspoon tandoori masala. Set aside.

In another small bowl, combine the onions, green chilli, cilantro, the juice from the other lime half, and the chaat masala. Set aside.

In a large skillet over medium-high heat, heat 1 teaspoon oil until it's shimmering. Add a frozen paratha and cook, flipping every minute or so, until the paratha starts to brown and puff up, 3 to 4 minutes. Press gently with a spatula to ensure that the paratha is browning evenly; transfer it to a plate and repeat with the other parathas, adding more oil as necessary.

Add another teaspoon of oil to the pan and pour about a quarter of the egg mixture into the center of the pan. When the egg spreads the same size as a paratha, quickly place a paratha on top of it. This lets them fuse together into one deliciously eggy-doughy disc. Cook for about a minute, then flip. Toast the other side until the paratha is crispy but still pliable. Repeat with the remaining three parathas and egg mixture, dividing the egg evenly.

Slice the chicken thighs into thin strips and set them aside on a plate. Pour over any leftover juices from the pan.

To assemble, place some sliced chicken on the eggy side of each paratha and top it with the onion-chilli mixture. Add a squeeze of lime juice and garnish with additional cilantro. Roll it up, take a big bite, and thank us later.

There won't be any leftovers, but if there are, store the chicken and parathas separately in the refrigerator, tightly covered, for up to 2 days.

VARIATION

PANEER KATHI ROLL

Substitute 1 pound of paneer, cut into 1½-inch cubes, for the chicken. Follow all the directions in the main recipe, baking the paneer until the edges are brown, 10 to 15 minutes. To serve, coarsely chop the paneer cubes into smaller pieces and, still being sure to mop up any juices from the sheet pan, sprinkle the paneer over the eggy paratha, garnish, roll it up, and enjoy.

MUMBAI TOASTIE

Makes 2 sandwiches

With the first bite I ever had of a club sandwich in America, I realized why street hawkers in Mumbai decided they could do better. In the West, a defining feature of a club sandwich is that extra layer of bread in the middle. But in India, we pull out all that limp salad-bar crap and swap it for thinly sliced boiled potatoes, beets, cucumbers, tomatoes, and chaat masala on buttered white bread. We then seal the toastie in a press, like a little Hot Pocket.

Unless you have a specialized toastie press (or a panini press) at home, you can achieve a similar effect in a cast-iron skillet with a heavy object pressed on top. If you really get into it, maybe find a busy street corner in your hometown and make yourself a fortune selling these things.

1 tablespoon unsalted butter, at room temperature

1 tablespoon Mint Chutney (page 272)

4 slices of the softest, whitest sandwich bread you can find (e.g., Wonder Bread)

1 medium Yukon Gold potato, boiled in salted water until tender and thinly sliced

1 small English cucumber, thinly sliced

1 hard-boiled egg, thinly sliced (optional)

1 medium cooked beet, thinly sliced (optional; see Note)

1 small Roma tomato, thinly sliced (optional)

Chaat masala (page 33), for sprinkling (optional)

½ cup shredded Cheddar cheese

Maggi ketchup, for serving (optional)

Spread both a thin layer of butter and a thin layer of chutney on both sides of each slice of bread. It can be a little tricky, but don't be afraid to get your fingers buttery—you can always lick them off later.

Layer each sandwich as follows: On the bottom piece of bread, place a potato layer, then cucumber, then egg (if using), then beet and tomato (if you're skipping the beets and/or tomato, finish with another layer of potatoes. Starting with the potato keeps the bread from becoming soggy when you toast it). As you layer, try to leave a little room around the edges of the bread, as you'll be pressing the sandwich and don't want the fillings to spill out. Sprinkle with a pinch of chaat masala, if you're so inclined. Top with the other slice of bread to form a sandwich.

If you own a panini press, this is a great time to bust it out. If you don't have a panini press, toast the sandwich in a nonstick skillet over medium-low heat, flipping once, until both sides are brown, about 2 minutes per side. After you flip the sandwich, place another pan on top of it (add some weight if the pan isn't very heavy) to help press the whole thing down. You're not trying to cook the filling here—if anything, the weird contrast between the hot exterior and the cool crunch of the fillings inside is part of what makes this dish so indescribably good.

Sprinkle a generous handful of shredded cheese over the sandwich as soon as it's toasted, then slice it into four squares. Serve warm, with Maggi ketchup on the side, if you'd like.

Note: ***Canned beets or the pre-cooked, vacuum-sealed ones you see in some groceries are perfect here—I recommend them over cooking one individual beet and slicing it up. If beets freak you out, just skip them.***

CRISPY MASALA FISH ROLL

Makes 4 rolls

This crispy masala fish roll, legendary at Chai Pani and Botiwalla for converting people who think they don't like fish, primarily uses ginger-garlic paste to nudge them toward the light. The paste forms a delicious crust on the fish—almost as if it was breaded, but without a grain of panko in sight. The combination of ginger-garlic paste and lime juice gives a nice tangy zing, which is rounded out with warm, fragrant notes from coriander, a pinch of heat from Kashmiri chilli, and beautiful color from turmeric.

This dish came about after a visit to a transcendental fish-fry shack in Hyderabad. The pre-fried fish was sitting out on the counter, and when we placed our order, it was tossed into a high-heat wok and flash-fried again until it was crispy AF. I loved how crunchy the fish was without the use of breading, and was determined to recreate the effect at home. This crispy fish technique can also be used with the Goan Fish Curry (page 194), or, if you want to swap the chicken for fish, with the Parsi Red Curry (page 191).

1 teaspoon coriander powder

1 teaspoon ground red chilli, such as Kashmiri (see page 18)

½ teaspoon turmeric powder

1 teaspoon kosher salt

2 tablespoons Ginger-Garlic Paste (page 276)

Juice of half a lime

2 tablespoons plus 1 cup neutral oil, such as grapeseed

1 pound flaky white fish fillets, such as tilapia, cod, or haddock, cut into strips about 1 inch wide (think fish fingers)

TO SERVE

4 store-bought naan (see page 84)

Unsalted butter, at room temperature

4 tablespoons Green Chutney (page 270)

Thinly sliced red onion

Maggi ketchup

Cilantro sprigs

In a large bowl, combine the coriander, ground chilli, turmeric, and salt. Stir in the ginger-garlic paste until well combined (it should be a vibrant red color), then stir in the lime juice and 2 tablespoons of the oil. Add the fish, turn it to coat, and let it sit in the marinade for at least 20 minutes and up to 1 hour.

Line a plate with paper towels and set it near the stove. In a large heavy-bottomed skillet, heat the remaining 1 cup oil over medium-high heat until shimmering. Working in batches to avoid overcrowding, arrange the fish strips in the oil (be careful not to splatter yourself with hot oil). Cook, turning once, until golden brown on both sides, 5 to 6 minutes. Transfer the fish to the prepared plate to absorb excess oil.

To serve, heat the naan in your toaster oven, on the griddle, or in a nonstick skillet. Swipe a thick pat of butter across the naan and assemble each roll in this order: chutney, fish, a sprinkling of onions, Maggi ketchup, and a few sprigs of cilantro. Wrap the naan up into a roll and, for the true street-style experience, wrap it tightly in waxed paper, like a gyro, before serving. Masala fish rolls are best eaten the day they're made.

Maggi
Hot & Sweet
TOMATO CHILI SAUCE

Why there's no fu-

Naan pisses me off.

Look: I know that naan is delicious. And much like pizza, even bad naan is good naan. But what drives me crazy is that automatic assumption that naan is some type of all-purpose, every-occasion "Indian food." Just like pizza is a regional specialty dish in Italy, naan is a region-specific flatbread that's rarely made at home.

Naan likely spread to India during the period between the 1200s and the 1500s via Islamists from Central Asia and Persia. Today, you're most likely to encounter fantastic naan in Punjab, Delhi, and Kashmir, many of whose residents are of Middle Eastern descent, and where wheat, conveniently, happens to flourish.

Even though naan in the United States is primarily associated with grilled and tandoori meats, it's used back home much like roti and chapati—as a general flatbread to mop up all kinds of dals, sauces, and gravies. Unlike rotis and chapatis, however, which are easy to make and don't require any type of baking skill, naan involves yeast, specific temperatures, ratios, and proportions. It would be more at home in a breadmaking book than a book about street food.

If you love you some naan—which, look, I get—there are some fantastic store-bought options for you. My preferred brand is Stonefire, which is widely available in the freezer section of grocery stores. To heat it up right at home, defrost it, get a cast-iron skillet blazing hot, and throw the naan in, bottom (flat) side down. After about 1 minute, flip it over and cook for another minute, and once it looks puffed, blistered, and charred, flip it back over and brush with melted ghee or butter. You're welcome.

-cking naan in here!
HONDA
REBEL

GOOD
MOOD

MASALA OMELET SANDO

Makes 2 sandwiches

Ubiquitous in Indian cafes, hotels, dorm rooms, bachelor pads, and street carts alike, the masala omelet is your everyday omelet graced with the magic of masala—in this case, a mixture of green chilli, turmeric, and coriander.

While the flavors are the same, this is not how the average masala omelet is made in India. Most people in India eat eggs, and Parsis, as I've mentioned elsewhere in this book, absolutely love them. The problem with the Indian approach to eggs is that we tend to cook the living daylights out of them. Runny eggs are simply not an option. Luckily, the Parsi side of me—in particular, the Anglicized Parsi side of me—appreciates soft-boiled, poached, and creamy-soft scrambled eggs, as well as their even sexier cousin, the French omelet. My masala omelet, I believe, combines the best of both worlds. With the heat and flavor of green chilli, the bite of onions, and copious amounts of butter, this gem of a breakfast pleases in a way no ordinary omelet can. Enjoy it as is or in sandwich form.

OMELET

3 large eggs

3 tablespoons salted butter

1 thinly sliced fresh Thai or serrano chilli (depending on your heat tolerance)

2 tablespoons finely diced red onion

Pinch of turmeric powder

½ teaspoon kosher salt

2 tablespoons coarsely chopped cilantro leaves

2 or 3 slices processed cheese, chopped (optional)

SANDWICH

Unsalted butter, at room temperature

4 slices of the softest, whitest sandwich bread you can find (e.g., Wonder Bread)

Maggi ketchup or regular ketchup, for serving

To make the omelet, whisk the eggs in a small bowl and set aside.

Heat a small nonstick skillet over medium-high heat. Once it's hot, add half of the butter. When the butter is sizzling, turn the heat down to medium-low and add the chillies and onions. Once the onions are brown and sizzling (after about 3 minutes), add the turmeric and salt to the pan and stir to combine. Stir in the rest of the butter and, when it melts, pour in the eggs. (I don't like to salt my eggs ahead of time, because it can cause water to separate out of the eggs and make them runnier, salting the ingredients in the pan rather than just the eggs.)

Temperature is key at this point: If the eggs sizzle immediately in the pan, turn the temperature down a little so that they cook a bit slower. This will scramble the eggs in the pan a bit and create soft curds, which is hard to do if the eggs are cooking too quickly.

As the eggs start to set, use a fork to draw the edges of the eggs out toward the edge of the pan. Lift the pan and tilt it so that the remaining uncooked egg streams out toward the edge of the pan, like you're making a crepe. Do this a few times over low heat, then turn the heat back up to medium and let the omelet finally set in the pan. While the surface is still a little soft-looking but not noticeably wet, sprinkle on the cilantro and cheese (if using) and fold the omelet in half. Turn the heat off completely and, after 30 seconds, slide the omelet onto a plate. If made correctly, the omelet will be set and light yellow in color, not browned.

You can eat the omelet as is, or make it into a sandwich like so: Cut the omelet in half and put one half on a well-buttered slice of bread. Top with another slice of buttered bread. Repeat with the other half omelet and slices of bread. Don't get fancy and try to toast the bread—in order to get the proper balance of egg to bread, everything should be very soft. It's very important that nothing comes between the egg and bread except butter: Cucumber slices, tomatoes, onions, and so on are strictly forbidden.

Serve with Maggi or regular ketchup. Masala omelets, plain or in sandwich form, are best eaten the day they're made.

BOTIWALLA LAMB BURGER

Makes 4 burgers

I really had a hard time with the idea of a hamburger when I first came to the United States. The ground meat part was familiar, but in India, ground meat is used to make kebabs (see page 175), which are seasoned with bright pops of ginger, garlic, masalas, and green chillies. So as I acclimated and slowly started mastering the American grill, I began to jazz up my burgers with some of the flavors I remembered from home.

My aha moment came when I was standing at Karim's in an alleyway in Old Delhi and realized that their melt-in-your-mouth seekh kebab, which is ethereally thin and cooked fast over high heat, would work perfectly as a burger patty. After a few experiments, I landed on this recipe, which is incredibly juicy and flavorful, and just thicker than a smashburger. I picked lamb specifically because its high fat content keeps the burger moist. Since they're thin, these patties cook quickly, and you want a nice sear on the outside without overcooking them, which is why having a hot pan is essential.

There's so much flavor packed into these burgers that you don't need lettuce and onions (though feel free to add them if you like)—just Maggi ketchup and mayo on a buttered bun are enough. This is often one of the first dishes a nervous customer tries at Botiwalla, and next thing you know they've turned into a hardcore Indian street food addict. It's also a gateway recipe for many at a backyard cookout—and far more satisfying than your average burger.

BURGERS

1 pound ground lamb, chilled

¼ cup finely diced red onion (from about half a medium onion)

¼ cup coarsely chopped cilantro leaves

1 finely chopped fresh Thai or serrano chilli (depending on your heat tolerance)

2 finely chopped garlic cloves

1 tablespoon peeled and finely chopped fresh ginger (about a 1-inch knob)

A few leaves of fresh mint, coarsely chopped

½ teaspoon Garam Masala (page 277, or use store-bought)

½ teaspoon ground red chilli, such as Kashmiri (see page 18)

½ teaspoon turmeric powder

½ teaspoon cumin powder

½ teaspoon coriander powder

Pinch of kosher salt

TO SERVE

4 pav, Hawaiian sweet rolls, or brioche hamburger buns

Unsalted butter, at room temperature

Maggi ketchup (or regular ketchup, if you must)

Lettuce (optional)

Thinly sliced red onions (optional)

Mayonnaise

To make the burgers, in a large bowl, combine all the ingredients and mix well with your hands to incorporate the aromatics and seasonings into the meat. Still using your hands, divide the mixture into four equal-size balls, each slightly larger than a clementine. Press into patties roughly 5 inches in diameter and ¼ inch thick.

Heat a large heavy-bottomed pan (cast iron is ideal) over high heat. Once the pan is hot, place the patties in—they should sizzle as soon as they hit the pan. (You may notice we're not adding any fat to the pan, because lamb is naturally fatty and you'll have plenty of grease coming off the burgers.) Cook for 2 to 3 minutes on each side, flipping once, until the bottom has a nice caramelized sear.

While the burgers cook, toast your pav, rolls, or buns. Ideally, you'll spread soft butter on the inside of the bun and toast it, butter side down, on another griddle or skillet, then flip it over and toast until you get a few brown spots on the top. Or you could take the easy way out and toast them in the toaster oven, but you'll be missing out on the perfect buttery-crispy-bun-to-soft-interior ratio. The choice is yours.

To assemble the burgers, put Maggi ketchup on the bottom bun, then lettuce (if using), then the patty, then onions (if using), and finally, a swipe of mayo on the top bun.

Lamb burgers are best made and eaten on the same day, though the uncooked lamb burger mixture can keep in the refrigerator for up to 3 days; just let it sit at room temperature for an hour or so before grilling to take the chill off.

FINGER SANDWICHES

My paternal grandmother, Viloo, was an Anglified Parsi to the core who loved having ladies over to play cards and drink tea. She almost always won, but to keep her victims in thrall so she could continue fleecing them, she served these delectable finger sandwiches, with milky Irani chai (page 266). These sandwiches were forbidden to me, as they were reserved strictly for her prey, but I always managed to sneak one or two out of her fridge.

These recipes seem borderline-ridiculously-simple, but it's not about the technique here—it's about the flavor combination of the chutneys with the butter or cheeses, and the soft, squishy white bread that holds it all together (there is no shame in using Wonder Bread here—in fact, it's preferred). Make one for yourself to have with a cup of tea or make 'em all as finger foods for a cocktail party, and you'll know why we had to include them in this book.

MINT CHUTNEY & CUCUMBER

Makes 2 sandwiches

In which we Indians took our first bite of a British-style cucumber-and-cream-cheese sandwich and said to ourselves, "You know what this needs? A little flavor." To get the cucumbers sliced thinly enough, a mandoline is ideal, but a regular knife works, too.

¼ cup cream cheese, at room temperature

3 tablespoons Mint Chutney (page 272)

4 slices of the softest, whitest sandwich bread you can find (e.g., Wonder Bread)

2 medium Persian or English seedless cucumbers, peeled (if desired) and sliced into very thin rounds

Freshly cracked black pepper

Pinch of sea salt

In a small bowl, mix the cream cheese and chutney together. Divide the mixture among the bread slices and spread it evenly to the edges of each slice. Cover two pieces of the bread completely with cucumber slices, overlapping each halfway with the next. Sprinkle a healthy crack of black pepper and a good dash of salt over the cucumber. Top with the other two chutney-and-cream-cheese-laden bread slices and press lightly so the sandwiches hold together. For a true Desi look, cut the crusts off. Cut the sandwiches diagonally in half and serve.

MINT CHUTNEY & BUTTER

Makes 2 sandwiches

You want the butter thick here—it's the marvelous combination of soft, creamy butter and sharp, minty chutney that makes this simple sandwich so magical.

4 slices of the softest, whitest sandwich bread you can find (e.g., Wonder Bread)

2 tablespoons salted butter, at room temperature

2 tablespoons Mint Chutney (page 272)

Generously spread one side of each of two slices of the bread with butter. Aim for a tablespoon per slice—you want a thick layer of butter.

Generously slather the chutney on one side of each of the other two slices of bread—again, going for about 1 tablespoon per slice.

Gently press one slice of buttered bread and one slice of chutney-ed bread together to form a sandwich. Trim the crusts off for true Desi elegance. Cut the sandwiches diagonally in half and serve. (Note that these sandwiches are also nice chilled in the fridge for a few hours before serving.)

SPICY TOMATO & CHEESE

Makes 4 sandwiches

This variation involves pre-toasting the bread to keep it from getting soggy and, unlike the other two, this sandwich is cut into strips, not triangles, before serving. The flavor combination here will be familiar to many Americans, though the mint chutney puts a twist in the pizza bagel vibe.

- 1 tablespoon salted butter, at room temperature
- 4 slices of the softest, whitest sandwich bread you can find (e.g., Wonder Bread)
- 1 tablespoon Mint Chutney (page 272)
- 1 or 2 firm medium Roma tomatoes
- 4 slices of white American cheese
- 1 to 2 Thai chillies or 2 to 3 serrano chillies (depending on your heat tolerance), thinly sliced
- Chaat masala (see page 33; optional)

Lightly butter all of the bread slices on one side. Toast them very lightly, butter side up, in a toaster oven or a hot skillet (if you're using a skillet, start butter side down and toast until both sides are lightly golden brown). Spread a thin layer of mint chutney on each slice of buttered toast.

Slice the tomatoes into rounds and cover each slice of toast with the rounds—a bit of overlap is okay. Lay a slice of cheese on top. Sprinkle the chilli slices on top of the cheese.

If you have a toaster oven, place the open-face sandwiches on the tray and toast until the cheese is bubbling and browned, 3 to 5 minutes. If you don't have a toaster oven, you can use a regular oven at 450°F.

Sprinkle with chaat masala (if using). Cut each bread slice into three strips, and serve hot.

MUMBAI-STYLE FRIED CHICKEN SANDO

Makes 4 sandos

I must give credit to my friend and fellow chef Asha Gomez for the basis of this recipe. She made probably the best fried chicken I'd ever had at our first (and still legendary) Brown In The South event, a rollicking collaborative dinner series I put together to help spotlight other Indian chefs who have made the American South their home. Asha served her spicy fried chicken with waffles and spiced honey; here, I've adapted it into sandwich form. Laced with fresh herbs and sprinkled with chaat masala and Kashmiri chilli powder, it's bursting with so much flavor and juiciness, I rarely feel the need for condiments beyond some sweet-and-sour pickles (though Maggi ketchup and mayo can both have a place here).

- 4 boneless, skinless chicken thighs (about 1½ pounds)
- 2 teaspoons ground red chilli, such as Kashmiri (see page 18)
- 1 cup buttermilk
- ½ cup coarsely chopped cilantro leaves
- ¼ cup coarsely chopped mint leaves
- 2 to 3 Thai chillies or 3 to 4 serrano chillies (depending on your heat tolerance), finely chopped
- 1 tablespoon plus 1 teaspoon kosher salt
- 1 teaspoon chaat masala (see page 33)
- 2 cups all-purpose flour
- 1 quart canola or other neutral oil, for frying
- Ghee or unsalted butter, for griddling
- 4 pav or Hawaiian sweet rolls
- Sweet-and-sour dill pickle rounds
- Maggi ketchup (optional)
- Mayonnaise (optional)

Rinse the chicken thighs and pat them dry. Use 1 teaspoon of the ground chilli to rub them, then place them in a large bowl. Set aside.

Combine the buttermilk, cilantro, mint, green chillies, and 1 tablespoon of the salt in a blender and puree until smooth. Pour the buttermilk mixture over the chicken and mix to coat the thighs well. Cover the bowl with plastic wrap and refrigerate for a minimum of 2 hours and up to 24 hours.

When you're ready to fry, mix the chaat masala and the remaining teaspoon of ground chilli together in a small bowl and set aside.

In a large bowl, stir together the flour and the remaining teaspoon of salt to combine.

Set a wire rack over a sheet pan to hold the chicken pieces once they're fried. (If you don't have a wire rack, line a plate with a few paper towels to help soak up the excess oil from the chicken.)

In a large heavy-bottomed pan that's big enough to hold a quart of oil (a large cast-iron skillet works well here), heat the oil over high heat until it reaches 350°F on an oil thermometer. Preheat the oven to 200°F.

Shake the excess buttermilk off each piece of chicken and dredge it in the flour mixture, coating it thoroughly and pressing the flour into the meat to ensure the ideal flour-to-chicken ratio.

Carefully lower each piece of chicken into the hot oil to avoid splattering. Don't crowd the pan—make sure there's 2 to 3 inches between each piece. (If you don't have a large enough pan to easily hold all the chicken at once, work in batches.) Once the chicken is in, don't touch it for 3 to 4 minutes.

Using tongs or a slotted spoon, carefully turn each piece and fry for another 3 to 4 minutes. The crust should be a deep golden brown and the internal temperature should reach 165°F.

Place the chicken on the wire rack and, while it's still hot and oily, sprinkle the chaat masala mixture liberally on all sides of it. Keep the chicken warm by placing the sheet pan in the oven for up to 30 minutes while you fry subsequent batches and/or prep the buns or anything else you are serving.

Just before serving, heat a small sauté pan over medium-high heat and melt a tablespoon or so of ghee or unsalted butter. Toast the pav, cut sides down, until golden-brown, about 2 minutes, adding more ghee or butter as needed to toast all the buns.

To assemble the sandwiches, place 3 to 4 pickle slices on the bottom bun, top with the chicken and the Maggi ketchup and/or mayonnaise (if using), and serve straight away, enjoying the spicy crunch!

KINGFISHER
PREMIUM
molina
PERFUMED PURE
POMADE
SAFETY MATCHES
Eagle

DESI PEEJA

Serves 2

What can I say? Indians love taking Western foods and making them our own (see also: the club sandwich), maybe because there's something inherently sexy about the foods' being Western. This is literally a shitty-sounding knockoff of pizza that has almost nothing in common with actual pizza except that it's round and has stuff on top. BUT. It's delicious! And it's so easy to make at home. If you're not sure where to start with cooking Indian food, this is about as simple as it gets.

The base is a store-bought paratha (check the freezer section of any South Asian grocer), so it's already better than pizza from the get-go. When I was a kid, peeja came topped with Maggi ketchup, grated processed cheese (i.e., white Velveeta), canned vegetables, and lots of chillies. My version still includes Maggi ketchup and shredded cheese (I've leveled up to Cheddar, though you can use Velveeta if you'd like), pickled jalapeños, frozen corn, bell peppers, and thinly sliced red onions. When it comes out of the oven all hot and bubbly, I sprinkle it with chaat masala. It's every college kid's 2 a.m. dream snack, stoned or not.

1 store-bought frozen paratha (or use naan; see page 84)
¼ cup Maggi ketchup
2 tablespoons sriracha
½ cup grated sharp white Cheddar cheese
½ green bell pepper, thinly sliced
¼ cup sweet corn kernels (thawed frozen is fine)
½ cup thinly sliced red onions
5 or 6 pickled jalapeño slices
Pinch of chaat masala (see page 33), to finish

Heat a nonstick or cast-iron pan over medium-low heat. Place the frozen paratha in the pan and toast for about 5 minutes, flipping frequently, until it's golden brown and crispy. Place on a sheet pan and set aside.

Turn on the broiler in your oven. (If you are actually in a dorm room right now, permission granted to use your toaster oven.)

In a small bowl, combine the Maggi ketchup and sriracha. Spread an even layer of this mixture onto the paratha, stopping about ½ inch from the edge.

Sprinkle half of the grated cheese on top and add the bell peppers, corn, onion, and pickled jalapeños in an even layer.

Sprinkle the other half of the grated cheese on top of everything and broil until the cheese is melted and starting to bubble, about 5 minutes.

Remove the peeja from the oven and sprinkle with chaat masala. Serve immediately. There won't be leftovers, but if there are, they will keep in the fridge, and can, naturally, be eaten cold the next morning (with an optional fried egg on top).

CAFES, CANTEENS & CHINESE FOOD

हिंदू हॉटेल
SINCE-1949
VIJAY HINDU HOTEL
प्रोप्रा. लक्ष्मणराव कुंडलिक
फरसाण
शेव, पापडी, चिवडा
अर्धा किलो /-
विजय हिंदू हॉटेल
भेळ
शेव, पापडी, चिवडा व मुरमुरे
अर्धा किलो /-
आमची नविन शाखा क्र.२
माणिकचंद कंपनी
पेट्रोलपंपाशेजारी नगर-
या नविन जागेत सुरु

This chapter is dedicated to three distinct but equally important subgenres of the greater Indian street food oeuvre: Irani cafe food; canteen and dhaba (truck stop) fare; and the world-beloved, infinitely adapted culinary juggernaut that is Chinese food—here, naturally, it's Desi-style Chinese. Shall we?

IRANI CAFES

Irani cafes aren't exactly street food purveyors in the strictest sense, given that they usually have seats, but they're not formal restaurants, either—they exist somewhere in the area between diner, coffee shop, and deli, with an important function as a casual central meeting point for Parsis and their pals. Irani cafes started popping up in Mumbai and nearby Pune in the late nineteenth and early twentieth centuries, courtesy of the Zoroastrian Irani immigrants who were fleeing persecution back home. They saw opening a little cafe (often with vaguely—or overtly—British-inspired décor) as their ticket to the Indian dream.

Most Irani cafes serve chai, along with sweet and savory snacks like dhansak (a hearty lentil and meat stew; see page 112) and farcha (an extra-eggy fried chicken—we Parsis freaking love our eggs—see page 107). In the 1960s, at their peak, there were something like 400 Irani cafes in Mumbai; today, that number has dwindled to about thirty, as the number of Parsis and Iranis in Mumbai has itself declined, and those who remain have moved on to more white-collar jobs. From among the few that remain, I've picked my favorite recipes for this chapter. Out of all the dishes in this book, these are the ones that are truest to my heritage, culture, and ancestry (just look at my name). What kind of Irani would I be if I didn't master and carry on the tradition that allowed my people to become a part of the fabric of India?

CANTEENS & DHABAS

The roadside truck stop, or dhaba, has a distinct mythology in India. Colorfully painted Tata trucks traverse the subcontinent from the high Himalayas in the north all the way down to the narrow tip of the southern peninsula and back, carrying everything from PVC piping to saffron. They make their way from the western coastal city of Mumbai up through the rapidly climbing mountain roads (ghats), traverse the arid Deccan Plateau, and wind back down to the coastal waters of Bengal in the east. And at every mile along the way (if not every quarter mile) is a dhaba.

Typically a tin shed with a few rope beds out front, a dhaba is a rest stop and refueling point. Often, dhabas also happen to serve some of the most delicious roadside food to be found in any country in the

world. I almost weep when I go into a gas station in America, thinking of the chole, chicken curry, and khichdi at rest stops back home. For many Indian truckers, these stops are the closest thing they have to home for months on end, and the food—hearty and comforting—helps them face the realities of life on the road.

Some dhabas and their cousins, canteens (essentially dhabas outside of truck stops), are beginning to offer dosas and their brethren, appam and uttapam. These pancake-like dishes have only recently become common as street foods. As a kid, I had to go to a South Indian resto to get a taste of the good stuff, but now, street vendors at little roadside cantinas as far north as Gujarat are making beautiful dosas on skillets fired by charcoal braziers. Fear not—most of these recipes use one mother batter that can be made in a blender and requires little or no proofing or shaping skills. But even if you're not in the market to master the art of Indian pancakes, there are plenty of cozy, soul-satisfying dishes to explore in this section.

DESI CHINESE

Desi Chinese food could be thought of as the Tex-Mex of India. If you paid attention in geography class, you may recall that India and China share a border that's thousands of miles long. As is too often the case when two cultures exist within shooting distance of each other, their people may not always get along, but their food almost always does.

So: Desi Chinese is the shotgun love child of two of the great and ancient cuisines of the world. Like many an orphan child, this cuisine has had to learn how to stand on its own and make its own way, and it has found a home among street vendors across India—showing the world that soy sauce, MSG, and sweet-and-sour chilli and vinegar work wonderfully with Indian flavors.

Many dhabas, canteens, and restaurants have at least a page or two of their menu devoted to delightfully (often indecipherably) named dishes like lung fung soup, American chop suey, and gobi manchurian, to name a few of my favorites. More people should get to know the delightful mash-up that is Indo-Chinese food. After one bite of gobi pepper fry or chilli paneer, you'll be planning next year's joint Diwali and Lunar New Year party.

FARCHA
(PARSI FRIED CHICKEN)

Serves 4 to 6

We don't really have a fried chicken culture in India, but the Parsis have a solid entry into the genre with this dish, farcha. Unlike crispy, crunchy American fried chicken, farcha uses an egg-based batter, which gives the meat a softer, more delicate—dare I even say lacy—outer layer. Eat this immediately after cooking it, or it will get a bit soggy. If for some reason you do have leftovers, use them to make a sandwich on plain white bread, with green chutney smeared across the whole thing.

MASALA PASTE

1 tablespoon toasted cumin seed
1 tablespoon turmeric powder
¼ cup loosely packed cilantro leaves
4 garlic cloves
One (2-inch) knob fresh ginger, peeled
1 to 2 Thai chillies or 2 to 3 serrano chillies (depending on your heat tolerance)
2 tablespoons freshly squeezed lime juice
Kosher salt
6 boneless, skinless chicken thighs
1 quart canola or other neutral oil, for frying
3 large eggs
1 cup all-purpose flour

TO SERVE

½ red onion, thinly sliced
1 teaspoon chaat masala (see page 33)
A few sprigs of cilantro, for garnish

To make the masala paste, in a food processor or blender, combine the cumin seeds, turmeric, cilantro, garlic, ginger, chillies, lime juice, and 1 teaspoon salt. Blend into a thick paste on high speed. If necessary, add a teaspoon or two of water to help the mixture blend smoothly, but don't let it get too runny.

Place the chicken thighs in a medium bowl, rub the masala paste onto them, coating each piece well, and marinate in the refrigerator for a minimum of 30 minutes and up to 4 hours. Set a wire rack over a sheet pan lined with paper towels to hold the chicken pieces once they are fried. If you don't have a wire rack, place a few paper towels on a plate to help soak up the excess oil from the chicken.

In a large heavy-bottomed pan that's big enough to hold a quart of oil (a large cast-iron skillet works well here), heat the oil over high until it reaches 350°F on an oil thermometer.

While the oil is heating, crack the eggs into a shallow bowl and beat until smooth, and place the flour in another shallow bowl or plate.

Dip each piece of chicken in the flour to coat on all sides; gently shake off any excess, then dip the chicken into the egg, coating it thoroughly on all sides and allowing any excess egg to drip off. Transfer the chicken to a clean plate.

Working in batches of two or three pieces at a time to avoid crowding, carefully add the chicken to the hot oil; gently spoon more oil over the top. Fry, flipping once, until each chicken thigh is golden and crisp and its internal temperature reaches 165°F, about 4 minutes per side. Remove the cooked chicken to the wire rack, and immediately sprinkle lightly with salt. (You can keep the chicken warm by placing the sheet pan in a 200°F oven while you cook the rest of the pieces, and for up to 30 minutes before serving.)

A few minutes before serving, combine the onions with the chaat masala in a small bowl, toss to coat, and set aside to let the flavors mingle. Serve the chicken hot with the chaat-macerated onions and garnished with cilantro sprigs. Any leftovers will keep, tightly covered in the refrigerator, for up to 5 days. See the headnote for an excellent suggestion for what to do with them.

THIS EATING HOUSE
PREMISES IS FIRE COMPLIANT
ISSION RESERVED
CUSTOMERS ARE REQUESTED TO
TAKE CARE OF THEIR BELONGINGS
PERSEPOLIS - IN - IRAN (YEAR 1930)
ONLY CASH

SORRY
NO TALKING TO CASHIER
NO SMOKING
NO FIGHTING
NO CREDIT
NO OUTSIDE FOOD
NO SITTING LONG
NO TALKING LOUD
NO SPITTING
NO BARGAINING
NO WATER TO OUTSIDERS
NO CHANGE
NO TELEPHONE
NO MATCH STICKS/LIGHTER
NO DISCUSSING GAMBLING
NO NEWSPAPER
NO COMBING HAIR
NO BEEF
NO LEG ON CHAIR
NO HARD LIQUOR ALLOWED
NO ADDRESS ENQUIRY
NO PHOTOGRAPHY
TOWN HALL - ASIATIC LIBRARY
KING EDWARD'S STATUE - KALA GHODA
zomato
top voted choice
IRANI CAFE
2015

AKURI

Serves 4 to 6

By this point, I've mentioned the Parsi love of eggs a few times, and this is another great example of a Parsi egg classic. Akuri is essentially spiced soft scrambled eggs, thematically similar to the masala omelet on page 87, but with the addition of tomatoes, which bring that sweet-sour flavor Parsis love.

Akuri wasn't served on the streets when I was growing up, but now it is, with dedicated egg wallas whipping up all kinds of egg dishes that would make even the most discerning Parsi proud. But street vendors usually cook their akuri too hot and fast; to do it right, make it at home, slowly and over very low heat.

The goal is to cook the eggs to a custard-like consistency. When the pan is too hot, egg proteins seize up and form spongy curds, which is how many folks think scrambled eggs are supposed to turn out. But I assure you: Once you try akuri and experience the velvety deliciousness of properly cooked soft scrambled eggs, you won't really be able to deal with a sad breakfast buffet again.

8 large eggs

2 tablespoons neutral oil, such as grapeseed

1 cup thinly sliced red onion (about 1 medium onion)

Kosher salt

Pinch of turmeric powder

1 to 2 Thai chillies or 2 to 3 serrano chillies, thinly sliced (depending on your heat tolerance)

1 cup coarsely chopped cilantro leaves and stems

½ cup coarsely chopped tomatoes, such as Roma

2 tablespoons unsalted butter, plus more to butter the bread

Pav, Hawaiian sweet rolls, or Chapati (page 212), for serving

In a large bowl, whisk the eggs well, getting a little bit of froth going. Set aside.

In a large nonstick pan over medium heat, heat the oil until shimmering. Add the onions and a pinch each of salt and turmeric and cook until the onions are soft and starting to brown at the edges, 5 to 7 minutes.

Add the green chillies, cilantro, tomatoes, and another pinch of salt and cook until the tomatoes have melted into the pan, their color has deepened a bit, and their water has evaporated, another 3 to 4 minutes.

Turn the heat down to low and give the pan a minute or two to cool a bit, then stir in the butter. When it has melted, pour in the eggs and sprinkle with another pinch of salt. (I don't like to put salt in my eggs ahead of time—it can cause water to separate out of the eggs and make them runnier, salting the ingredients in the pan rather than the eggs themselves.) Let the eggs spread out to the edges of the pan. If you hear the eggs sizzle, the pan is too hot—take it off the heat for a minute.

As soon as the eggs have filled the base of the pan, stir them gently with a rubber spatula, scraping the edges in toward the middle of the pan and letting the runny part flow out to the sides. Use the spatula to continuously stir the eggs, repeatedly folding the cooked part of the egg over the runny part. (If you have to take the pan off the heat to slow down the cooking, depending on the quirks of your stove, do so.)

Slowly and surely the eggs will start to firm up into a soft custard that's jiggly and moist looking but not runny. This process can take anywhere from 4 to 7 minutes depending on what kind of pan you're using and the heat level; it might feel like a lot longer than it should, but I promise, the texture of these eggs makes it worthwhile.

Serve the akuri with buttered soft bread: pav, Hawaiian rolls, or chapati.

KHEEMA PAV (AKA SLOPPY JAI)

Serves 4

Every culture has its own ground meat dish that's heavily spiced and tenderized and made into a hash, ragù, or sausage-type item; this helps make use of humbler cuts of meat. Kheema is the Parsi version, reconstructed from a sixteenth-century Persian recipe and gussied up with all the flavor-bomb goodness we know how to throw at you (which is a lot).

When I was coming up with the first menu at Chai Pani, I was looking for as many crossover dishes as I could find—things that I knew would appeal to an American palate. In Parsi houses and restaurants, kheema is traditionally served with chapati, roti, or pav on the side. Inspired by this tradition, and by the iconic sloppy Joe, I decided to pile lamb kheema directly onto a bun and slather it with chutney, and voilà—the sloppy Jai was born.

In order for the filling to not be a soggy mess that makes the bun fall apart, I use yogurt liberally to thicken and bind the filling mixture. Sloppy Jai has become one of our signature dishes, and I consider it the gateway dish for anyone on the fence about Indian street food.

2 tablespoons neutral oil, such as grapeseed

1 tablespoon cumin seed

2 cups diced red onion (about 2 medium onions)

1 tablespoon peeled and finely chopped fresh ginger (about a 1-inch knob)

2 finely chopped fresh Thai or serrano chillies (depending on your heat tolerance)

2 tablespoons Ginger-Garlic Paste (page 276)

Kosher salt

2 teaspoons coriander powder

2 teaspoons cumin powder

1 teaspoon turmeric powder

1 teaspoon ground red chilli, such as Kashmiri (see page 18)

¼ cup coarsely chopped cilantro

1 pound ground lamb

½ cup full-fat plain yogurt

1 (14½-ounce) can crushed tomatoes

1 teaspoon sugar

1 teaspoon distilled white vinegar

1 teaspoon Garam Masala (page 277, or use store-bought)

TO ASSEMBLE

Unsalted butter, at room temperature

4 pav or Hawaiian sweet rolls

4 teaspoons Sweet Yogurt Sauce (page 273)

4 teaspoons Green Chutney (page 270)

Chopped cilantro, for garnish

Diced red onion, for garnish

In a large sauté pan over medium heat, heat the oil until it shimmers. Add the cumin and let the seeds sizzle in the oil for a few seconds until aromatic, then add the diced red onion. Cook for 2 to 3 minutes, stirring frequently, then add the ginger, green chilli, ginger-garlic paste, and a healthy pinch of kosher salt.

Now, cooking the onions as described in this paragraph really matters. This step takes time and patience, and it may require finessing the heat level. Stir the onions into the oil frequently but not constantly, keeping them in an even layer. Make sure they're sizzling but not scorching, melting into each other, and not frying. As the water cooks out of the onions, they will eventually start to resemble a marmalade with a rich bourbon color. This is good! The goal is to get the onions so jammy and reduced that they almost become one with the sauce (as opposed to being an ingredient in the sauce). Keep an eye on the heat; if the onions are starting to crisp on the edges, turn the heat down and add a teaspoon or two of water to stop the frying. This slow, careful reduction is an important Indian cooking technique that shows up across multiple recipes in this book.

After about 10 minutes, when the onions reach the state described above, stir in the coriander, cumin, turmeric, ground red chilli, and coarsely chopped cilantro, and add 1 tablespoon of water to deglaze the pan and help the spices incorporate into the onion mixture. Cook for about 1 minute more.

Add the ground lamb and break it up with your spatula. Cook, stirring frequently, until it's golden brown and fully cooked, 5 to 7 minutes. Stir in the yogurt and continue cooking for about 5 minutes, until the lamb is glossy.

Add the crushed tomato, sugar, vinegar, garam masala, and another pinch of salt. Turn the heat down to medium low and cook for about 10 minutes, stirring frequently, until the tomatoes are cooked down and there's a sheen of oil on the surface of the lamb mixture. You're looking for the mixture to be somewhat loose but not so soupy that it can't sit comfortably on a bun. Taste for seasoning and add salt if needed.

To assemble, spread butter on both cut sides of the pav or Hawaiian roll and toast it, butter side down, on a nonstick skillet over medium-high heat (you can also use a toaster oven if you don't want to get another pan dirty). Pile the sloppy Jai mixture high on the bottom bun, drizzle with sweet yogurt sauce and green chutney, and garnish with chopped cilantro and diced red onions. Top with the other half of the pav or Hawaiian roll and serve immediately. Leftover sloppy Jai keeps, covered in the refrigerator, for up to 5 days. Reheat gently in a pan over medium-low heat, stirring in a teaspoon or two of water to loosen the mixture up if necessary.

WITHOUT JOINT

SALLI CHICKEN

Serves 4 to 6

Many Parsi dishes are considered modern-day classics in India, and salli chicken is absolutely up there on the wall of fame as an iconic Parsi dish beloved throughout the country. Salli *is the Persian word for "potato," which is, I would say, probably the second-biggest block (after eggs) of the Parsi food pyramid. (Eggs and potatoes together is its own megalith, but we'll get to that later.) Here, the word specifically refers to the matchstick potatoes this chicken dish is served with; you should be able to find these in the snack aisle of any American grocery store, though crushed-up plain potato chips are a fine alternative. (Parsis have been sprinkling potato chips on top of things for forever.)*

I love having this recipe in this book, because it's one of the few dishes that's done in a style that predates the colonial exchange that brought tomatoes to India. The gravy is made entirely of onions and spices, which is how all gravies worked before tomatoes arrived via the Portuguese. Goat is the traditional protein, but as chicken became popularized in India, it has slowly replaced goat as the meat of choice in this recipe. Feel free to use any bone-in dark meat here (drumsticks, wings, etc.). If the addition of salli seems odd, think of it as a saucier version of steak frites . . . with chicken.

1½ tablespoons neutral oil, such as grapeseed
1 medium red onion, thinly sliced
1 teaspoon cumin seed
1 cinnamon stick, broken into 2 or 3 pieces
6 cloves
½ teaspoon whole black peppercorns
4 green cardamom pods
1½ teaspoons kosher salt
1 tablespoon Ginger-Garlic Paste (page 276)
2 finely chopped fresh Thai or serrano chillies (depending on your heat tolerance)
1 or 2 whole dried red chillies (see page 18)
1 pound bone-in, skin-on chicken thighs
2 cups hot water

TO SERVE
Cilantro
Thinly sliced red onions
Store-bought potato sticks
Chapati (page 212)

In a large heavy-bottomed skillet over high heat, heat the oil until shimmering. Add the onion, cumin seeds, cinnamon stick, cloves, peppercorns, cardamom pods, and ½ teaspoon of the salt. Turn the heat down to medium-high and sauté, stirring occasionally, until the onions are beginning to soften, 2 to 3 minutes. Stir in the ginger-garlic paste, fresh chillies, and dried chillies and sauté for another minute or so.

Continue stirring the onions frequently (but not constantly) into the oil, keeping them in an even layer. Make sure they're sizzling but not scorching, melting into each other, and not frying. As the water cooks out of the onions, they will eventually start to resemble a marmalade with a rich bourbon color. This is good! The goal is to get the onions so jammy and reduced that they almost become one with the sauce (as opposed to being an ingredient in the sauce). Keep an eye on the heat; if the onions are starting to crisp on the edges, turn the heat down and add a teaspoon or two of water to stop the frying. After about 10 minutes, when the onions reach the state described above, add the chicken and the remaining teaspoon of salt and really stir it around so the spices and onions get all over the chicken. Cook the chicken, flipping it as necessary, until it's browned on all sides, 5 to 7 minutes.

Add the hot water to the pan and bring to a boil, then turn the heat down to a low simmer and cover the pan. Cook, stirring occasionally, until the meat starts to separate from the bone when you poke at it, 30 to 40 minutes. At this point, you should have a gravy-esque sauce made primarily of onions: It should be a rich brown, with a thick consistency (similar to beef bourguignon or coq au vin) that you can mop up with a chapati. Transfer the chicken and sauce to a serving platter. (If the sauce seems too thin, remove the chicken to the serving platter and bring the sauce to a boil over medium-high heat. Reduce the sauce until it reaches that gravy-like consistency, then pour it over the chicken.)

Garnish with the cilantro, red onions, and potato sticks, and serve hot with chapati. Any leftovers will keep, tightly covered in the refrigerator, for up to 4 days.

DHANSAK

Serves 4 to 6

Dhansak is a hearty Parsi stew that combines not one, not two, but three different kinds of lentils, a whole bunch of vegetables, and a bit of meat (traditionally goat, though I like chicken), slowly cooked together into a perfect one-pot meal.

This particular recipe is my mom's adaptation—a lighter version of the original. Traditional recipes call for heavier lentils like brown masoor, but Mom prefers a mix of toor dal (split yellow lentils), masoor dal (split pink lentils), and yellow mung dal. (If you can only find one or two out of the three, it's okay; just use what you have.) She's also reduced the amount of spices to make the dish lighter on the palate and to allow the vegetal nature of, well, the vegetables, come through more clearly.

Dhansak is traditionally served with caramelized basmati rice (i.e., rice cooked with a bit of brown sugar) and Kachumber (page 115), but you can eat it with plain basmati rice (see page 276) or mop it up with a chapati or even a slice of white bread. You can easily omit the chicken to make this a vegetarian entrée as well.

3 cups mixed lentils, such as toor dal, masoor dal, and yellow mung dal

MASALA

1 teaspoon coriander seed

½ teaspoon cumin seed

6 cloves

1 teaspoon whole black peppercorns

1 cinnamon stick, broken into 2 or 3 pieces

2 black cardamom pods

3 whole dried red chillies, such as Kashmiri (see page 18)

1 pound boneless, skinless chicken thighs, cut into 2-inch pieces

Pinch of turmeric powder

Pinch of ground red chilli, such as Kashmiri (see page 18)

Kosher salt

2 tablespoons neutral oil, such as grapeseed

2 teaspoons Ginger-Garlic Paste (page 276)

1 tablespoon tamarind paste (see page 19)

1 tablespoon powdered jaggery (see page 20) or dark brown sugar

½ teaspoon turmeric powder

1 cup chopped eggplant (any variety will work)

1 cup chopped peeled pumpkin or winter squash

2 cups chopped spinach

2 medium Roma tomatoes, chopped

1 small red onion, chopped

1 finely chopped fresh Thai or serrano chilli (depending on your heat tolerance)

5 cups hot water, plus more as needed

Rice or bread, for serving

Put the lentils in a large heavy-bottomed pot or fine-mesh strainer. Rinse them three or four times with cold water, until the water runs clear, stirring them lightly with your hand while rinsing, then draining the water completely. Cover the dal with 2 to 3 inches of water and soak at room temperature for at least 15 minutes (and ideally 30 minutes).

To make the masala, in a dry skillet over medium heat, toast the coriander, cumin, cloves, peppercorns, cinnamon, cardamom, and dried red chillies until fragrant, about 2 minutes. Let the toasted spices cool and then grind them to a coarse powder in your dedicated coffee or spice grinder (see page 35).

Place the chicken pieces in a large bowl and sprinkle with a pinch each of turmeric, ground red chilli, and salt, and set aside.

In a large heavy-bottomed pot or Dutch oven, heat the oil over medium heat until shimmering. Add the ginger-garlic paste, and stir and scrape until it starts to brown, 30 to 60 seconds. Add the tamarind paste, all but ½ teaspoon of the masala, the jaggery, the turmeric, and 1 teaspoon salt, and stir to combine.

Add the eggplant, pumpkin, spinach, tomatoes, onion, and green chilli and stir for 1 minute to coat the vegetables evenly with the masala. Add 4 cups of the hot water, then drain the dal and add it to the pot as well.

Stir well and bring the mixture to a boil over medium-high heat. Reduce the heat and simmer, uncovered, for 30 to 45 minutes, depending on the mix of lentils you're using. You'll know it's ready when the lentils start breaking down and the vegetables mash easily when pressed with a spoon. You should have a thick, soupy mixture, with some lentils broken down and some still holding their shape—it should resemble oatmeal.

And now: Puree this sucker. My mom didn't have a blender, so she just mashed it through a colander, but today, we are graced with immersion blenders, which are perfect for this. (If you don't have one, work in batches in your countertop blender.) Roughly puree until the vegetables are mostly incorporated but the mixture isn't homogenous. The dhansak should still have some texture.

Stir in the remaining 1 cup hot water and add the chicken pieces. Cover partially and cook over medium-low heat, stirring occasionally, until the chicken is cooked through and falling apart, 20 to 25 minutes. (It's important to cook over low heat here because we don't want the lentils to dry out or overcook.) If necessary, add ¼ cup of hot water at a time to maintain the stew's consistency while the chicken cooks. Err on the side of too loose rather than too thick.

Taste for seasoning, adding more salt if needed. Stir in the remaining ½ teaspoon masala and serve hot with rice or bread. Leftover dhansak keeps in the refrigerator, tightly covered, for up to 4 days.

KACHUMBER

Serves 4

Kachumber is a fresh, light dish that blurs the line between a Parsi-style salad and salsa fresca. By itself, the flavors aren't groundbreaking, but when paired with heartier, spicier dishes like the Shrimp Patia on page 197 or the Dhansak on page 112 (plus all manners of dals and curries), it provides a very welcome dose of fresh, cooling, crunchy flavor. It's similar to Persian shirazi salad, but with the Parsi twist of swapping parsley for cilantro.

I like to use Persian cucumbers because they stay firm and are less watery. Although the name of the salad refers to the act of chopping things into little pieces (the bad guy in a Hindi movie might say, "I'll make a kachumber out of you!"), don't slice the vegetables so finely that they disintegrate. Keep all of the veggies about the same size, and dress the salad just before serving.

3 small Persian cucumbers or 1 small English seedless cucumber

2 medium Roma tomatoes

½ medium red onion

¾ cup loosely packed, coarsely chopped cilantro leaves

1 to 2 finely chopped fresh Thai or serrano chillies (depending on your heat tolerance)

Kosher salt

Juice of ½ lime

Halve the cucumbers lengthwise, then slice the halves into 3 or 4 strips (depending on the cucumbers' width), and slice into quarter-moon pieces about ¼ inch thick. You should have about 1½ cups of cucumber slices.

Slice the tomatoes in half lengthwise and use a spoon to scoop out the seeds and fleshy part of the tomatoes; discard these. Chop the tomatoes into pieces about the same size as the cucumbers. You should have about ¾ cup of chopped tomatoes.

Chop the onion into pieces roughly the same size as the cucumber and tomato. You should have about ½ cup of chopped onion.

In a medium bowl, combine the cucumbers, tomatoes, onion, cilantro, and chilli and mix together. Hold in the refrigerator until ready to serve.

To serve, mix in a generous pinch of salt and the lime juice. Serve chilled or at room temperature the same day you make it.

ANYTHING PUFFS

Makes 8 puffs

The British and French brought puff pastry to India, and Parsis in particular created a variety of "puffs" stuffed with whatever was on hand, often kheema (ground spicy lamb hash), paneer, and/or caramelized onions. Indian puffs are jazzed up with cashews, currants, mint, cilantro, and a touch of chilli heat, and are at their best when served with Maggi ketchup.

- 2 tablespoons extra-virgin olive oil
- 2 tablespoons unsalted butter
- 1 small yellow onion, thinly sliced
- ½ teaspoon kosher salt
- 2 cups Paneer (page 274, or use store-bought), crumbled
- ½ cup coarsely chopped cashews
- ¼ cup currants or raisins
- 3 mint leaves, finely chopped
- ¼ cup finely chopped cilantro

TADKA

- 3 tablespoons vegetable oil
- ¼ teaspoon turmeric powder
- ¼ teaspoon ground red chilli, such as Kashmiri (see page 18)
- ½ teaspoon ajwain or caraway seed
- 3 or 4 curry leaves (optional)

- All-purpose flour, for dusting
- 2 sheets frozen puff pastry (such as Dufour), thawed
- Maggi ketchup, for serving

First, caramelize the onion. Don't rush the process! This is where the flavor comes from. In a large pan over medium-high heat, heat the olive oil until it shimmers. Add the butter and the sliced onion. Stir to coat the onion slices with butter and oil, then spread them evenly across the pan. Turn the heat down to medium and cook, stirring frequently, until the onion slices begin to soften, about 10 minutes.

Add the salt, then stir and spread the onions evenly across the pan again. Cook, stirring occasionally and scraping the bottom of the pan, until the onions are a deep golden brown, another 15 to 20 minutes. If the onions start to stick to the bottom of the pan, add a couple of teaspoons of water. Once the onions are a burnished brown and taste good enough to eat on their own, remove the pan from the heat and set aside to cool.

To make the filling, in a medium bowl, combine the paneer, cashews, currants, mint, cilantro, and cooled caramelized onions. Set aside.

To make the tadka, in a small saucepan over medium-high heat, heat the vegetable oil until it shimmers. Add the turmeric, ground red chilli, ajwain seeds, and curry leaves (if using) and stir together. Sizzle for 30 seconds, stirring constantly, until the spices are heady and aromatic, then remove the pan from the heat and pour the tadka over the paneer mixture. Stir to combine and allow to cool slightly.

Preheat the oven to 400°F.

Dust a clean work surface or a sheet of parchment paper with a little bit of flour, then unroll one of the puff pastry sheets. Cut the sheet into roughly 4-by-5-inch rectangles (they don't have to be perfectly measured, as you'll be folding them over to make triangles anyway). Repeat with the remaining puff pastry—you should have 8 rectangles.

Line a sheet pan with parchment paper. To fill the pastries, add 2 tablespoons of paneer filling to the center of each puff pastry rectangle. Fold one corner to meet the opposite corner of the rectangle to form a triangle. Press the edges together and use a fork to pinch them closed, or add your own decorative twist. Set onto the lined sheet pan and repeat with the remaining pastry rectangles.

Bake until the pastry triangles have fully puffed and are golden brown and crispy, about 20 minutes. Serve hot or at room temperature, with Maggi ketchup. Leftover puffs keep in the refrigerator, tightly covered, for up to 5 days. Reheat them in the toaster oven or regular oven to resurrect their golden crispiness.

Hot &
Sweet
TOMATO CHILI SAUCE

PARSI SAMOSAS

Makes 12 samosas

Hands down, my favorite nostalgic dish (that only my mom can make perfectly) are these Parsi-style kheema samosas. The major differences between this style of samosa and other meat samosas are the heavy use of mint in the lamb mix, the lack of any other spices beyond the aromatics present in garam masala, and the thin, crispy patti (strip) it's wrapped in. And unlike the big, bulging samosas many Americans are familiar with, these samosas are folded into neat, skinny little triangles.

When my mother cooks these, she insists on making her own wrappers before carefully folding and frying each batch. I love these samosas but not enough to put all that work in, so I recommend using store-bought wonton wrappers (ideally square ones, though round will work, too; you'll just have more of a half-moon-shaped samosa than a triangle).

This kheema filling can also be used in the Anything Puffs on page 116. Note that the filling can be made up to two days ahead and refrigerated—the filling is easier to work with when cold, so I recommend making it a day in advance if you can. Serve these with Maggi ketchup, or the Green Chutney or Tamarind Chutney on pages 270 and 271, respectively.

FILLING

1 tablespoon neutral oil, such as grapeseed

2 medium white onions, finely chopped

¼ cup Ginger-Garlic Paste (page 276)

½ pound Roma tomatoes, finely diced

1 pound ground lamb

2 teaspoons kosher salt

2 to 3 fresh Thai or serrano chillies (depending on your heat tolerance), finely chopped

½ cup finely chopped fresh mint

½ cup finely chopped cilantro leaves and stems

1 tablespoon Garam Masala (page 277, or use store-bought)

12 (3-inch) wonton wrappers

2 to 3 cups canola or other neutral oil, for frying

Maggi ketchup, for serving (optional)

Green Chutney (page 270), for serving (optional)

Tamarind Chutney (page 271), for serving (optional)

To make the filling, in a large nonstick skillet over medium-high heat, heat the oil until shimmering. Add the onions and cook, stirring frequently, until translucent and very lightly browned around the edges, 5 to 7 minutes. Add the ginger-garlic paste and fry until the mixture is lightly brown at the edges, about 3 minutes.

Add the tomatoes and cook until most of the water has evaporated from the tomatoes, 6 to 8 minutes. Add the lamb and salt and cook, breaking up the meat with your spatula, until the meat is browned and somewhat dry, 5 to 7 minutes.

Turn the heat down to medium-low and add the chillies, mint, cilantro, and garam masala. Stir to wilt the herbs and incorporate all the flavors, about 2 minutes. Transfer to a bowl and allow to cool to room temperature.

Trim your wrappers so they're no more than 3 inches across. If you can only find larger 5- to 6-inch egg-roll-sized wrappers, cut them in half on the diagonal to get two triangular samosas out of one wrapper.

Place 1 to 1½ tablespoons of cooled filling onto the bottom half of a wrapper. Moisten the edges of the wrapper with a bit of room-temperature water. Fold over and press firmly, ensuring the edges are completely sealed. If you're using squares, fold diagonally into a triangle shape; if you're using circles, fold in half. Repeat with the remaining wrappers until all the filling is used.

To fry the samosas, in a large heavy pot, heat the oil over high heat until it reaches 325°F. (If you're doubling the recipe for a large batch, preheat the oven to 200°F to keep the finished samosas warm.) Set a wire rack over a sheet pan to drain the samosas as they come out of the cooking oil, or use a plate lined with paper towels.

Working in batches so the samosas aren't crowded, carefully slide the samosas one by one into the hot oil. Fry the samosas until they're uniformly golden brown, 3 to 5 minutes; turn with a slotted spoon every minute or so to cook them evenly.

Remove the samosas from the oil with metal tongs or a slotted spoon and place them on the wire rack or lined plate. Bring the oil back up to 325°F between batches to ensure all the samosas are cooked evenly.

Serve hot with your choice of Maggi ketchup and/or green or tamarind chutneys (if using). Freeze unfried samosas in a single layer on a sheet pan, then transfer them to a freezer bag for up to 3 months. Fry directly from frozen, adding 1 to 2 minutes to the frying time.

CHOLE, PUNJABI STYLE

Serves 4 to 6

I didn't grow up eating chole—a richly spiced chickpea stew—since chickpeas are more of a North Indian thing, and not so prominent in Maharashtra, where I'm from. If you're Punjabi, chole would be a meal unto itself, served with roti or kulcha (a soft leavened flatbread similar to naan). But chole has made its way into the chaat lexicon in Mumbai and elsewhere, where it's become an accompaniment to chaat dishes such as aloo tikki chaat and samosa tikki.

Why? I'm not entirely sure, but I can confirm that chole has gone from being a side act to a highly requested solo star at my restaurants. And it's actually no wonder: This is a complex dish in terms of flavors, and one of the rare instances where using more spices is actually better. The sweetness of the tomatoes, the tang of the chole masala, the earthy nuttiness of the chickpeas—they all come together beautifully in a dish that can be easily mopped up with perfectly cooked basmati rice (or your carb of choice). It's nice to make your own chole masala so you have control over the spice levels, but you can also buy premade versions at many Indian groceries (if you do, ignore the first section of the ingredient list and the first step of the instructions).

CHOLE MASALA

1 tablespoon coriander seed

1 teaspoon cumin seed

1 teaspoon fennel seed

1 teaspoon whole black peppercorns

One (2-inch) cinnamon stick

1 black cardamom pod

4 cloves

2 dried red chillies, such as Kashmiri (see page 18)

1 teaspoon amchoor (optional; see Note)

CHOLE

6 cups fully cooked chickpeas (about four 15-ounce cans)

1 tea bag black tea (make sure the tea bag is sturdy)

¼ cup canola oil

1 teaspoon cumin seed

¼ teaspoon hing (optional)

2 cups diced red onion (about 2 medium onions)

1 tablespoon plus 1½ teaspoons kosher salt, plus more for seasoning

2 tablespoons Ginger-Garlic Paste (page 276)

2 teaspoons turmeric powder

½ cup canned crushed tomatoes

1 tablespoon plus 1½ teaspoons coriander powder

2 teaspoons cumin powder

1 cup hot water, plus more as needed

1 tablespoon plus 1½ teaspoons chole masala (homemade or store-bought)

1 teaspoon Garam Masala (page 277, or use store-bought)

Thinly sliced red onion, for serving

Lime wedges, for serving

Perfect Basmati Rice (page 276), for serving

To make the chole masala, heat a small skillet over medium heat and dry-toast all of the spices except for the amchoor until fragrant, 1 to 2 minutes. Let cool slightly, then pulse in a coffee grinder dedicated to spices (see page 35). Add the amchoor (if using) and mix well. Store in an airtight container; it keeps well for several weeks.

To make the chole, drain the chickpeas and rinse them well to remove excess starch and skins. In a small pot, bring 4 cups of water to a boil, turn off the heat, and steep the tea bag for 3 to 4 minutes. Remove the tea bag and set aside this tea-water.

In a large heavy-bottomed pot over high heat, heat the canola oil until shimmering. Add the cumin seeds and let them sputter for 30 seconds. Add the hing (if using), diced onions, and 1½ teaspoons of the salt and stir well to combine.

Continued

SRIKARUPPUSAMYTHUNAI
D.THIRUKUMARAN
வாழ்க
D.தர்ஷிகா
வளமுடன்
N
P
TN.28
BA7322

CHOLE, PUNJABI STYLE

Continued

Cooking the onions properly takes time, attention, and patience. Stir the onions into the oil frequently but not constantly, keeping them in an even layer. Make sure they're sizzling but not scorching, melting into each other, and not frying. As the water cooks out of the onions, they will eventually start to resemble a marmalade with a rich bourbon color. This is good! The goal is to get the onions so jammy and reduced that they almost become one with the sauce (as opposed to being an ingredient in the sauce). Keep an eye on the heat; if the onions are starting to crisp on the edges, turn the heat down and add a teaspoon or two of water to stop the frying.

When the jammy/marmalade-y state is reached, add the ginger-garlic paste and mix in well. Cook for 1 to 2 minutes, stirring often. Stir in the turmeric and cook for 1 minute, stirring continuously.

Add the crushed tomato, coriander powder, cumin powder, the remaining 1 tablespoon salt, and the hot water. Stir well to combine, raise the heat to medium-high, and bring to a boil.

Once the mixture is boiling, lower the heat to medium, cover, and cook, stirring occasionally, 7 to 10 minutes, until the tomatoes are glossy and have deepened in color from bright orange-red to a darker red, and the oil starts to separate from the edges.

Add the chickpeas, chole masala, and reserved tea-water. Bring back to a boil, stirring occasionally. Once the liquid is boiling, lower the heat to medium and simmer, uncovered, for 5 to 10 minutes, stirring occasionally, until the liquid is reduced by a quarter of its volume, thickening the chole slightly. Don't let it get too thick—you want the consistency of a chunky soup. The mixture will continue to thicken as it cools, but if you think you've overdone it, thin it out by adding hot water ¼ cup at a time. Stir in the garam masala and taste for seasoning.

Serve with thinly sliced onions and a wedge or two of fresh lime, over basmati rice. Leftover chole keeps, tightly covered in the refrigerator, for up to 5 days.

Note: *Amchoor, or dried green mango powder, adds tanginess and acidity to this and many other Indian dishes. If you don't have it to add to your chole masala, be sure to finish the chole with an extra squeeze of fresh lime instead.*

Amul
PASTEURISED
BUTTER
PULL
Amul
BUTTER
PASTEURISED
500 g

PAV BHAJI

Serves 4 to 6

Cooked in butter and zinging with masala, this dish is arguably one of Mumbai's greatest street food inventions. And, through a series of culinary and cultural dominos falling, one of the most iconic street dishes of Mumbai can trace its origins back to . . . Abraham Lincoln?

Let's back up. During the American Civil War, as cotton production in the South screeched to a halt, demand for Indian cotton skyrocketed. Factory workers in Mumbai labored around the clock, and after the tiffin wallas stopped delivering their prepacked meals for the day, street vendors stepped in to feed the hungry workers throughout the night.

Those enterprising vendors needed something hearty and affordable to offer, hence the invention of bhaji, or hash, which is made from potatoes, bell peppers, onions, tomatoes, spices, and lots and lots of butter, all smashed together on a giant griddle, or tawa. Since there was no way for these hawkers to also make fresh roti on the spot, they started buying pav (the Portuguese word for "bread") from the Franciscan monks who had bakeries nearby and were often working in the wee hours, too.

As with any beloved dish, there are countless variations of pav bhaji, a lot of them depending on the vegetables and bread you have on hand (for example, I have successfully used hot dog buns in lieu of Hawaiian rolls). Feel free to play around with the exact mix of vegetables and spices, but no matter what, do not *skimp on the amount of butter—this dish is intended to be completely decadent.*

Kosher salt

4 cups diced Yukon Gold potatoes (about 4 large potatoes)

1 cup diced carrots (about 2 large carrots)

4 cups coarsely chopped cauliflower (about 1 medium head of cauliflower)

12 tablespoons (1½ sticks) unsalted butter, plus 2 tablespoons for serving

1½ cups diced red onion (about 1 large onion)

1 heaping teaspoon fennel seed

¾ cup diced green bell pepper (about 1 large pepper)

2 tablespoons Ginger-Garlic Paste (page 276)

1 Thai chilli or 2 serrano chillies (depending on your heat tolerance), finely chopped

1 tablespoon coarsely chopped cilantro stems (optional)

1 teaspoon ground red chilli, such as Kashmiri (see page 18)

1 teaspoon cumin powder

1 teaspoon coriander powder

½ teaspoon turmeric powder

1½ cups canned crushed tomatoes or 2 medium Roma tomatoes, diced

Juice of 1 lime

1 teaspoon chaat masala (see page 33)

4 to 6 pav or Hawaiian sweet rolls, for serving

1 tablespoon coarsely chopped cilantro leaves, for garnish (optional)

Fill a large pot with water and bring to a boil over high heat. Add 1 tablespoon salt, along with the potatoes, carrots, and cauliflower and cook until the vegetables are soft, about 20 minutes. Drain the water and use a potato masher to mash the vegetables into a thick paste. Set aside.

In a large sauté pan over medium-high heat, melt 8 tablespoons (1 stick) of the butter. Add the onions and a pinch of salt, and cook until the onions are soft and lightly golden, 7 to 10 minutes.

Add the fennel seeds and bell pepper, stirring to incorporate, and cook until the pepper begins to soften, about 5 minutes. Add the ginger-garlic paste and a pinch more salt. Sauté for another 5 to 10 minutes, stirring often, until everything is golden and caramelized.

Add the green chilli and the cilantro stems and continue to sauté, stirring often, until browned, another 5 minutes. Add the ground red chilli, cumin, coriander, and turmeric, stirring to combine.

Add the tomatoes and cook, stirring occasionally, until the tomatoes are glossy and the oil starts to separate from the edges of the pan, about 10 minutes.

Add the reserved vegetable mash and the lime juice and mix everything together, then add the chaat masala and stir to incorporate. Add 4 tablespoons (½ stick) of butter, stirring until it has melted and is fully incorporated. Taste, and adjust the salt as needed.

Just before you're ready to serve, heat a small sauté pan over medium-high heat and add the last 2 tablespoons butter. When it's melted, toast your pav cut side down in the buttered pan until golden brown, about 2 minutes.

Assemble the bhaji on the toasted pav, garnish each with a pinch of cilantro if you like, and serve. Leftover bhaji keeps, tightly covered in the refrigerator, for up to 4 days.

RICE & MOONG KHICHADI

Serves 4 to 6

Khichadi is at once one of the humblest and one of the most revered dishes in all of India. There are references to it in ancient Vedic texts, and in Ayurvedic lore, mung beans are considered a complete food that balances all of the doshas, which are the energy principles that govern our bodies and health.

A simple khichadi with just salt and a hint of turmeric is often the first food fed to a baby, and it's also a comforting food for the elderly. It's always there if you're noticing a cold coming on, or have indigestion, or you just want a simple, nourishing meal. Khichadi is a dish for the poorest of the poor, but it can also be served to kings.

In fact, this is the dish I served the prime minister of India, Narendra Modi, during his state visit to the US in 2023. Khichadi is a staple in his home state of Gujarat, and I couldn't think of a more fitting way to honor his visit than with one of the most foundational foods of Indian cuisine. We maharaja-ed it up for him with all kinds of fancy bits, but what follows is a simple, easy version that I could eat every day.

Feel free to use basmati rice here if you don't have short-grain rice, and serve this one-pot meal with store-bought mango or lime pickle for the full effect.

1 cup moong dal (hulled and split mung beans, also known as yellow mung dal)

1 cup short-grain white rice, such as Sona Masoori

2 tablespoons ghee, plus more as needed and for serving

1 teaspoon cumin seed

1 teaspoon minced fresh ginger (about a ½-inch knob)

1 teaspoon minced garlic (2 to 3 cloves)

1 to 2 Thai chillies or 2 to 3 serrano chillies (depending on your heat tolerance), finely chopped

¼ cup finely diced white onion (about ½ medium onion)

8 to 10 curry leaves (optional)

¼ teaspoon turmeric powder

¼ teaspoon hing (optional)

½ cup very finely chopped Roma tomatoes (about 2 medium tomatoes)

Kosher salt

Hot water, as needed

Ghee (optional)

Mango or lime pickle (optional)

Separately wash the moong dal and the rice: Place in two large bowls and cover with water. Stir the submerged dal and rice gently with your hand, drain separately through a fine-mesh sieve, and return to the bowls. Repeat the process two or three times with fresh water each time, rinsing and draining until the rinse water runs clear.

Return the rinsed dal and rice to their separate bowls, cover each with 2 to 3 inches of water, and let soak on the countertop for 15 to 30 minutes.

In a large heavy-bottomed pot over medium-high heat, heat the 2 tablespoons ghee until it's shimmering. Add the cumin seeds and, as soon as they begin to wiggle, add the ginger; sauté for about a minute. Add the garlic, chilli, onion, and curry leaves (if using). Sauté, stirring frequently to prevent burning, until the onions are soft, translucent, and just starting to brown on the edges, about 4 minutes. Add the turmeric and hing (if using) and stir for another minute. Add the tomatoes and cook until soft, 3 to 4 minutes.

Drain the moong dal and add it to the pot with the masala. Cook, stirring, for 2 to 3 minutes—this toasting step gives the dal a bit of a nuttier flavor. If the dal is sticking to the pot or the masala isn't sizzling, add an extra teaspoon of ghee.

Drain the rice and add it to the pot, mixing well. Add 6 cups of water and 2 teaspoons of salt. Bring to a boil over medium-high heat, then turn the heat down to medium-low and cover. Cook, stirring occasionally and skimming any foam that rises to the top with a ladle, for 20 to 25 minutes, until the rice grains are cooked through and the mixture is thick and soft. The finished khichadi should resemble a smooth porridge.

Khichadi thickens as it cooks, so add ¼ cup of hot water at the end if necessary to thin it out a bit. Taste, and adjust the salt as needed. Serve with a dollop of ghee on top of each bowl (if using) and a garnish of mango or lime pickle (if using). Leftover khichadi keeps, tightly covered in the refrigerator, for up to 5 days.

UPMA

Serves 4 to 6

Upma is usually served as a savory breakfast, or as a filling anytime snack at dhabas—particularly in the central and southern states. It belongs to the genre of what I'll call "breakfast all day" foods. Imagine a savory oatmeal (though made with semolina flour, or sooji), and you have the general idea. Upma is nutritious and filling (and contains none of the sugar that fills most American cereals), which is why it—like poha and khichadi—does double duty as a breakfast and a meal that can be eaten any time of day. This recipe is easy and comforting, and I wanted to include it because upma is exactly the type of dish that's in danger of disappearing as the Indian breakfast palate becomes increasingly westernized. If you can't find fine sooji, coarse is okay, but your upma might not be as fluffy.

2 cups fine sooji (see headnote)

3 tablespoons neutral oil, such as grapeseed

2 teaspoons mustard seed

10 curry leaves (optional)

1 tablespoon minced garlic (2 to 3 cloves)

1 tablespoon peeled and minced fresh ginger (about a 1-inch knob)

1 to 2 Thai chillies or 2 to 3 serrano chillies (depending on your heat tolerance), finely chopped

1 teaspoon cumin seed

¼ teaspoon hing (see page 22; optional)

¼ cup peanuts or split cashews (optional)

½ cup finely diced white onion (about ½ medium onion)

2 teaspoons kosher salt

Heat a large heavy-bottomed pot over medium heat and add the sooji; stir constantly, roasting until the color starts to darken to a light golden blond. (It should feel slightly crunchy when pressed between your fingers.) It's important to keep stirring and watch attentively, because sooji can burn in the blink of an eye, and you'll have to toss the whole thing. This toasting process can take up to 5 minutes, so be patient.

Remove the toasted sooji from the pot. Wipe the pot clean and place it over medium-high heat. Add the oil and heat until shimmering. Add the mustard seeds; when they start to wiggle and pop, turn the heat down to medium to avoid burning. (Make sure the oil is hot enough that the mustard seeds actually start to pop—otherwise they're not flavoring the oil!) Add the curry leaves, if using (they'll spit as you add them, so stand back), garlic, ginger, chillies, cumin, hing (if using), and nuts (if using), and stir for about 1 minute, until the curry leaves have stopped crackling. Add the onions and cook, stirring frequently, until they're soft and translucent, about 3 minutes (try to avoid browning).

Bring a separate pot with 4 cups of water to a boil. Add the boiling water and the salt to the pot with the spice mixture; stir to incorporate. Bring to a rapid boil over high heat.

Slowly start pouring the roasted sooji into the pot with the masala mixture and water, stirring while you go. Don't dump the entire thing in at once, because it will clump. The sooji will start to thicken; as it does so, turn the heat down to medium-low. Keep stirring for 1 to 2 minutes, smoothing out any lumps and making sure the semolina is fully incorporated in the liquid. Turn the heat to low, cover the pot, and cook, undisturbed, until all the water is absorbed and the upma resembles fluffy grits, 4 to 5 minutes.

Serve hot. Leftover upma keeps, tightly covered in the refrigerator, for up to 3 days. Reheat in a pot over medium-low heat, stirring in another teaspoon or two of water to loosen up the upma if necessary.

BAINGAN BHARTA

Serves 4 to 6

A traditional North Indian baingan bharta involves smoked eggplant mashed into a paste with raw onions, green chillies, and spices, and served almost like a dip with flatbread. Countless variations abound, and this one, imbued with ghee and heavy cream, is what you'd whip up if a sultan stopped by. It's inspired by the utterly decadent version served at Pakwan, my favorite Indo-Pakistan dive, in the Tenderloin in San Francisco.

Eggplant is polarizing, but this dish will make even the haters into believers. How can it not? Roasting the eggplant neutralizes the slimy texture that some people are offended by, and the slight bitterness is completely counterbalanced by the decadence of the dairy and the slow-cooked tomatoes. You can also "smoke" the eggplant employing the Dunghar technique that we describe in detail in the Auntie Hack on page 229, though this step isn't required.

EGGPLANT

4 Italian eggplants, cut in half lengthwise

8 garlic cloves

½ teaspoon kosher salt

½ teaspoon turmeric powder

½ teaspoon ground red chilli, such as Kashmiri (see page 18)

¼ cup neutral oil, such as grapeseed

¼ cup ghee or melted butter

1 tablespoon cumin seed

1 tablespoon ginger powder

1 to 2 fresh Thai or serrano chillies (depending on your heat tolerance), coarsely chopped

3 cups finely diced red onion (about 2 large onions)

1 tablespoon coarsely chopped cilantro stems (optional)

Kosher salt

1 teaspoon cumin powder

1 teaspoon coriander powder

½ teaspoon turmeric powder

½ teaspoon ground red chilli, such as Kashmiri (see page 18)

One (28-ounce) can crushed tomatoes

1 teaspoon Garam Masala (page 277, or use store-bought)

¼ cup heavy cream

Fresh Chapati (page 212) or store-bought naan (see page 84), for serving

To roast the eggplant, line a sheet pan with aluminum foil and preheat the oven to 500°F. Poke 4 or 5 evenly spaced holes into the cut side of the eggplant and press a garlic clove into one of these holes, so that every eggplant half has a garlic stud.

In a small bowl, mix together the salt, turmeric, ground red chilli, and oil. Brush some of the mixture onto the cut surface of each eggplant half.

Place the eggplants on the lined sheet pan, skin side down, and roast until their skin is wrinkled, 20 to 30 minutes. Turn the oven temperature down to 400°F and roast for another 20 minutes, until the flesh is soft and brown. Scoop the flesh and garlic out of each eggplant half into a large bowl; discard the skins. If you're choosing to employ the Dunghar auntie hack to smoke the eggplant, now is the time; if not, set the eggplant aside.

In a large heavy-bottomed pot over high heat, heat the ghee or butter until shimmering. Add the cumin seeds. As soon as the seeds start to brown, 30 to 60 seconds, stir in the ginger and green chillies. Add the onion and the cilantro stems (if using) and a pinch of salt and cook, stirring occasionally, until the onions are soft, brown, and nearly caramelized, 20 to 30 minutes.

Add the cumin powder, coriander, turmeric, and ground red chilli. Stir to incorporate for 1 minute. Add the crushed tomatoes and lower the heat to medium. Simmer, stirring frequently, for 10 to 15 minutes.

Add the eggplant (smoked or not) and the garam masala into the tomato mixture. Cook, stirring frequently, until the tomatoes are glossy and the oil starts to separate from the edges, about 20 minutes.

With an immersion blender or potato masher, begin to mash the mixture into a coarse puree, keeping some chunks of eggplant for texture. Add the heavy cream and salt to taste. Serve with chapati or naan.

Leftover baingan bharta keeps, tightly covered in the refrigerator, for up to 4 days.

APPAM ✤ DOSA ✤ RAVA DOSA ✤ UTTAPAM

Pancakes Came First

Sure, the advent of bread is foundational to the formation of human society, but you know what gets overlooked when we talk about the historic development of mankind in relation to our carbs? Pancakes. Pancakes, or at least flatbread-esque proto-pancakes, were invented first, helping us evolve one more step beyond our monkey brethren.

Imagine, for a moment, your ancestors chewing on some grains and realizing that these little seed-like objects somehow, almost magically, provided them with an extra jolt of energy. Now imagine the next generation of your ancestors realizing that they could graduate from merely chewing on those grains to actually soaking and pounding them into a batter to make them even easier to eat and digest. And then, maybe someone poured (or spilled) some of the batter onto a hot stone near the fire, and it smelled really good. Hence pancakes, which were far easier for our Stone Age ancestors to figure out than the more sophisticated processes of milling flour and baking bread, which followed in due course.

Humans have been mashing up grains for a long, long time—there's archaeological evidence of 30,000-year-old pancakes made out of cattails and ferns. For slightly more modern iterations, look no farther than Ethiopia, where teff—a hard millet that's nearly impossible to turn into flour but relatively easy to soak and pound into a batter—is the basis for injera, a staple pancake. In South India, urad dal is similarly near-impossible to grind into flour, but it can be soaked, blitzed into a batter, and cooked into the beloved fermented crepe uttapam. (Given the 2,000-year-old trade routes between India and East Africa, I have spent many a late night speculating about the injera-to-uttapam pipeline. My findings will be published in a future report.)

In homage to these carbs and the rabbit holes they've sent me down, I have recipes for both dosas and uttapams on pages 140 to 146. Not only are these pancakes delicious, they're a direct link to the history of early humans' relationship with seeds and grains, which eventually led to the advent of agriculture, which eventually led us to where we are today—nerding out about pancakes in the pages of this book.

APPAM (AKA HOPPERS)

Serves 4

While dosas steal the spotlight in the South Indian fermented pancake canon, their lesser known cousins, appam and uttapam, are more home cook–friendly and versatile. Dosas, due to their technical nature and the specialized cooking equipment they require, are often eaten outside the home, but appam and uttapam are made at home on the reg.

While uttapams are often topped with vegetables, almost like pizza, appam's basic function is to be used as a bread. It's like a South Indian injera—a delicious, spongy, sour-sweet blank slate with which to mop up curries, gravies, and more. And it's incredibly easy to make, requiring no soaking or grinding of anything. I like to serve appam with the Arangaon Chicken on page 130 or the Butternut Squash & Green Bean Coconut Curry on page 204.

In Sri Lanka, where these pancakes are more energetically known by the Anglicized name "hoppers," a common variation is to make them with a fried egg cracked directly on top of the batter and allowed to set for a minute or two. You can think of them as a savory pancake, with a bit of natural sweetness from the coconut, and enjoy them with eggs and bacon on the side; butter and jam on top; or—a personal favorite of mine—slices of sweet mango when it's in season.

Traditional appams are made in a concave pan similar to a wok, so the end product is curved, but that's the evolution of a shape meant to hold things (like the aforementioned eggs). It's not necessary to make a curved appam—I've had plenty of entirely delicious flat ones in my day.

2 cups rice flour
½ cup all-purpose flour
2 teaspoons kosher salt
1½ cups warm water
1½ teaspoons instant yeast
1 cup full-fat coconut milk, plus 1 to 2 tablespoons, as needed
Neutral oil, such as grapeseed, for greasing the pan

Turn the oven on to its lowest temperature (a warmer function is great for this), and once it gets there, turn it off. The point in doing this is to create a warm place (approximately 100°F) for the yeast in the batter to rise.

In a large bowl, combine the rice flour, all-purpose flour, and salt. Slowly pour in the water while whisking the dry ingredients to make a thick, stiff batter. Whisk in the yeast, and place the bowl in the warm oven, leaving the door cracked slightly ajar. Depending on the warmth and humidity of your kitchen, the batter should increase in volume by about a third in approximately 30 minutes. If it doesn't, let it sit a little longer, and/or try to find somewhere a little warmer to put it.

Once the batter has fermented, whisk in the coconut milk, then repeat the fermentation process by turning the oven back on to its lowest temperature, then turning it back off when it reaches that temperature. Place the bowl with the batter back in the slightly warm oven with the door slightly ajar for about 45 minutes to an hour. It won't rise much, but it should start to look a little fluffy and frothy, with small air bubbles on the surface.

Remove the bowl from the oven and give it a whisk to even out the batter. It should have the consistency of thin pancake batter; add another tablespoon or two of coconut milk if necessary to thin it out.

If you have a favorite pancake- or crepe-making pan, use it now. Otherwise, heat a large nonstick skillet with a well-fitting lid over medium heat. A well-seasoned cast-iron pan can also work, provided it has a lid. Drizzle a tiny little bit of oil into the pan, then wipe it off with a paper towel—the goal is to use as little oil as possible.

Pour in about ¼ cup of batter, tilting the pan in a circular motion until the batter reaches the edges. Cover with the lid, allowing the appam to lightly brown on the bottom and steam on top. Cook for about 2 minutes, or until the top is completely set, with lots of tiny bubbles, and the bottom lifts easily from the pan. Do not flip it! The appam should be about ¼ inch thick and slightly spongy in the middle, with thin, crepe-like edges. Repeat with the remaining batter.

As they finish cooking, wrap appam in a towel or place in an airtight container where they can stay warm. Remember—appam are meant to be spongy, not crispy. Eat as is, or alongside any of the dishes mentioned in the headnote.

Leftovers keep, tightly covered in the refrigerator, for 2 to 3 days. Appam can be revived in the microwave or quickly warmed in the same skillet you cooked them in.

DOSA BATTER

Makes 4 cups of batter

This is the master recipe for the batter you'll use to make dosas and uttapams, and their variations, across pages 142 to 146. It might seem like a lot of prep, but it only really takes minutes of active time—you just need to plan ahead to build in time to soak the grains and allow the batter to rise. You can do the soaking in the evening and make the batter before bed, and by the next morning, you'll have batter that lasts for days—it's worth it.

While dosa batter ferments beautifully when it's somewhere warm and tropical, at home you might have to mess with it a little more to get the perfect temperature. I've developed a little hack (included below), using the oven to try to mimic the heat-and-humidity conditions of South India. If it's very warm where you live, you may not need to do this—play around until you find a technique that works for you.

- 1½ cups short grain rice (ideally parboiled/idli rice, though Sona Masoori rice works, too)
- ½ cup split urad dal (husked split black lentils; see Note)
- 1 tablespoon channa dal (split chickpeas; optional)
- ½ teaspoon fenugreek seed (optional)
- 2 teaspoons kosher salt

Rinse the rice and place it in a large bowl. Cover it with 2 to 3 inches of water and soak at room temperature for 4 to 6 hours.

Rinse the urad dal and place it in a large bowl. Cover with 2 to 3 inches of water and add the channa dal, if using. (The channa dal helps with the color of the batter, but it's not strictly necessary.) Add the fenugreek seeds here, as well, if you're using them. Soak at room temperature for 4 to 6 hours.

After soaking, pour off the excess water from the rice and dal (you don't have to drain the rice and dal, just pour away whatever's on top).

Place the dal in a blender and pour in ½ cup of fresh water. Blend on high speed until completely smooth, about 1 minute—it may froth a bit while you're blending, which is normal. Rub a bit of the dal batter between your fingers—there shouldn't be any grittiness, and if there is, keep blending until smooth.

Transfer the dal batter to a large heatproof container (a stockpot or Dutch oven works well for this). You want to make sure the batter has room to rise, because it will increase in volume by a third.

Place the rice in the blender (it doesn't need to be rinsed) and pour in ⅔ cup of fresh water. Blend on high speed until completely smooth, about 2 minutes. Rub a bit of this rice batter between your fingers—there shouldn't be any grittiness, so blend more if there is. Pour the rice batter into the same bowl as the dal batter. Add the salt, then use your hands to stir the batters together to combine. (According to auntie lore, the bacteria and warmth from your hand helps jump-start the fermentation process.) The batter should be smooth and thick, like a milkshake or thick pancake batter. If it seems too thick, add a few tablespoons of water at a time, using your hand to mix it in.

Cover the container with plastic wrap, poking a few holes in the top. Place the container somewhere warm (about 100°F). The hack I've developed at home is to turn the oven to its lowest temperature (a warmer function, if your oven has it, is great for this), and, once it gets there, cut the heat. Put the container in the oven and let it sit, with the door closed, for a minimum of 8 hours and up to 12 hours.

Depending on the warmth and humidity of your kitchen, the batter should rise by a quarter to a third in volume overnight. Even if it doesn't rise too much, check if it looks aerated and fluffy—if it does, you're ready. If it doesn't, let it sit for a few more hours, and/or try to find somewhere a little warmer.

Once the batter is fermented, you can pour it into an airtight container and store it in the refrigerator for up to a week, bringing it to room temperature before cooking, but the dosas and uttapams taste best when the batter is fresh.

Note: ***Somewhat confusingly, husked split black lentils are actually white in the bag. Just look for lentils labeled urad dal/black lentils, appearances aside. Be aware that many South Asian grocers also sell non-husked urad dal, which is black in appearance; make sure you are buying the husked version.***

PLAIN DOSA

Makes 8 dosas

From the 1960s onward, as samosas, naan, butter chicken, saag paneer, and vindaloo started entering Western consciousness as mainstream Indian foods, North Indian cuisine came to dominate palates in Europe and America. But over the last twenty years, more Americans have been introduced to the pleasure of the dosa, thanks to the South Indian restaurants that have popped up in major cities.

Once you become a master of the heat of the griddle, you'll find these recipes delicious and relatively foolproof. Think of the dosa and its cousin, the uttapam, as savory crepes or pancakes, with toppings limited only by your imagination.

The best cooking vessel for dosas is a tawa—a large, heavy, extremely smooth griddle made of carbon steel, common across India. If you don't have that, you can use a very smooth cast-iron skillet (a nice one—the cheaper brands just aren't smooth enough), a crepe pan, or a griddle. I can't recommend making dosas in a nonstick pan, as tempting as it might seem, because the dosa just slides around and doesn't actually cook properly. Choose a heavy-bottomed pan: You want the pan to get very hot then maintain its temperature over a lower heat.

You'll also need a ladle (ideally metal, ideally 3 ounces) with a rounded cup. The rounded cup is essential to smooth the batter across the surface of the griddle. The flatter the bottom of your ladle, the harder it is to spread evenly. If you plan to cook a lot of dosas, this small and inexpensive tool is a very worthwhile investment.

4 cups Dosa Batter (page 140)

4 tablespoons (½ stick) cold unsalted butter (needs to be in stick form)

Coconut Chutney (page 272), for serving

Mom's Quick 'n' Easy Potatoes (page 207), for serving

Heat a heavy-bottomed pan with a smooth surface (see headnote) over high heat until very hot: A drop of water should sizzle immediately on its surface.

Once the pan is nice and hot, turn the heat down to medium-high and rub the surface with a few swirls of a stick of butter. With a damp paper towel, wipe off the butter. (In India, they use a halved onion for this step, which you're welcome to try as well.) You want just to season the pan—if there's any excess butter, the dosa won't stick and won't cook right, becoming more like a scramble.

Using your metal ladle with a rounded cup, pour one ladleful of batter into the middle of the pan.

Let the dosa sit for about 10 seconds and then, using light pressure, place the rounded part of the ladle in the middle of the batter and start spreading out in a spiral motion, pushing the batter out to the edges, trying to get it as thin as possible without tearing it. Do not go back and forth in different directions—once you pick a direction, commit to it and finish making the spiral in that way. Don't backtrack or attempt to smooth out any lumpy parts—it will tear the dosa. (If you do have lumpy parts, your best bet is to wait until the dosa is further set, then scrape them off before serving—or don't, and it will still taste just fine.)

Once the dosa spreads out, it will start to form little air bubbles around the edges. These bubbles should form within maybe 15 seconds of the batter hitting the pan—if they don't, it means your pan isn't hot enough. Once the bubbles appear, use your stick of butter to butter the surface of the dosa, starting from the edges and working your way in. The batter may seem a little undercooked, getting pushed down from the pressure of the butter, but that's okay—it takes 3 to 5 minutes to cook fully.

Once the white part of the top of the dosa looks fully set, use a fish spatula or other thin-edged metal spatula to release the dosa from the pan. It should come away easily without sticking if you've used enough butter. Fold the dosa over itself to form a semicircle and set aside while you cook the remaining batter.

Before you start the next dosa, wipe off any excess butter and stuck dough from the pan with a wet paper towel. It's really important that the pan is totally clean so the next dosa doesn't stick or tear. (In India, dosa vendors have a bucket of water with a straw broom in it, which they use to scrub the tawa clean between each batch.)

If it seems like the pan is getting dry and the dosas are starting to stick, you can grease the pan with more butter and wipe it off again with a damp paper towel, but you shouldn't have to do this between each dosa.

Serve with coconut chutney and potatoes. Dosas are best eaten the day they're made.

VARIATIONS ON PLAIN DOSAS

Cacio e pepe dosa: After applying butter to the top of the dosa, sprinkle freshly ground black pepper and grated Parmesan over it as well. This flavor combo is insanely good: The salty parm works perfectly with the tang of fermented dosa batter.

Pancetta and parm dosa: When I visited Modena, Italy, there was a guy making paper-thin crepes, topped with cheese and melted lardo. It was so wrong for an Indian but so right for me, and I had to re-create it at home. You can either sprinkle cooked pancetta along the top of the dosa as it sets; or cook up some raw pancetta until it's crispy, set the crispy bits off to the side, use the grease from the pork to cook the dosa, then top the finished product with said crispy bits and some grated Parmesan.

RAVA DOSA

Makes 4 dosas

You'll probably make this more often than the plain dosa, because unlike plain dosas, rava dosas are instantaneous. They're made of sooji (fine semolina flour) that's mixed with rice and all-purpose flours to make a thin, lacy, delightfully crispy variation. Rava dosas might not get as much attention as their more traditional brethren, but they're definitely more fun, loaded up as they are with onions, green chillies, and cilantro. As with plain dosas, the pan matters: Choose a smooth-surfaced, heavy-bottomed pan that will hold heat well and won't let the dosas stick.

½ cup sooji (fine semolina flour)
½ cup rice flour
¼ cup all-purpose flour
½ teaspoon kosher salt, plus more as needed
½ teaspoon cumin seed
¼ teaspoon freshly ground black pepper
1 teaspoon finely minced fresh Thai or serrano chilli (depending on your heat tolerance)
¼ cup finely chopped red onion
2 tablespoons finely chopped cilantro leaves
1 teaspoon finely minced fresh ginger (about a ½-inch knob)
5 finely chopped curry leaves (optional)
2½ cups water, plus more as needed
2 teaspoons plain full-fat yogurt
¼ cup neutral oil, such as grapeseed
Coconut Chutney (page 272), for serving
Dry Garlic Chutney (page 273), for serving

In a large bowl, combine the sooji, rice flour, all-purpose flour, salt, cumin seeds, black pepper, green chilli, red onion, cilantro, ginger, and curry leaves (if using) and mix with your hands. Whisk in the 2½ cups of water to make a batter. The semolina flour won't dissolve into the liquid the way the other ingredients will, so this batter will be gritty; that's okay. You want a very thin, runny batter, more like crepe batter than pancake batter, so add a tablespoon more water if needed.

Mix in the yogurt and whisk to combine. Taste the batter for salt and add more if needed. Set the batter aside for 15 to 30 minutes.

Heat your pan over high heat until very hot; a drop of water should immediately sizzle on its surface.

Turn the heat down to medium-high and add about a tablespoon of the oil to coat the surface. With a damp paper towel, wipe off the oil. You want to just season the pan—if there's any excess oil, the dosa won't stick and won't cook right.

Using a 3-ounce metal ladle with a rounded cup, pour one ladleful of batter into the pan, working from the outside in a spiral shape toward the middle. Try to make a very thin layer across the surface of the pan, like a crepe.

Turn the heat to medium-low, then use your fingertips or a pastry brush to spread a few more drops of oil along the surface of the dosa, making sure to get the edges. Unlike a regular dosa, as this one continues to cook, the edges will start to peel off on their own. Cook until the edges are curled and brown and the dosa is lacy and crisp, 3 to 5 minutes.

Fold the rava dosa over twice into a triangular shape, like it's a handkerchief. Serve it hot, with coconut chutney and dry garlic chutney, while it's still crispy—as it cools, the dosa will soften.

Repeat with the remaining batter, whisking it well before each pour, as the semolina and vegetables will settle.

Before you start the next dosa, wipe off any excess oil and stuck dough from the pan with a wet paper towel. It's really important that the pan is totally clean so the next dosa won't stick or tear. (In India, dosa vendors have a bucket of water with a straw broom in it and use the broom to scrub the tawa clean between batches.)

If it seems like the pan is getting dry and the dosas are starting to stick, you can grease the pan with more oil and wipe it off again with a damp paper towel—but you shouldn't have to do this between every dosa.

Rava dosas are best eaten the day they're made.

UTTAPAM & ITS VARIATIONS

Makes about 8 uttapams

If I had to take a wild guess, based purely on their level of complexity, I'd say that the invention of uttapams predates that of dosas. Thick, fluffy, vegetable-and-aromatics-studded uttapams are as easy to make as pouring a pancake, and don't demand the tight technique required to make a dosa. Uttapams are delicious and forgiving, so if you're looking for a good first use for all that batter you made on page 140, this is it.

¼ cup neutral oil, such as grapeseed, plus more as needed for frying

4 cups Dosa Batter (page 140)

1 tablespoon finely minced fresh Thai or serrano chilli (depending on your heat tolerance)

½ cup finely chopped red onion

¼ cup finely chopped cilantro leaves

2 teaspoons peeled and finely minced fresh ginger (about a 1-inch knob)

10 finely chopped curry leaves (optional)

Kosher salt

Coconut Chutney (page 272), for serving

Heat a large cast-iron skillet or griddle over high heat until it's smoking hot. Coat the pan's surface with about a tablespoon of the oil, then wipe off the oil with a damp paper towel.

Using a ladle, pour 3 to 4 ounces of batter in the middle of the pan. Tilt the pan to spread the batter to the size of a standard American diner pancake, about 6 inches.

Within a minute, bubbles should form on the edges of the batter. Turn the heat down to medium-high at this point and drizzle a teaspoon or so of oil around the edges and over the top of the uttapam.

Sprinkle a portion each of the chilli, onion, cilantro, ginger, and curry leaves (if using) over the uttapam. Hit it with a sprinkle of salt and drizzle a bit more oil over the top while you're at it.

After cooking for about 2 minutes, lift up one edge of the uttapam with a fish spatula or other thin-edged metal spatula, and see if the bottom is brown and crispy. Unlike a pancake, you want your uttapam to be dark golden brown, like well-done toast. If it looks good and burnished, flip it over and cook on the other side for about 1 minute—you're just giving a little sear to the veggies on top. Do not press down! This is not a smashburger.

Repeat with the remaining batter and ingredients, and serve hot, with coconut chutney on the side. You can keep finished uttapam warm in a 200°F oven until all are ready. If you happen to live in Hawaii or L.A., grab a banana leaf to serve the finished product on.

UTTAPAM VARIATIONS

Tomato-cheese uttapam, aka **Uttapam Pie:** This is the most popular variation at Chai Pani. Follow the directions above, but instead of cilantro and curry leaves, sprinkle the uttapam with 2 tablespoons of coarsely chopped Roma tomatoes and ¼ cup shredded mozzarella cheese: Make it cheesy! Once it's brown on the bottom, carefully flip it and cook, cheese side down, until the mozzarella forms a gorgeously caramelized crust. Serve hot.

Omelet Uuttapam: Somewhere, Lord Shiva is rolling his eyes at the sight of a Parsi desecrating yet another one of India's culinary treasures by putting an egg on it. What can I say? I gotta put an egg on it.

Whisk 8 eggs in a bowl (if you're cooking fewer than eight uttapams, scale down to one egg per uttapam). Follow the directions above, but omit the ginger and curry leaves. As you pick the uttapam up to flip it, pour a few tablespoons of egg into the skillet, sprinkle in a pinch each of salt and pepper, then flip the uttapam wet side down into the egg, so that the uttapam and omelet fuse together (this is similar to the kathi roll technique on page 78). Cook for 1 minute, until the egg is set, and serve hot.

BERS. M.
MEDNAGAR.
26928783.

AVON

ROADSIDE HAKKA NOODLES

Serves 2 to 4

In the tradition of Singapore or Hong Kong–style street noodle hawkers, India's version of stir-fried noodles is easy, and it's a straight-up banger. Our instant noodle of choice is the dried Maggi noodle, which is nearly as beloved in India as Maggi tomato sauce (aka ketchup). Simply cook the noodles in water with their seasoning packet, and in a separate pot cook up the vegetables with a bunch of spices and some soy sauce. Combine the contents of both pots to make a thick, salty noodle-y treat (you can thank me later, after you can't eat another bite).

- 2 packages Maggi instant noodles (preferably masala flavor), including seasoning packets
- 3 tablespoons vegetable oil
- 7 or 8 curry leaves (optional)
- ½ small red onion, thinly sliced
- 1 medium carrot, thinly sliced
- 1 small green or red bell pepper, thinly sliced
- 1 finely chopped fresh Thai or serrano chilli (depending on your heat tolerance)
- 3 tablespoons soy sauce
- 2 tablespoons chilli-garlic sauce (such as Huy Fong)
- 1 teaspoon rice wine vinegar
- ¼ teaspoon sugar
- Kosher salt
- 3 green onions, thinly sliced, for garnish

Fill a large pot with about 2 quarts of water, add one of the noodle seasoning packets, and bring to a boil. Once the water is boiling, break both of the dried noodle blocks into 3 or 4 pieces and add to the pot. Cook the noodles for 2 minutes, then drain them in a strainer and set aside.

In a wok or large sauté pan, heat the oil. Once hot, add the curry leaves (if using) and onion. Fry for a minute, until aromatic, then add the carrot, bell pepper, and chilli, and the second noodle seasoning packet. Sauté the vegetables for 3 to 4 minutes, until lightly cooked. Do not overcook them—they should be slightly crunchy.

In a small bowl, combine the soy sauce, chilli-garlic sauce, vinegar, and sugar. Add to the wok and toss to coat the vegetables. Add the noodles and toss them with the vegetables until everything is fully mixed and the noodles are well coated. Taste and adjust the seasonings to your liking. Transfer the noodles to a serving bowl and garnish with green onion.

Leftovers keep, tightly covered in the refrigerator, for up to 5 days.

MAGGI POINT NOODLES

Serves 2 to 4

High in the foothills of the Himalayas, about a one-hour drive from my mother's hometown of Dehradun, lies the mist-shrouded town of Mussoorie. It was a hill station favored by the British, who went there to escape the summer heat, as well as the summer home of the Nepalese royal family. Mussoorie has a large Nepalese population and is home to one of my favorite Desi Chinese restaurants, Kalsang.

Every few minutes along the road that climbs up the mountain from Dehradun to Mussoorie—wherever there's an outcropping with a view—there are these tiny shacks known as Maggi Points. These are basically rest stops, offering travelers a hot cup of chai and a bowl of instant Maggi noodles (and, for the young and frisky, a convenient place to make out).

This recipe pays homage to the Maggi Point noodles of my youth and, accordingly, is something you might be able to whip up in a dorm room. You can swap out any of the vegetables or throw an egg on top, but the most important thing is to get good Maggi noodles. You want the two-minute instant noodles, ideally the masala flavor; these are available on Amazon and they last forever. If you can't get Maggi specifically, most brands of instant noodles or ramen will work. Just pick a flavor that has a bit of zing, because the seasoning packets are very much called into action here.

The frozen vegetable mix called for here is fairly common in many groceries, but if you can't find it, swap it out for another frozen vegetable mix or just use ¼ cup more of the other vegetables listed.

- 2 tablespoons neutral oil, such as grapeseed
- 1 tablespoon peeled and minced fresh ginger (about a 1-inch knob)
- 1 tablespoon minced garlic (2 to 3 cloves)
- 1 to 2 Thai chillies or 2 to 3 serrano chillies (depending on your heat tolerance), finely chopped
- 8 to 10 curry leaves (optional)
- 1 tablespoon coarsely chopped cilantro stems
- ½ cup thinly sliced red onion (about ½ medium onion)
- Kosher salt
- ¼ cup thinly sliced green bell pepper
- ¼ cup thawed frozen mixed vegetables (corn, peas, and carrots)
- 2 packages Maggi instant noodles (preferably masala flavor), including seasoning packets
- 1 teaspoon rice wine vinegar
- 1 teaspoon soy sauce
- Coarsely chopped cilantro, for serving
- Lime wedges, for serving

Over high heat, bring a large pot of about 8 cups of water to a boil.

While the water comes to a boil, in a large heavy-bottomed pan with high walls (a carbon-steel wok is good here), heat the oil over medium-high heat until shimmering.

Add the ginger and stir for a minute. Add the garlic, green chillies, curry leaves (if using), and cilantro stems and stir for another minute, until the curry leaves stop popping. Stir in the onion and a pinch of salt and cook until the onion is soft and brown, about 5 minutes. Stir in the bell peppers and sauté until crisp-tender, 2 to 3 minutes. Stir in the corn-pea-carrot mixture and cook for another minute.

Add one Maggi seasoning packet to the boiling water. Break both bricks of noodles into the boiling water and cook according to package directions (as their name implies, it should take about 2 minutes).

Add the other seasoning packet to the vegetables in the pan and stir to combine. Deglaze the pan with the rice wine vinegar, then stir in the soy sauce. At this point, your noodles should be done. Don't bother straining them—bring the pot next to the pan with the vegetables (the pan should still be on the heat) and use a pair of tongs to transfer the noodles directly into the pan (it's okay if they're dripping liquid). Fold the noodles into the veggies, stirring vigorously for about 1 minute to cook off some of the water without breaking the noodles.

Once the noodles look drier and are well coated with the vegetable mix, they're ready to eat. Finish with a pinch of salt, a handful of chopped cilantro, and a squeeze of fresh lime juice.

Leftovers keep, tightly covered in the refrigerator, for up to 5 days.

CHILLI CHICKEN

Serves 4

A discerning reader will quickly realize, as you start flipping back and forth between recipes in this section, that there's a lot of sweet-and-sour sauce and a lot of bell peppers and onions: Embrace it for what it is. In India, chilli chicken and its vegetarian counterpart, Gobi Pepper Fry (page 155), are eaten as a little street snack—no sides, just straight-up. Feel free to go that route if it speaks to you, or steam up a pot of white rice to make it a meal.

VEGETABLES

1 tablespoon neutral oil, such as grapeseed

½ large red onion, cut into 1-inch pieces

½ large green bell pepper, cut into 1-inch pieces

Kosher salt

SAUCE

2 teaspoons neutral oil, such as grapeseed

1 tablespoon peeled and minced garlic (2 to 3 cloves)

1 tablespoon minced fresh ginger (about a 1-inch knob)

1 Thai or 2 serrano chillies (depending on your heat tolerance), finely chopped

10 fresh curry leaves (optional)

½ teaspoon coriander powder

¼ teaspoon ground red chilli, such as Kashmiri (see page 18)

1½ tablespoons rice wine vinegar

1 tablespoon soy sauce

2 tablespoons sweet chilli sauce (such as Maggi or Mae Ploy)

CHICKEN

2 pounds boneless, skinless chicken thighs, cut into 2-inch pieces

1 tablespoon plus 1½ teaspoons Ginger-Garlic Paste (page 276)

2 tablespoons soy sauce

1 teaspoon freshly ground black pepper

1 teaspoon ground red chilli, such as Kashmiri (see page 18)

1 teaspoon kosher salt

½ teaspoon Ajinomoto MSG (see Note)

1 large egg, whisked

⅓ cup all-purpose flour

⅓ cup cornstarch

4 to 6 cups canola or other neutral oil, for frying

Perfect Basmati Rice (page 276), for serving (optional)

Finely shredded green cabbage, for serving (optional)

To make the veggies, heat the oil in a large saucepan over medium-high heat until shimmering. Add the onions and bell peppers and a pinch of salt. Sauté the vegetables for 3 to 4 minutes—the goal is to get them slightly cooked but not soft. Set the vegetables aside in a small bowl, keeping as much of the cooking oil in the pan as you can (do not wash it).

To make the sauce, add the 2 teaspoons oil to the same pan. Bring the heat back up to medium-high and, once the oil is shimmering, add the garlic and ginger and cook until the garlic starts to brown on the edges, 30 to 60 seconds. Add the green chillies and the curry leaves (if using). The curry leaves will pop and sputter for a few seconds, and once the sputtering stops and they start to darken, add the coriander and ground red chilli and mix well for another minute.

Stir in the rice wine vinegar, soy sauce, and sweet chilli sauce and cook, stirring occasionally, until the sauce starts to bubble, 3 to 5 minutes. Turn the heat down to medium-low and add ¼ cup of water. Stir for another minute and adjust the heat to keep the sauce at a simmer. Taste for seasoning and add a splash of whatever you think it needs. (I usually don't add any salt to the sauce because the soy sauce is salty enough. But if you feel like it needs a bit more salt, add to taste now, because it's hard to season the dish once it's assembled.) Set the sauce aside in the pan.

To make the chicken, in a large bowl, combine the chicken with the ginger-garlic paste, soy sauce, black pepper, red chilli, salt, MSG, and egg. Mix well until all the chicken is fully coated. In a small bowl, combine the flour and cornstarch until well mixed, then add to the chicken and mix again until everything is evenly distributed and well combined.

In a large heavy-bottomed pot suitable for deep-frying, heat the canola oil to 350°F (an oil thermometer is your friend here). Place a wire rack over a sheet pan or line a plate with paper towels and place it next to the stove.

Carefully add the chicken to the hot oil, working in batches if necessary to avoid overcrowding. Cook until golden brown and crispy, or until a meat thermometer inserted into the thickest part of a nugget reads 165°F, 6 to 7 minutes.

As the chicken is done, transfer it from the oil to the wire rack or paper towel–lined plate to drain excess oil.

Now the easy part—assembly! Reheat the sauce over medium-high heat until bubbling, then add the reserved vegetables and the fried chicken, stirring gently so you don't knock the batter off the chicken. Give it a minute and it's ready to serve.

If you like, serve with white rice and/or shredded cabbage. Chilli chicken is best eaten the day it's made.

Note: *As a kid, I didn't know what MSG was, but I definitely knew what Ajinomoto was, recognizing the label from my mom's shopping trips. To my mother, along with many other home and restaurant cooks in India, Ajinomoto was just a different type of salt, similar to how you might think of Himalayan pink salt or smoked salt today.*

I don't want to get lost in the sauce over the great MSG debate, but from where I stand—and if there's anything you know about me by now, it's that I research deeply—I have no problem using it in moderation in certain Desi Chinese recipes. The way black rock salt adds a particular type of saline umami that is synonymous with chaat for me, MSG adds a meaty umami that works perfectly in this dish and several others. The choice is, as always, totally up to you, but that's my two cents.

GOBI PEPPER FRY

Serves 4

This is a thematic variation on the chilli chicken fry on page 152—something crispy coated in garlicky, sweet, peppery sauce. But to give Gobi Pepper Fry its due, it's not simply substituting cauliflower for chicken—this is a different recipe, with its own distinct sauce and its own distinct crunch.

SAUCE

1 cup canned crushed tomatoes

½ cup soy sauce

¼ cup distilled white vinegar

2 tablespoons plus 1½ teaspoons sugar

2 teaspoons freshly ground black pepper

2 teaspoons kosher salt

½ teaspoon Ajinomoto MSG (see Note on page 153)

CAULIFLOWER

1 cup cornstarch

1 teaspoon kosher salt

2½ cups medium-size cauliflower florets (about half of a medium head)

4 to 6 cups canola oil, for frying, plus 2 tablespoons for the finishing sauce

4 tablespoons Ginger-Garlic Paste (page 276)

6 to 10 fresh curry leaves (optional)

Freshly cracked black pepper, for serving

Perfect Basmati Rice (page 276), for serving (optional)

Finely shredded green cabbage, for serving (optional)

To make the sauce, combine the tomatoes, soy sauce, vinegar, sugar, pepper, salt, and MSG in a bowl and whisk well. The sauce can be made up to 3 days in advance and held in the refrigerator.

To make the cauliflower, combine the cornstarch and salt in a medium bowl and dredge the florets in this mixture until they're thoroughly coated. (You can also put the salted cornstarch in a zip-top bag with the florets and shake to coat.)

Before you cook the cauliflower, preheat the oven to 200°F and place a wire rack over a sheet pan. In a large heavy-bottomed pot suitable for deep-frying, heat the 4 to 6 cups of oil to 350°F (an oil thermometer is your friend here). Carefully add the cauliflower to the hot oil, working in batches if necessary to avoid overcrowding. Cook until golden brown and crispy, 5 to 7 minutes. Remove from the oil to the rack.

Heat 1 tablespoon of the oil in a medium saucepan over medium-high heat until shimmering.

Add 2 tablespoons of the ginger-garlic paste and sauté until the paste starts to brown, 30 to 60 seconds. Add half of the curry leaves (if using)—which will crackle and pop—and stir for 1 minute.

Add half of the sauce (about 1 cup) and half of the fried cauliflower. Coat the florets in the sauce and sauté over medium heat, stirring gently, until the cauliflower is dry and the sauce is caramelized, 4 to 6 minutes.

Transfer the finished cauliflower to a heatproof serving dish and place it in the oven to keep it warm. Wipe the pan clean and repeat with the remaining 1 tablespoon oil, ginger-garlic paste, curry leaves, sauce, and fried cauliflower, adding it to the serving dish when it's done.

Garnish with black pepper and serve with white rice and/or shredded cabbage if you like. Gobi pepper fry is best eaten the day it's made.

TAMARIND-GLAZED SPARE RIBS

Serves 4 to 6

While I was still in my "meat whisperer" days in San Francisco, I was emboldened to cook pretty much everything meat-related—except ribs. I'd never had them in India, and I had some notion that they could only be cooked low and slow, so they never really entered my repertoire.

Around this time, my daughter, Aria, and I spent a lot of time watching Iron Chef, *both the OG Japanese version and the more Hollywood-ified American one. I distinctly remember my jaw hitting the floor when chef Michael Symon announced he would cook ribs in 45 minutes. As the judges were whispering among themselves about the impending disaster of tough ribs, Michael, with a flourish, dropped the ribs he'd been cooking in the oven into the deep-fryer for the last few minutes, then coated them with a sticky-sweet glaze. The rest, as they say, is history.*

I have shamelessly ripped off that technique at my restaurants, not because I'm trying to save time, but because it leads to some of the crispiest, juiciest ribs ever created: just the way I like them.

As an aside, Michael was always one of Aria's favorite chefs, and in life's funny way of bringing things full circle, he cooked with me as part of his show at both Chai Pani and my then-BBQ restaurant, Buxton Hall. One of the highlights of my culinary life was standing with Aria and Michael as we all three raised our hands in the air and recreated the Chairman's famous downward chop, yelling out, "ALLEZ CUISINE!"

MARINADE

½ cup soy sauce
½ cup red wine vinegar
½ cup honey
½ cup tamarind paste (see page 19) or Tamarind Chutney (page 271)
2 tablespoons peeled and minced fresh ginger (about a 2-inch knob)
2 to 3 Thai chillies or 3 to 4 serrano chillies (depending on your heat tolerance), finely chopped
2 teaspoons finely chopped lemongrass (optional)

RIBS

1 (4- to 5-pound) rack St. Louis–style pork spare ribs
1 tablespoon sesame oil
1 teaspoon kosher salt
½ teaspoon ground red chilli, such as Kashmiri (see page 18)
½ teaspoon turmeric powder
6 garlic cloves, coarsely chopped
One (2-inch) knob of ginger, peeled and thinly sliced
1 cinnamon stick, broken into 2 to 3 pieces
1 star anise, crushed with a heavy pan (optional)
3 or 4 whole cloves
1 teaspoon whole black peppercorns
6 cups canola oil, for frying
Toasted sesame seeds, for garnish (optional)
Finely chopped green onions, for garnish (optional)
Coarsely chopped cilantro leaves, for garnish (optional)
Fried curry leaves, for garnish (optional)

To make the marinade, combine all the ingredients in a small bowl and mix well. Set aside.

To make the ribs, preheat the oven to 425°F. Trim the excess fat from the ribs on the meat side, then cut the rack into single ribs. Place in a casserole dish and toss with the sesame oil to coat lightly.

In a small bowl, mix the salt, ground red chilli, and turmeric, and toss the ribs with this spice mix, coating evenly.

Place the ribs on a rimmed sheet pan, spacing them to separate, and roast for 15 minutes. Pull the sheet pan from the oven and pour about two-thirds of the marinade over the ribs, then scatter the garlic, ginger, cinnamon, star anise (if using), cloves, and peppercorns over them. (Reserve the remaining marinade for the glaze.)

Turn the oven down to 350°F. Cover the sheet pan with aluminum foil, return the ribs to the oven, and cook for about 1 hour. The ribs won't be falling off the bone or anything at this point, but they'll be cooked. Remove the pan from the oven and leave the foil on while you let things cool for 15 minutes or so. Uncover the pan and remove the ribs from the braising liquid; discard the liquid.

Continued

TAMARIND-GLAZED SPARE RIBS

Continued

At this point, you can store the ribs in the refrigerator until you're ready to fry them, up to 3 or 4 days.

To fry the ribs, heat the canola oil to 350°F in a large heavy-bottomed pot suitable for deep-frying; use an oil thermometer to ensure the correct temperature. While the oil is coming to temperature, heat the remaining marinade in a large wide saucepan over medium-low heat until simmering.

This next part goes fast—the ribs are already cooked, and we're just softening them up so they're primed to suck up the glaze we're about to hit them with.

Working in batches to avoid overcrowding, add the ribs to the hot oil for about 2 minutes, until the outside is charred and crispy.

As the ribs finish frying, take them out of the oil and drop them into the pan with the glaze; turn to coat well. (Dunking hot ribs into the sauce guarantees maximum sauce absorption.) Repeat until all the ribs are fried and coated.

Plate the ribs and garnish with sesame seeds, green onions, cilantro, and/or curry leaves if you like. Serve hot.

The ribs are best eaten the day they're made, but leftovers will keep, tightly covered in the refrigerator, for up to 3 days.

CHICKEN LOLLIPOPS

Serves 4

As fun to eat as they are to make, these little French chicken drumettes are marinated in the Indian idea of what constitutes a Chinese marinade, which involves soy sauce, Mae Ploy sweet chilli sauce, and rice wine vinegar (along with curry leaves and fresh green chillies, of course).

The hack is the cornstarch, which gives the lollipops a delightfully crispy texture to go with their explosively sweet-sour-spicy sauce. They're best when deep-fried, so the directions below are for deep-frying. They can also be either pan-fried with less oil than we call for below, dry-roasted in the oven, or perfectly crisped up in an air fryer.

2 pounds cut chicken wings (see Note, page 162)

SAUCE

2 teaspoons neutral oil, such as grapeseed

1 tablespoon minced garlic (2 to 3 cloves)

1 tablespoon peeled and minced fresh ginger (about a 1-inch knob)

1 teaspoon minced fresh Thai or serrano chilli (depending on your heat tolerance)

10 curry leaves (optional)

¼ teaspoon ground red chilli, such as Kashmiri (see page 18)

½ teaspoon coriander powder

1½ tablespoons rice wine vinegar, plus more to taste

1 tablespoon soy sauce, plus more to taste

2 tablespoons sweet chilli sauce (such as Mae Ploy or Maggi), plus more to taste

Kosher salt (optional)

2 tablespoons Ginger-Garlic Paste (page 276)

1 teaspoon ground red chilli, such as Kashmiri (see page 18)

½ teaspoon kosher salt

4 to 6 cups canola oil, for frying

1 cup cornstarch

Shredded green cabbage, for serving (optional)

The first order of business is to peel the skin off of each chicken wing (see photographs, page 162). The easiest way to do this on the drumette is to use a sharp paring knife to cut around the skinny part of the bone, so you can easily pull the skin away from the drumette. Then cut through the skin on the flat wing part and use your fingers to peel the skin off and discard it. Don't sweat the technique too much—just try to separate the drumette and flat parts neatly and get the skin off both sides without butchering the meat.

Stand each drumette on a cutting board with the meat part down and bone part up, and use a paring knife to push or scrape the meat of the drumstick down toward the cutting board. It should look like a lollipop, the meat pushed down toward the bottom in a bulbous orb, with an exposed white bone sticking out. Repeat with all the drumettes.

For the wing part, there are two bones: a large one and a small skinny one. Pick either end and perform the same scraping motion, pushing all the meat down toward the bottom. When you're finished, both bones will be sticking out; break off the skinnier one by twisting it until it pulls loose at both ends, and discard it. Repeat this process with all the flat wing parts.

At this point, you should have a bunch of lollipop-looking parts. The hard work is done. Set the wings aside while you make the sauce.

To make the sauce, heat the neutral oil in a large heavy-bottomed saucepan over medium-high heat until shimmering. Add the garlic and ginger and cook, stirring, until the garlic starts to brown on the edges, 60 to 90 seconds. Add the green chillies and the curry leaves (if using). The curry leaves will pop and sputter for a few seconds, and once the sputtering stops and they start to darken, add the ground red chilli and coriander and mix well for another minute.

Stir in the rice wine vinegar, soy sauce, and sweet chilli sauce and cook, stirring occasionally, until the sauce starts to bubble, 3 to 5 minutes. Turn the heat down to medium-low and add ¼ cup of water. Stir for another minute and adjust the heat to keep the sauce at a simmer. Taste for seasoning (sweet/sour/spicy) and add a splash of whatever you think it needs. We didn't add any salt to the sauce because the soy sauce is salty. But feel free to add salt or more soy sauce to taste. Set the sauce aside in the pan.

To fry the drumettes, combine the ginger-garlic paste, ground red chilli, and salt in a small bowl and rub this paste into the meaty part of the lollipops.

Continued

CHICKEN LOLLIPOPS

Continued

In a large heavy-bottomed pot suitable for deep-frying, heat the canola oil to 350°F on an oil thermometer.

Put the cornstarch in a small bowl. Holding a lollipop by the bone, dredge the head in the cornstarch and shake off excess. Lower the lollipop head-first into the hot oil, and repeat, working in batches to avoid overcrowding. Cook the lollipops until they're golden brown and crispy, 8 to 10 minutes (or until a meat thermometer inserted into the thickest part of the meat reads 165°F).

As the lollipops come out of the oil, drop them into the pan with the chilli sauce and turn to coat well. (Dunking them hot into the sauce guarantees maximum sauce absorption.)

When the lollipops are all fried and coated with chilli sauce, serve them on a bed of shredded cabbage if you like. Eat with your hands.

Chicken lollipops are best eaten the day they're made, but leftovers will keep, tightly covered in the refrigerator, for up to 3 days.

Note: ***Cut chicken wings have both the wing and the drumstick intact, but not the wing tip. If you can't find them, just buy whole wings and remove the tip joint with a sharp knife.***

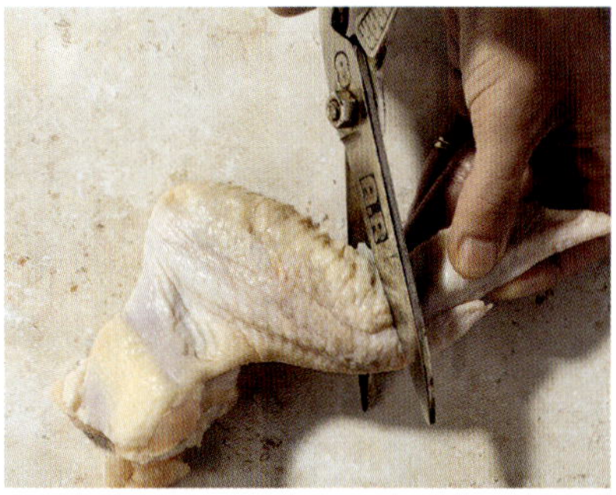
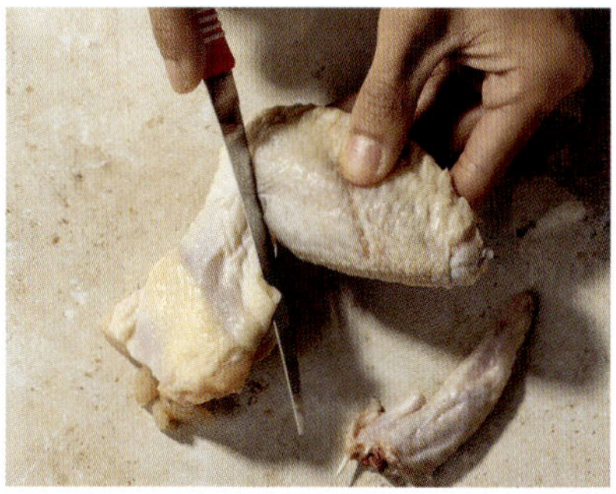
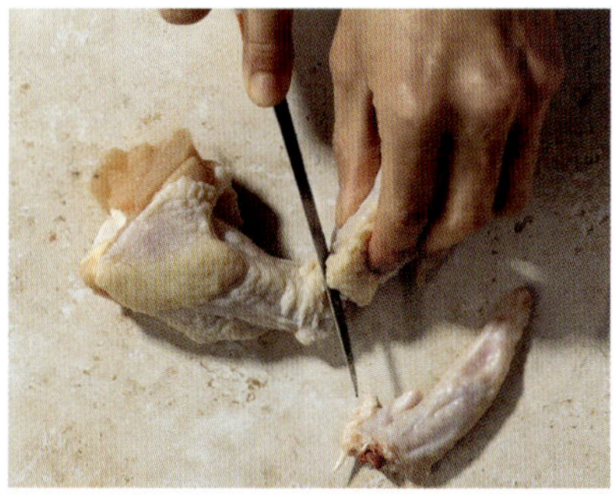

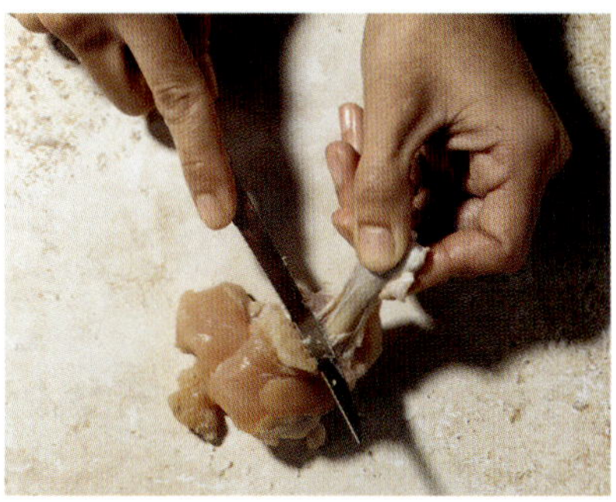

GRILL (SIGRI)

AKA NIGHT MOVES

For a mostly vegetarian country, India has a fantastic reputation for grilled and tandoori meats (most of which are sold on the streets after dark, which is why we've been semi-jokingly referring to this chapter as "night moves").

The typical grill, or sigri, is a long, narrow charcoal brazier that probably made its way from the Middle East to Afghanistan and down to northern India during the Mughal Empire (1500s to 1800s). The tandoor, which is essentially a clay convection oven, likely made its way to India around the same time, where it was primarily used for making breads such as the ever-popular naan. But sometime in the early 1900s, meats also started getting cooked in the tandoor, and the technique became popular in contemporary Indian cuisine. But while early tandoori-grilling enthusiasts were grilling up all kinds of exotic game meats (peacock, anyone?), today's omnivores favor chicken, beef, lamb, and goat.

I truly believe that no nation has perfected the art of flavor on the grill the way India has. When I moved to the US, it was a bit of a shock to me to see how Americans grilled. The idea of a hamburger patty—with absolutely no seasoning—being cooked on a propane grill and shoved into a bland bun blew my mind, in a bad way. What a waste of perfectly good meat!

If there's one superpower I have, it's grilling at home, quickly, efficiently, and with an explosion of flavor. Yes, we're gonna make tandoori chicken. Not having tandoori chicken in this chapter would be like leaving Tom Cruise out of the *Mission Impossible* franchise. Do note that, while recipe titles with the word "tandoori" in front technically signify foods cooked in a tandoor oven, we're not doing that. But the flavor profile of yogurt and ground Kashmiri red chilli has become synonymous with these dishes, so we're using the term in reference to our method of replicating that typical tandoori flavor at home, on the grill.

But lest you think the tando bird is India's only contribution to America's obsession with smoke and fire, you're also going to learn how to make the most succulent lamb chops, finely spiced ground meats, delicate flaky fish, and juiciest pork chops on the grill, as God intended.

TANDOORI CHICKEN

Serves 4 to 6

Nothing in Indian cooking has quite captured the imagination of Westerners like the tandoor—that 900°F clay oven in which the Indian equivalent of roast chicken—albeit roast chicken with mind- and palate-blowing flavor—is cooked.

Clay ovens have been around in the Middle East since antiquity. The tool was likely brought to India by some combination and cross-cultural pollination of Moguls, Persians, Turks, and Afghans. As far as I can tell, in every other culture the clay or brick oven is used almost exclusively to cook flat breads (even the Italians predominantly cook pizza in their brick ovens). But sometime around the turn of the twentieth century, the Indian tandoor became synonymous with tandoori chicken, lamb chops, paneer tikka, and assorted variations.

Hand in hand with the tandoor is the classic tandoori look and flavor, epitomized by the glow-in-the-dark red chicken popularized by modern-day tandoori chicken joints. More often than not, that luminescent red is achieved with the liberal use of (much cheaper and more convenient) food coloring, instead of the original Kashmiri chillies, which are renowned for their flavor and color.

A proper tandoori chicken is an absolute revelation of flavor and texture. Perfectly grilled with little bits of char on the outside, it also has succulent tender flesh on the inside and is zingy with the warm, slow heat of red chillies and the tang of yogurt and lime juice. With fenugreek leaves interplaying with the aromatics of garam masala, it truly is a magical dish. No wonder it's India's number one culinary export to the rest of the world.

I don't expect many of you to have a tandoor at home, so this recipe has been adapted for a home oven. You might have an instinct to use a grill because of its live-fire component, but unless you have a very specific kind of grill like a Big Green Egg (which is essentially a variation on the idea of a tandoor), an oven is better suited to getting a result that's close to the original.

MARINADE

1 tablespoon Ginger-Garlic Paste (page 276)

1 tablespoon freshly squeezed lime juice, plus more to taste

½ cup full-fat Greek yogurt (see Notes, page 168)

1 teaspoon ground red chilli, such as Kashmiri (see page 18)

2 tablespoons tandoori masala (see page 33)

1 tablespoon green chilli paste (see Notes, page 168)

½ teaspoon kosher salt, plus more to taste

2 tablespoons neutral oil, such as grapeseed

2 pounds bone-in chicken thighs and legs

Neutral oil, such as grapeseed, for the wire rack

FOR BASTING

¼ cup ghee or butter

1 teaspoon ground red chilli, such as Kashmiri (see page 18)

¼ teaspoon fenugreek leaves (optional)

Thinly sliced red onions, for serving

Freshly squeezed lime juice, for serving

Chaat masala (see page 33), for serving

Store-bought naan, for serving (see page 84)

Butter, for the naan

To make the marinade, combine all the ingredients in a large bowl. Whisk (or use your hand) to make sure everything is well incorporated. Taste for acidity and salt and add lime juice or salt as needed.

Into the meat of each piece of chicken, cut deep slits about 2 inches apart, pushing your knife tip down to the bone. Pat the chicken dry and add it to the marinade, ensuring that it's fully coated and that some marinade gets into the slits. Marinate for a minimum of 30 minutes and up to 6 hours.

When you're ready to cook the chicken, heat the oven to its highest cooking temperature (usually around 500°F—do not set it to broil). If you have a convection fan option, turn it on.

Oil a wire rack (if you have one) and place it over a sheet pan lined with aluminum foil (this catches the drippings and makes cleanup easy). If you don't have a wire rack, it's okay—just line the sheet pan with aluminum

Continued

TANDOORI CHICKEN

Continued

> ### SUPER SPECIAL SECRET SPICE BLEND
>
> *While we discuss several masalas throughout this book, there is one spice blend worth mentioning. Indians' unique approach to grilling meat involves seasoning almost any cut with salt, turmeric powder, and ground red chilli. This trifecta is used regardless of what other spices or masalas might come later. The salt seasons and helps tenderize the meat (particularly important for things like goat); the turmeric adds both flavor and an antibacterial component; and the chilli powder adds a base layer of heat so that you don't end up with a dish where the curry tastes spicy but the protein itself is bland. We don't really have a name for this meat rub, but we do tell you to do it in many of the recipes in this chapter and the next, so we're calling your attention to it here.*

foil and oil it well. Place the chicken pieces on the rack or pan as far apart as you can so that each piece gets the maximum amount of heat circulation. Roast for 20 minutes.

When the chicken goes in the oven, make the basting oil. In a small saucepan over low heat, heat the ghee or butter until it's warm and liquid. Sprinkle in the ground chilli and fenugreek (if using). Every 6 to 7 minutes, pull the sheet pan out and baste the chicken with this chilli-infused ghee before returning it to the oven.

When the 20 minutes have elapsed, set the oven to broil and continue cooking the chicken for another 3 to 5 minutes; this gives it some color and a light char on top. Check for doneness: An instant-read thermometer inserted into the thickest part of the meat (avoiding the bone) should read 165°F.

While the chicken broils, stir together the thinly sliced red onions, a few squeezes of fresh lime juice, and a pinch of chaat masala. Heat the naan. Serve the chicken with the macerated onions and a side of hot buttered naan.

Leftover tandoori chicken keeps, tightly covered in the refrigerator, for up to 3 days.

Notes: ***Regular yogurt has too much water, which makes a marinade thin when it sits for a while—that's why we call for Greek yogurt here. If you don't have Greek yogurt but you do have regular yogurt, no worries—put about ⅔ cup of regular yogurt in a mesh strainer and suspend it over a bowl overnight in the fridge. The water will slowly drip out, and by the next day you'll have a deliciously thick yogurt similar in texture to the Greek stuff.***

To make green chilli paste, smash or blitz 3 to 4 fresh green chillies (Thai or serrano, depending on your heat tolerance) in a mortar and pestle or small food processor with a teaspoon or so of water and a pinch of kosher salt until you have a thick paste.

TANDOORI LAMB CHOPS

Serves 4 to 6

The Indian lamb chop traditionally is not a medium-rare cut of New Zealand's grass-fed finest. We are more apt to cook the living daylights out of a leg of mutton from a ewe that has given her all before being sent to the final pasture in the sky. But I do love a classic American-style lamb chop, and in this recipe, we will get the best of both worlds by tenderizing our lamb chops, adding flavor and charring them into the finest lamb chops you've ever tasted.

My version takes it back to how meats were traditionally cooked in the Indo-Pakistan-Afghan-Persian hodgepodge: on a grill. (Or in an oven, if you don't have a grill.) We replace the stain-your-hands-red dye with ground red Kashmiri chilli powder. Kashmiri is the beautiful, vibrant, citrusy, not-too-high-on-the-Scoville-scale chilli pepper that originally gave this dish its beautiful orange hue.

PS: We like a double-cut chop taken from the rack for a main course, but single-rib chops cut from the rack make great appetizer-size lamb lollipops!

1 tablespoon green chilli paste (see Note, page 168)
2 tablespoons Ginger-Garlic Paste (page 276)
1 tablespoon freshly squeezed lime juice, plus more for serving
1 tablespoon distilled white vinegar
1½ teaspoons ground red chilli, such as Kashmiri (see page 18)
1 teaspoon turmeric powder
1 teaspoon kosher salt
1 tablespoon tandoori masala (see page 33)
8 to 10 bone-in thick-cut lamb chops, cut from 2 racks of lamb (2½ to 3 pounds total)
Thinly sliced red onions, for serving
Chaat masala (see page 33), for serving
Store-bought naan, for serving (see page 84)
Butter, for the naan
Raita, for serving (page 274; optional)

In a large bowl, combine the green chilli paste, ginger-garlic paste, lime juice, vinegar, ground red chilli, turmeric, salt, and tandoori masala. Stir together to create a paste.

Add the lamb chops to the bowl and mix them around in the paste with your hands, making sure they are fully coated. Really get in there—don't be shy.

Heat a grill (or grill pan) over medium-high heat until a drop of water sizzles when sprinkled over it. Grill the lamb chops for 2 to 3 minutes per side, until an instant-read thermometer inserted into the thickest part of the chops registers 120°F for rare or 130°F for medium-rare. Rest the chops for about 10 minutes before serving.

While the lamb rests, stir together a handful of thinly sliced red onions, a few squeezes of fresh lime juice, and a pinch of chaat masala. Heat the naan.

Serve the lamb with the macerated onions and a side of hot buttered naan and raita (if using). Leftovers keep, tightly covered in the refrigerator, for up to 4 days.

TANDOORI SALMON

Serves 4

This dish was in regular rotation on weekends in the early days of Chai Pani.

Salmon with a high fat content is best for roasting. King and sockeye salmon are absolutely at the top of the salmon flavor chain, with their high oil content and succulent, flaky flesh. Depending on where you live, you may be more likely to find farmed Atlantic salmon at your grocery store; this is not always a bad thing, since many fish farms today are more sustainable than those of years past. Ask at the seafood counter about the provenance of the fish, or look at the label if it's prepackaged. (If you're shopping at a place where no one has any idea where the fish or meat comes from, you need to switch to a different grocery store.)

Eagle-eyed readers will notice that the ingredients and preparation for this tandoori marinade are very similar to those in the recipe for Tandoori Chicken on page 167. Whichever one you're making, my advice is to make extra marinade for use in the other recipe later in the week—I love a good two-for-one! Tandoori marinade can be made ahead of time, and because of the high acidity from the yogurt and lime juice, it can be stored for up to a week.

MARINADE

1 teaspoon Ginger-Garlic Paste (page 276)

1 tablespoon freshly squeezed lime juice, plus more to taste

½ cup full-fat Greek yogurt (see Note, page 168)

1 teaspoon ground red chilli, such as Kashmiri (see page 18)

1 tablespoon tandoori masala (see page 33)

¼ teaspoon kosher salt, plus more to taste

1 tablespoon neutral oil, such as grapeseed

4 garlic cloves

4 thick center-cut salmon fillets or 1 large belly piece (skin on), approximately 2 pounds total

Kosher salt

Oil, for the pan

Thinly sliced red onions, for serving

Freshly squeezed lime juice, for serving

Chaat masala (see page 33), for serving

Store-bought naan, for serving (see page 84)

Butter, for the naan

Heat the oven to 325°F. Because of its delicate texture, salmon needs to be cooked at a lower temperature. (If you've noticed some white stuff coming out the sides when you're cooking salmon, that's a protein called albumen. When salmon is cooked at too high a temperature, the muscle fibers seize up and squeeze out albumen.)

To make the marinade, combine the ginger-garlic paste, lime juice, yogurt, ground red chilli, tandoori masala, salt, and oil in a small bowl. Whisk (or mix with your hand) to make sure everything is well incorporated. Taste for acidity and salt and add lime juice or salt as needed.

Cut each garlic clove into 3 or 4 slices lengthwise. Pat the salmon dry and season very lightly with salt on both sides. Pierce the flesh with the tip of a slice of garlic and push it all the way down so the slice is almost completely embedded in the salmon. Continue with the remaining garlic, using 3 to 4 slices per fillet. (This is a little uncle hack I figured out to get some extra flavor into the flesh of the fish. The garlic slices steam inside the fish while it's cooking and, if you like garlic as much as I do, it adds a lovely pop of flavor when you bite into a piece.)

Rub the marinade into the top and sides of the salmon, spreading it evenly in a very thin layer. If you don't use up all of the marinade, that's okay: It'll keep in a sealed container for up to a week and can be used on tandoori chicken or lamb chops (page 167 and page 171).

Line a sheet pan with aluminum foil. Lightly oil the foil and sprinkle a bit of salt across it; this helps prevent the salmon from sticking. Place the salmon skin side down and roast on the oven's middle rack for about 15 minutes, or until the internal temperature reaches 120°F to 125°F for medium-rare.

Move the tray to the top rack in the oven and turn on the broiler. Broil until the top of the salmon is seared and bubbling, about 2 minutes. I like my salmon pink in the center, but you can leave it in there for another minute or two if you like yours more thoroughly cooked.

While the salmon broils, stir together a handful of thinly sliced red onions, a few squeezes of fresh lime juice, and a pinch of chaat masala. Heat the naan in the toaster oven or in the lower section of the oven while the salmon is broiling.

Serve the salmon with the macerated onions and a side of hot buttered naan.

Leftovers keep, tightly covered in the refrigerator, for up to 2 days.

Premchand
Premchand
JUMBO
Premchand
JUMBO
DHANA DAL

SEEKH KEBABS

Makes 6 kebabs

The word "seekh" means the skewer upon which the meat is pierced and grilled. So a seekh kebab, by definition, is meat on a skewer cooked over an open flame. Kebabs themselves were a part of the Indian royal diet as far back as 1200 CE, though over time, as the Mughal Empire grew to influence almost all of India, kebabs and seekh-style cooking became ubiquitous throughout the subcontinent. Seekh kebabs are everywhere today, and they're hugely popular in Delhi, Lucknow, and Hyderabad.

This particular recipe is my variation on the traditional technique, in which onions, garlic, ginger, and mint are ground very finely, to nearly a puree, and mixed with lamb meat. The idea is that the kebab should almost melt in your mouth—a nod to the days when emperors were so decadent that they wanted meat they could eat without chewing. My palate, however, leans toward lamb with more texture—and the occasional burst of garlicky flavor—so I don't chop everything quite so finely. My version has the added benefit of holding up better on the grill, though you can also cook these on a griddle or in a large, blazing-hot cast-iron pan on the stovetop. You'll also need six 10-inch metal or wooden skewers.

Serve these hot off the grill with naan and accompaniments.

2 teaspoons cumin powder
2 teaspoons ground red chilli, such as Kashmiri (see page 18)
2 teaspoons turmeric powder
1 tablespoon kosher salt
1 tablespoon finely chopped mint leaves
¼ cup finely chopped cilantro leaves
¼ cup finely diced red onions (from about ½ medium onion)
2 finely chopped fresh Thai or serrano chillies (depending on your heat tolerance)
4 finely chopped garlic cloves
One (2-inch) knob fresh ginger, peeled and finely chopped
3 pounds ground lamb or beef, chilled
Naan (store-bought is fine) or chapati (page 212), for serving (optional)
Julienned red onions, for serving (optional)
Finely chopped mint and/or cilantro, for serving (optional)
Green Chutney (page 270), for serving (optional)
Rosemary Grilled Onions (page 176), for serving (optional)

In a large bowl, combine the cumin, ground red chilli, turmeric, salt, mint, cilantro, red onions, green chillies, garlic, and ginger, and stir to combine. Add the lamb or beef and mix well with your hands (it's helpful if the meat is cold, so the fat doesn't melt and get all over your hands).

Refrigerate for at least 1 hour or up to 4 hours—the kebabs form more easily when the meat is cold. If you're using wooden skewers, soak them in water for 15 to 30 minutes before grilling.

Form the kebabs with your hands, rolling the meat into six equal-size balls, each slightly larger than a golf ball. Pierce the tip of each skewer through the middle of a ball and use your hands to smooth the ball into an oblong kebab that runs down the length of the skewer. It should be 4 to 6 inches long, and though you should try to keep an even thickness on all sides, don't worry too much about getting it perfect—it'll grill up just fine.

Heat the grill to as high as it goes (if you're using a griddle or cast-iron pan, heat it over high heat). Kebabs are meant to be cooked fast—there should be an audible sizzle when the meat hits the grill. Once the grill surface is ripping hot, turn the flame down to medium-high and add the kebabs, turning occasionally, until brown on all sides, 7 to 10 minutes.

Slide the meat off the skewer before plating and serving hot with accompaniments of your choice: naan, red onions, fresh herbs, chutney, or grilled onions. Leftovers keep, tightly covered in the refrigerator, for up to 4 days.

ROSEMARY GRILLED ONIONS

Serves 4

Whenever I'm grilling, I'm conscious that I've got a live-fire heat source going, and I look for ways to get other dishes done with minimal effort. This particular recipe is great because you don't really need to measure anything, and you're just using passive grill time to make a delicious side for grilled lamb and other meats.

When I was growing up, it wasn't unusual to see both a big pot sitting on a wood-fired stove and a bunch of root vegetables shoved into the embers beneath it to roast. Those veggies could be eaten as an accompaniment to whatever was in the pot or stored for later. So while this recipe isn't particularly Indian in flavor profile, it pairs well with those flavors, and it captures the same idea: to make as many things as possible with a single fire.

2 large red onions, unpeeled
Kosher salt
Freshly ground black pepper
2 teaspoons unsalted butter
2 sprigs fresh rosemary
Olive oil

Setting each onion on its stem end, slice halfway down from the top of the root end, making an X shape. Don't cut all the way through. Using your fingers, pry the onions open a little bit without splitting them in two.

Sprinkle salt and pepper into each wedge, stick a teaspoon of butter and a sprig of fresh rosemary in there, and drizzle the whole thing with a teaspoon or so of olive oil.

Wrap each onion tightly in aluminum foil and place it on the grill, preferably while you're cooking something else on it. Turn the onions occasionally and roast until they are soft to the touch when pressed, about 30 minutes.

To serve, unwrap the onions and peel off the outer layers. Serve hot as an accompaniment to grilled meats or kebabs. Leftovers keep, tightly covered in the refrigerator, for up to 5 days.

PANEER TIKKA

Serves 4

This is the vegetarian counterpoint to the tandoori chicken, lamb, and salmon recipes on pages 167 to 172, using paneer instead of meat. Although we have a recipe for homemade paneer on page 274, I actually recommend using the store-bought stuff here, as it's been pressed to get rid of moisture and it easily slices into cubes. If for some reason you can't find fresh paneer in the store, halloumi is a fine alternative.

It's important that the vegetables in these skewers aren't cut wider than the paneer cubes; otherwise the cheese won't touch the cooking surface. Also, while you can cook most tandoori meats on the stovetop if you don't have a grill, for this one, I actually prefer the oven-cooked method: It's less work, and you don't lose the runny marinade between the grill grates. I'm including directions for both techniques; play around and see what works best for you.

Serve these tikkas as is with just a squeeze of fresh lime, slide them into a paratha to make a tikka roll, or drop them atop the Desi Salad on page 49.

½ cup plain full-fat yogurt

1½ tablespoons freshly squeezed lime juice

2 garlic cloves, minced

1 teaspoon coarsely chopped cilantro leaves

1 tablespoon tandoori masala (see page 33)

1 teaspoon ground red chilli, such as Kashmiri (see page 18)

Pinch of kosher salt

Pinch of coarsely ground black pepper

1 pound store-bought paneer, cut into 1½-inch cubes

½ green bell pepper, cut into 1-inch pieces

¼ large red onion, cut into 1-inch pieces

Neutral oil, for grilling

You'll need six 10-inch metal or wooden skewers; if you're using wooden skewers, soak them in water for 15 to 30 minutes before you use them.

In a large bowl, combine the yogurt, lime juice, garlic, cilantro, tandoori masala, ground red chilli, salt, and pepper. Stir together to combine. Taste and adjust the seasoning to your liking. Add the paneer, bell pepper, and onion to the marinade and toss to coat completely.

Thread the paneer and veggies onto the skewers, alternating between the paneer, onion, and bell pepper and being careful not to crowd the ingredients.

If you're using a grill, heat the grill as high as it goes—crank the burners up to maximum heat, leave the lid down, and let this thing get very hot. We're trying to replicate the heat and convection effect of a clay oven—we'll never get all the way there, but we can try. Make sure the grates are well oiled, and drizzle oil over the skewers before you put them on the grill to keep them from sticking.

Get the skewers onto the grill quickly and cover to retain the heat. Cook for 3 to 5 minutes, until the paneer takes on some char, then uncover and flip. (The skewers should come off the grill easily if the grates are well seasoned and you've used some oil.) Paneer is fully cooked, so your main goal here is to get that nice char on the outside of the cheese and vegetables.

If you're using the oven, the same rules apply about getting the oven very hot—crank it up to its maximum temperature, and if you have a convection setting, turn it on. Place the paneer skewers 1 to 2 inches apart on an aluminum foil–lined sheet pan and drizzle with oil. Cook on the middle rack until the paneer starts browning, about 7 minutes, then flip the skewers and cook until the paneer is evenly browned on all sides and no wetness from the marinade remains, another 7 to 10 minutes.

Slide the paneer and veggies off each skewer before plating, and serve hot (see serving suggestions in the headnote). Leftovers keep, tightly covered in the refrigerator, for up to 4 days.

LAMB BOTI KEBABS

Serves 4

A boti is a chunk of meat; that's all. When, in what I thought was a flash of genius, I named my grill-based restaurant Botiwalla, I didn't realize that I'd spend the rest of my life explaining to my customers that a boti is just a piece of meat. It seems that Americans tend to think of kebabs as chunks of meat, whereas in India, a kebab can be meat in either ground form (as it is in the Seekh Kebab recipe on page 175) or chunk form.

This is likely a much earlier form of cooking meat over fire than the more sophisticated ground meat versions. Grilled meat techniques in India come primarily from Persia and Afghanistan, and many kebab recipes tend to be fairly one-note, flavor-wise. When casting about for a kebab recipe with a different flavor profile that still read as Indian, I discovered a South Indian treatment involving black pepper, curry leaves, and the surprise addition of soy sauce that's apparently a holdover from early Polynesian incursions into the region. I love that the flavors in this recipe tell of a different type of trade—not one driven by European colonial exploration but by Asians exploring the Indian Ocean. This masala will keep, tightly covered in the refrigerator, for up to four weeks, and it serves as a delicious marinade for all kinds of grilled meats and veggies.

4 tablespoons canola oil

2 cups coarsely chopped red onion (about 2 medium onions)

½ cup fresh or dried curry leaves

2 tablespoons peeled and finely chopped fresh ginger (about a 2-inch knob)

2 tablespoons finely chopped garlic (about 6 cloves)

2 to 3 finely chopped fresh Thai or serrano chillies (depending on your heat tolerance)

1 tablespoon tamarind paste (see page 19)

1 teaspoon sugar

¼ cup soy sauce

¼ cup distilled white vinegar

2 tablespoons coarsely ground black pepper

2 teaspoons kosher salt, plus more to taste

One (3-pound) boneless lamb shoulder

Store-bought naan or Chapati (page 212), for serving

Raita (page 274), for serving

In a large nonstick skillet over high heat, heat 2 tablespoons of the oil until shimmering. Add the onions and turn the heat down to medium, lightly frying the onions until they're translucent and the edges are slightly brown, 3 to 5 minutes.

Add the curry leaves, ginger, garlic, and chillies and stir for 1 to 2 minutes. Keep the heat at medium-low; you don't want the onions or garlic to overcook.

Add the tamarind paste, sugar, soy sauce, vinegar, black pepper, and salt. Stir thoroughly to combine and cook for 1 to 2 minutes. Remove from the heat.

After the onion mixture has cooled, scrape it into a mini food processor or blender and blend it into a coarse paste.

Cut the lamb into small even pieces, about 2 inches each.

Season the lamb liberally with salt. Let it sit at room temperature for 10 minutes, so that the salt begins to tenderize the meat, then generously apply the masala; you should use about 1 cup of the masala for the three pounds of meat.

Let the meat marinate, in the refrigerator, for at least 30 minutes and up to 6 hours. You'll need six 10-inch metal or wood skewers for grilling; if you're using wood skewers, submerge them in water for 15 to 30 minutes before you load them up.

Thread the meat onto the skewers—you should be able to fit 5 to 6 pieces on each skewer—and brush with the remaining 2 tablespoons of oil.

Heat the grill as hot as it goes, or, if you're using a griddle or a cast-iron pan, heat it over high heat until it's sizzling hot. Kebabs are meant to be cooked fast—there should be an audible sizzle when the meat hits the grill or the pan surface. Once the surface is ripping hot, turn the flame down to medium-high and grill the kebabs, turning occasionally, until the meat is browned on all sides and medium rare inside, 7 to 9 minutes. You are looking for an internal temperature of around 130°F.

Slide the meat off the skewers and serve hot, placing the meat either directly into naan or chapati to make handheld sandwiches or alongside the bread, with raita for dunking. Leftovers keep, tightly covered in the refrigerator, for up to 4 days.

MASALA PORK CHOPS

Serves 2

What are pork chops doing in an Indian cookbook, you ask? The answer is simple: nostalgia. As Parsis we are carnivores, unfettered by the various religion-based dietary restraints Hindus, Jews, Muslims, and others navigate. Not only can we eat meat with abandon, we can eat ALL the meats—chicken, goat, lamb, beef, pork, fish, shellfish. If it flies, walks, or swims, it's (literally) fair game!

Back in India, the butcher shops in my part of town stood alone in a small dusty field, away from all other businesses and were given a wide berth by Hindu vegetarians. The building was divided into four rooms, each with its own entrance. One room sold pork and was run by a Christian family. (When Portuguese missionaries arrived in Goa in the 1600s and started converting Hindus to Christianity, they introduced pork into the local diet, sealing the conversion of the local population and ensuring they couldn't subsequently be converted to Judaism or Islam, or even back to Hinduism.) The Muslims sold beef in a different room, and non-vegetarian Hindus sold goat meat in the third room. The last room sold chicken and eggs.

The cook at my grandparents' bed-and-breakfast made the best pork chops I can remember, using a simple rub of turmeric, ground red chilli, salt, and ginger-garlic paste. I ate so many pork chops in one sitting that I actually broke out in meat sweats. I've cheffed up his recipe a bit, but the extra effort is entirely worth it.

I like to cook these thick pork chops low and slow, a time-tested method for juicy, tender meat, as any BBQ pitmaster will tell you. (Cooking at high heat causes the muscle fibers in meat to quickly shrink and tighten, squeezing out moisture and drying out the meat; don't do this.) I also like to roast these chops (and most other cuts of meat or fish) on a wire rack that fits perfectly into a sheet pan; the rack elevates the meat and allows heat to circulate all around it. That way, you don't end up with a piece of meat that's beautifully brown on top but soggy on the bottom because it's been resting directly on the pan.

2 thick (1½ inches or more) bone-in, rib-cut pork chops

1¼ teaspoons kosher salt

½ teaspoon sugar

½ teaspoon turmeric powder

½ teaspoon ground red chilli, such as Kashmiri (see page 18)

½ teaspoon neutral oil, such as grapeseed, plus more for searing the pork

2 teaspoons Ginger-Garlic Paste (page 276)

2 tablespoons unsalted butter or ghee

Pat the pork chops dry with paper towels. Season well with 1 teaspoon of the salt and the sugar, sprinkling liberally on all sides.

Rest the chops on a wire rack set over a sheet pan in the refrigerator for at least 8 hours or overnight. Resting the pork this way does two things: It allows osmosis to draw the salt and sugar into the tissues for better flavor, and it reduces moisture, allowing a great crust to form during the pan-searing step. Lifting the chops off the pan or plate ensures it dries on both sides. If you don't have a wire rack, do as Indians do, and jugaad yourself a solution by laying a few chopsticks across a plate to elevate the meat.

Once the chops have rested, mix the turmeric and ground red chilli together in a small bowl and rub it all over the meat.

In a small bowl, mix together the remaining ¼ teaspoon salt with the oil and ginger-garlic paste. Rub this all over the meat. You don't want a thick crust of ginger-garlic paste, so really rub it in there, spreading the paste evenly and avoiding excessive clumps.

To cook the chops, we're going to use the reverse-sear method that has been popularized by some food nerd guys I follow. While it's a bit more time-consuming, it gives the best results if you're looking for a juicy interior with a lovely crust.

Preheat the oven to 250°F. Line a sheet pan with foil and place a wire rack above the sheet. Put the chops on the rack and cook until the interior temperature reaches 120°F, about 30 minutes.

In a large cast-iron or stainless-steel skillet, heat about 1 teaspoon of oil until shimmering over high heat. Place the chops in the pan and sear, flipping once, for about 1 minute on each side.

Turn the heat down to medium-high and add the butter or ghee on the side of the pan closest to you. Spoon the melted butter over the top of the chops as they cook for the next 2 minutes or so (tilt the pan towards you a bit to get at the butter), flipping the chops once or twice to baste both sides. If you want to get extra cheffy, use tongs to stand the chops on their edges to melt off some of the fat cap there.

The chops are done when an instant-read thermometer stuck into the thickest part of the chop reads between 130°F and 140°F, which is the sweet spot for medium.

Set a wire rack over a pan or plate and rest the chops for 5 to 7 minutes until they're ready to eat. Serve with your choice of sides, such as Apple Sabji on page 203, Masala Green Beans on page 201, or Rosemary Grilled Onions on page 176. Leftover pork keeps, tightly covered in the refrigerator, for up to 3 days.

CHICKEN TIKKA ROLLS

Makes 6 rolls

Grilled meat (or paneer) served with naan on the side and an accompaniment of onions, chilli, and cilantro is the most common way to order chicken tikka in India. A premade wrap is a somewhat newfangled concoction, but it's becoming increasingly popular in India as more and more city workers want food on the go. Enter the tikka roll, which combines all those delicious flavors into one easy-to-eat handheld meal.

With their big flavors and short cooking time, these rolls are a great alternative to grilling burgers and dogs at your next backyard barbecue. This recipe is for chicken, but you can also use boneless leg of lamb, sirloin, or cubed paneer, or go big and do a mix of all four, letting people assemble their own roll with all the fixings.

A quick note on the name: "Tikka" as it relates to chicken describes a boneless piece of white meat typically cooked in a tandoor oven or on a sigri (open charcoal brazier). The same goes for paneer. But if lamb or, God forbid (literally, for Hindus), beef get the same treatment, they're typically referred to as boti. (Hence my restaurant chain that specializes in grilled chunks of meat, Botiwalla.)

Note: ***You'll need six 10-inch metal or wooden skewers. If you're using wooden ones, put them in water to soak for 15 to 30 minutes before you load them up.***

CHICKEN

2 pounds boneless, skinless chicken breasts, cut into 1½-by-1½-inch chunks

2 tablespoons Ginger-Garlic Paste (page 276)

1 teaspoon kosher salt

4 teaspoons tandoori masala (see page 33)

1 teaspoon ground red chilli, such as Kashmiri (see page 18)

¼ teaspoon Garam Masala (page 277, or use store-bought)

2 tablespoons full-fat Greek yogurt

1 tablespoon neutral oil, such as grapeseed

1 teaspoon distilled white vinegar

Juice of 1 lime

Canola oil or cooking spray, for grilling

6 store-bought naan or flatbread of choice (such as pita or lavash)

Ghee or butter, for brushing on the flatbread

1 small red onion, thinly sliced

¼ cup coarsely chopped cilantro

¼ cup Green Chutney (page 270)

In a large bowl, combine the chicken with the ginger-garlic paste, salt, tandoori masala, ground red chilli, garam masala, yogurt, oil, white vinegar, and lime juice and stir to combine. Marinate in the fridge for at least 1 hour and up to 4 hours.

Make sure your grill grates are clean, then heat your grill to high heat (at least 500°F) with the lid off: The idea is to grill hot and fast. Taking the lid off gets the grates hot enough that the chicken sears when it hits them. If you're using a charcoal grill, make sure you have enough charcoal to be able to maintain a high heat the whole time; if you're using gas, keep the flames on high.

Thread the chicken onto the skewers, leaving about an inch of space on the top and bottom of each skewer. Pack the chicken tightly—don't leave space between the chunks.

Brush the grill grates with canola oil and drizzle oil over each skewer (or spritz with nonstick cooking spray). Arrange all the skewers across the hottest part of your grill, then leave them the hell alone. They should sizzle audibly. If the flames are actually leaping up to meet the chicken, turn them down—you do want a high heat, but you don't want to incinerate dinner.

At the 2- to 3-minute mark, give the skewers a gentle wiggle. If they move easily without sticking, that means they're ready to flip. (If they stick, your grill is likely not seasoned—or you didn't use enough oil on the grates. Regardless, the chicken still needs to be flipped.) Cook on the other side until the internal temperature reads 165°F on a meat thermometer. Set aside on a warm spot.

Place the bread on the hot part of the grill (if using naan, place the flat side down first). Brush the top of each flatbread with ghee or butter. After about 1 minute, flip, and toast for another minute.

To assemble the rolls, slide the contents of the skewer onto the top (buttered) side of the flatbread. Sprinkle a generous amount of red onions and cilantro over the chicken, then drizzle with about 2 teaspoons of green chutney. Wrap the roll up tightly and serve hot.

To serve the rolls street style, wrap two-thirds of the roll in waxed paper or aluminum foil (so nothing falls out). If you're serving a large group, you can serve the skewers and flatbread separately, along with bowls of each topping, and allow people to assemble their own rolls.

DELUXE
BHOLA

M.G.
ROAD

MG WINGS

Serves 4 to 6

Our iconic MG Road Bar & Lounge (RIP), which was named after India's great spiritual and political leader (a teetotaler and vegan, naturally), served these wings during its heyday of pop-ups and late-night dance parties. From Pork Katsu Karaoke to MG Roadhouse to Punk Wok, MG hosted some of the most memorable concepts—and some of the most exciting food to be had in the Southeast after 9 p.m.—and these wings were always in heavy rotation. Ideally, they should be double fried, but to spare your stovetop, here's a version that can be made in the oven or in an air fryer in one step.

MARINADE

- 1 tablespoon jaggery syrup (see Notes), cane syrup, maple syrup, or honey
- 1 tablespoon soy sauce (dark preferred but regular is fine)
- 1 teaspoon freshly squeezed lime juice
- 2 fresh Thai or serrano chillies (depending on your heat tolerance), finely chopped
- 2 garlic cloves, finely chopped
- 1 teaspoon freshly ground black pepper
- 1 teaspoon red chilli flakes, such as Kashmiri (see page 18)
- ¼ teaspoon Garam Masala (page 277, or use store-bought)
- 1 tablespoon olive oil or grapeseed oil, plus more for the pan

- 2 pounds chicken wings, rinsed and patted dry

WING DUST

- 1 tablespoon roasted rice powder (optional; see Notes)
- ½ teaspoon ground red chilli, such as Kashmiri (see page 18)
- ¼ teaspoon coriander powder (roasted preferred)
- ¼ teaspoon freshly ground black pepper
- ¼ teaspoon chaat masala (see page 33)
- ¼ teaspoon kosher salt
- Thinly sliced fresh Thai or serrano chillies (depending on your heat tolerance), for garnish (optional)
- Cilantro sprigs, for garnish (optional)
- Fried curry leaves, for garnish (optional)
- Lime wedges, for garnish (optional)
- Store-bought ranch dressing or Raita (page 274), for serving (optional)

To make the marinade, combine the jaggery syrup, soy sauce, lime juice, green chillies, garlic, pepper, chilli flakes, garam masala, and oil in a large bowl and mix well until incorporated. Add the chicken wings and mix until they are fully coated. Place everything in a large plastic zip-top bag, scraping all the marinade into the bag and sealing most of the top, leaving an inch or so open. Push all the wings to the bottom of the bag and roll it up to force all the remaining air out of the bag through the small opening, then completely seal the bag. Refrigerate for at least 1 hour and up to 6 hours.

Once the chicken has marinated, preheat the oven to 450°F (if you have a convection oven, now is a good time to use it; heat to 425°F).

Line a sheet pan with aluminum foil and lightly brush it with olive or grapeseed oil so the wings don't stick. Place the wings in an even layer, spaced apart with the skin sides facing up. Roast on the middle rack until a thermometer inserted into the thickest part of the wing reads 175°F, 15 to 20 minutes. If you're using an air fryer—which would be brilliant—follow the manufacturer's instructions.

While the chicken cooks, make the wing dust. In a large bowl, combine the rice powder (if using), ground red chilli, coriander, pepper, chaat masala, and salt and stir together until combined. Once the wings are cooked, toss them right into the wing dust, turning them to coat evenly and shaking off any extra dust before serving.

Serve hot, garnished with fresh green chilli slices, cilantro sprigs, fried curry leaves, and/or lime wedges and with ranch dressing or raita on the side for dipping.

Ungarnished wings keep well for 2 to 3 days in the refrigerator and can be reheated in an oven or air fryer.

Notes: *To make jaggery syrup, crush jaggery chunks into powder by wrapping them in a kitchen towel and smashing them with a heavy pan, then boiling the powder with a bit of water to make a thick syrup. One cup powdered jaggery plus ¼ cup water will give you about a cup of syrup, which will keep, stored in an airtight glass jar, for months in your refrigerator. (Some Indian grocery stores sell powdered jaggery.)*

Roasted rice powder is exactly what it sounds like—slow-roasted raw sticky rice that's ground into a fine powder. Typically used in Thai and Vietnamese cuisines, it can be found online or at most Asian grocery stores. Though it's optional, I love the nutty flavor and slightly crunchy texture it gives the wings.

GHAR KA KHANA (HOME COOKING)

Despite the title, the recipes in this chapter aren't necessarily *only* eaten at home. All across India, little roadside stalls and rest stops—or sometimes just an entrepreneurial auntie who's opened up her home to lunch service—will whip up these types of homestyle dishes for travelers and for neighbors too busy to cook for themselves. *Cozy* and *rustic* are the key words here—most of these dishes have heavy comfort-food vibes.

This chapter is where I'm revealing some of my actual family recipes—not the stuff on the menu at Chai Pani but the old-school curries, stews, and dals that my mom and grandmother cook when I go back to India. It's also where I'm including a few of my own creations that delight my wife and daughter in my own home kitchen (think butternut squash and green bean coconut curry). And, because no homestyle cooking chapter would be complete without our daily bread, this is also where you'll find chapati and its sexier cousins, parathas and stuffed parathas.

PARSI RED CURRY

Serves 4

Since the Parsis settled in Gujarat and eventually in Mumbai (see page 104), there's not a lot of coconut in our cooking. In fact, most of central India, despite the long coastline that wraps around the subcontinent, prefers to use dried coconut instead of fresh coconut milk. Having said all that, when I think of a classic curry, I, along with most of the Western world, think about coconut milk. (For more on that, see page 192.)

The result of that is this recipe, which I more or less made up. I've freely gathered bits and pieces of Parsi ingredients, traditional coastal ingredients, and my own taste preferences into a catchall curry that works equally well with chicken, shrimp, and meaty, oily fish. It's creamy and mild, with a beautiful ocher color when finished, in contrast to the deep brick red we associate with vindaloos and chicken tikka masala. And it comes together quickly, requiring only white rice to make a full meal.

CHICKEN

2 pounds boneless, skinless chicken thighs
Neutral oil, such as grapeseed
Pinch of kosher salt
Pinch of turmeric powder
Pinch of ground red chilli, such as Kashmiri (see page 18)

MASALA PASTE

1 cinnamon stick, broken into 2 or 3 pieces
3 or 4 cardamom pods
3 or 4 cloves
1 tablespoon cumin seed
1 tablespoon coriander seed
1½ teaspoons sesame seeds
1 tablespoon whole black peppercorns
5 or 6 garlic cloves
¼ cup peeled and coarsely chopped fresh ginger
1 cup coarsely chopped white onion
1 tablespoon ground red chilli, such as Kashmiri (see page 18)
1 teaspoon kosher salt
¼ cup vegetable oil, plus more as needed
One (28-ounce) can crushed tomatoes
One (13.5-ounce) can full-fat coconut milk

Perfect Basmati Rice (page 276), for serving (optional)

Preheat the oven to 450°F.

Drizzle the chicken with a little neutral oil and sprinkle with a healthy pinch each of salt, turmeric, and ground red chilli, turning with your hands to coat. Place the chicken on a sheet pan and bake for about 15 minutes, until the internal temperature reaches 165°F on a meat thermometer. Remove the pan from the oven and tent it lightly with foil to keep the chicken warm.

While the chicken cooks, make the masala paste. In a small sauté pan over medium heat, toast the cinnamon, cardamom, cloves, cumin, coriander, sesame seeds, and black peppercorns until fragrant, 2 to 3 minutes. Set aside until cool enough to handle.

With a mortar and pestle or in a mini food processor, combine the garlic, ginger, onion, ground red chilli, salt, and toasted spices and blend until a thick paste forms. (If you're using a processor, you may need to add a few teaspoons of water to help the mixture grind properly.)

In a large heavy-bottomed pot or Dutch oven, heat the vegetable oil over medium-high heat until shimmering. Add the masala paste to the hot pan and cook for 1 minute, then turn the heat down to medium and continue cooking, stirring occasionally, for another 7 to 10 minutes. It's important that this masala is cooked well; otherwise it will taste like raw onions. If you need to add a touch more oil, feel free—you're essentially frying this paste, so it should sizzle rather than steam. Start tasting around the 7-minute mark—if there's any raw flavor, keep cooking until the masala has deepened in color and aroma and tastes lightly caramelized, and the onions have released their sugars and broken down completely into the paste.

Add the crushed tomatoes and cook, stirring occasionally, until the tomatoes are glossy and the oil starts to separate around the edges, 5 to 7 minutes. Add the coconut milk and stir to incorporate.

Cut the chicken into bite-size chunks and add it to the pan, then scrape in the juices from the sheet pan. Simmer on low heat for another 5 minutes, stirring occasionally, to allow the flavors to combine.

Serve the curry warm, by itself or over freshly steamed basmati rice. Leftover curry keeps, tightly covered in the refrigerator, for up to 4 days.

A CURRY BY ANY OTHER NAME

In the way that Americans use the word "sushi" as shorthand for Japanese food, "curry" has become synonymous with Indian cuisine around the world. While I have strong feelings about naan standing in for all the other (superior) Indian breads (see page 84), I actually don't have a problem with curry serving as the poster child of Indian cuisine. Gravies and sauces are essential components of cooking in India, and while different regions may have different foundational ingredients, their purpose is the same—a delicious spiced sauce with a rich mouthfeel that pairs well with rice or bread.

Still, I do wonder: Where does "curry" come from, and how has this one (albeit multifaceted) dish come to bear the weight of an entire cuisine? The etymology of the word curry has been debated by scholars, and as far as I can tell from aggregating multiple arguments, the root word is probably kari, the Tamil word for "sauce"—though even that is up for debate (other theories maintain that "kari" refers alternately to black pepper or neem leaves, which look similar to curry leaves).

In terms of the "where" of curry, all signs point toward South India, where coconut milk–based gravies are often flavored with curry leaves as well as turmeric, red chilli, and sometimes a hint of cinnamon. Given the ubiquity of curry in many Tamil and other South Indian dishes, the proliferation of trade from the southern coast, and the eventual British presence there, it seems only natural that this particular combination of ingredients would form the basis of what many people consider "curry" today.

But even if we can't pinpoint the exact origin of curry itself (some say the first recipe is from Madras, others Andra, others still Kerala—as with many such things, the exact origins are murky), we should be able to agree that true curry is a region-specific dish. Other sauces and gravies might look or smell like a curry, but in my opinion without four core ingredients—coconut milk, curry leaves, turmeric, and red chilli—they are not truly so.

Emphasis here is on the word "core"—I could spend a lifetime arguing with aunties about which spices constitute a "real" curry, but the truth is that at this point, it matters little. Curry has gone global, and it comes in forms from the pasty yellow curry powder the Brits love to the root vegetable–heavy stylings popular in Japan. So if calling a delicious sauce a curry is what gets you to love Indian food, hey, I won't be the one to stop you!

We have a few examples of curries and close-to-curries in this book—the Parsi Red Curry on page 191, the Goan Fish Curry on page 194 (which doesn't have cinnamon but has everything else), and the Arangaon Chicken on page 130 (which uses desiccated coconut instead of coconut milk, but I'm squeezing it in here anyway). Try them all and see if there's one that speaks to you, official curry cred or no.

GOAN FISH CURRY

Serves 4

As has been discussed ad nauseam, including by me on the preceding pages, the most overused—and yet confusing—word in Indian cuisine is "curry." That single word has launched a thousand arguments that all, inevitably, land us back at the fact of colonialism. I'm hesitant to even call this dish a curry, but it would be a great injustice to my memories of traveling through South India to avoid it for semantics.

To me, this dish has all the essential elements of a good coconut-based curry—garlic, black peppercorns, chillies, and curry leaves—each infusing its headiness into the sweetness of coconut milk that's been laced with tamarind or lime. Add some firm, oily fish, and you've got the Malabar Coast on your plate.

It's important to blend the garlic and spices into a coarse paste—you want them to be well incorporated, so keep adding water to the blender until you get there. Frying this paste is where the real magic happens, and you don't want any big chunks getting in the way. Note that the chilli is where the heat comes from in this spice blend, so go as easy or hard as you'd like with it. While mackerel is the traditional fish of choice around Goa, you can also use white fish like grouper or cod—any firm-fleshed fish works.

FISH

Pinch of ground red chilli, such as Kashmiri (see page 18)

Pinch of turmeric powder

Pinch of kosher salt

1 pound mackerel fillets (or use a firm-fleshed white fish such as grouper or cod), cut into 2-inch pieces

GARLIC-SPICE BLEND

2 teaspoons coriander seed

1 teaspoon cumin seed

1 tablespoon whole black peppercorns

6 whole dried red chillies, such as Kashmiri (see page 18), or 2 to 3 fresh Thai or serrano chillies (depending on your heat tolerance)

½ teaspoon turmeric powder

6 to 8 garlic cloves

¼ cup vegetable oil, plus more as needed

1 medium white onion, finely diced (about 1 cup)

Kosher salt

8 to 10 fresh or dried curry leaves (optional)

2 cups full-fat coconut milk

2 to 3 cups hot water

1 tablespoon homemade or store-bought tamarind paste (see page 19) or 2 tablespoons freshly squeezed lime juice

Perfect Basmati Rice (page 276), for serving

Cilantro sprigs, for garnish

Lime wedges, for garnish

Rub a pinch each of ground red chilli, turmeric, and salt into the fish, and set aside.

To make the garlic-spice blend, toast the coriander seeds, cumin seeds, black peppercorns, and dried or fresh chillies in a small skillet over medium-high heat until aromatic, 2 to 3 minutes. Let cool, then place the toasted spices in a mini food processor or blender along with the turmeric, garlic, and ¼ cup of water and blitz until you have a coarse paste with no large chunks or lumps.

In a large heavy-bottomed pot over medium-high heat, heat the oil until it's shimmering. Add the onion and a pinch of salt and cook until the onion starts to turn golden around the edges, 3 to 5 minutes.

Add the garlic-spice paste and another healthy pinch of salt to the onion. (You may need to add another glug or two of oil to the pan so there's enough to make a nice sizzle when the paste hits the pan.) Fry the paste, stirring occasionally, for 2 to 3 minutes. Add the curry leaves (if using) and continue cooking until most of the liquid has evaporated from the paste and the onion is golden brown, about 5 minutes.

Add the coconut milk and stir well. Once the coconut milk is bubbling, add 2 cups of the hot water (or, if you like a thinner/soupier curry, add up to 3 cups). Stir in the tamarind paste or lime juice.

Add the seasoned fish and stir gently to spread the pieces throughout the sauce. Cook until the fish is flaky and falling apart, 5 to 7 minutes depending on how thick the fish pieces are (start checking for doneness around the 4-minute mark to be sure you don't overcook). Taste for salt and adjust as necessary.

Serve over rice with a sprig of cilantro and a squeeze of fresh lime.

Leftover curry keeps, tightly covered in the refrigerator, for up to 2 days.

S.J. & S.P. FAMILY TRUST AHMEDABAD-21

SHRIMP PATIA

Serves 4

This seafood curry of sorts demonstrates, better than any other dish I can think of, the Parsi predilection for sweet-and-sour flavors. The Persians would have used palm vinegar to add acidity, but over time this has given way to tamarind and jaggery—two ingredients that have indelibly influenced the cooking of Gujarat, where the Parsis first settled. The result is a tangy, fragrant stew that my mom would often whip up for lunch when she didn't have much time.

In general, curries like this are paired with dal, a combination that's arguably the rice and beans of India. The curry brings a punch of flavor and umami to an otherwise very simple dish of dal. Although shrimp patia is delicious on its own or just with freshly steamed rice (see page 276), for the full experience, I recommend pairing it with My Grandma's Dal on page 199.

SHRIMP

1 pound medium (41/50 count) shrimp, peeled and deveined

Pinch of kosher salt

Pinch of turmeric powder

Pinch of ground red chilli, such as Kashmiri (see page 18)

MASALA PASTE

1 teaspoon cumin seed

5 to 8 whole dried red chillies, such as Kashmiri (see page 18)

5 garlic cloves

½ teaspoon turmeric powder

2 tablespoons neutral oil, such as grapeseed

2½ cups finely diced red onion (from about 2 medium onions)

Kosher salt

2 cups coarsely chopped ripe, juicy Roma or heirloom tomatoes (about 3 tomatoes)

2 tablespoons powdered jaggery (see page 20) or dark brown sugar

½ cup homemade or store-bought tamarind paste (page 19)

1 cup hot water, or more as needed

½ cup coarsely chopped cilantro

Perfect Basmati Rice (page 276), for serving (optional)

My Grandma's Dal (page 199), for serving (optional)

Rinse the shrimp well, pat dry, and season with a healthy pinch each of salt, turmeric, and ground red chilli. Set aside.

To make the masala paste, combine the cumin, dried chillies, and garlic in a small sauté pan over medium heat and toast for 2 to 3 minutes, stirring occasionally, until the cumin is aromatic and the garlic has a few brown spots. Set aside until cool enough to handle.

Combine the toasted spices and turmeric in a mini food processor or mortar and pestle. If using a processor, you may need to add a few teaspoons of water to help the mixture grind properly. Pound or pulse into a thick paste and set aside.

In a large heavy-bottomed pot or Dutch oven, heat the oil over medium heat until shimmering. Add the onions and a healthy pinch of salt and cook, stirring occasionally, until the onions are soft and slightly brown around the edges, 3 to 5 minutes. Add the masala paste and sauté it with the onions until everything is golden brown and well combined, another 3 to 5 minutes.

Add the tomatoes, jaggery, another pinch of salt, and the tamarind paste. Cook, stirring occasionally, for 3 to 4 minutes, so the flavors can meld. Add the hot water and bring the mixture to a boil, cooking for 1 to 2 minutes more, so all the flavors can meld.

Decrease the heat to medium and add the cilantro and seasoned shrimp. Cook until the shrimp is opaque, 3 to 5 minutes. Check for seasoning and add more salt if necessary.

Serve with rice and dal if you like. Leftover shrimp patia keeps, tightly covered in the refrigerator, for up to 2 days.

MY GRANDMA'S DAL

Serves 4 to 6

India is the land of a thousand dals, and this recipe is my buoy in the vast sea of lentils washing across the subcontinent. My maternal grandparents, Shubudra and Kumar, grew basmati rice (along with wheat and sugarcane) in the fields outside of Dehradun, in the foothills of the Himalayas. I'd spend my summers on the farm with them to escape the heat of the Deccan Plateau.

Although they did occasionally eat meat, their day-to-day diet was almost exclusively vegetarian. I can close my eyes and remember sitting cross-legged on my grandma's screened-in veranda, eating rice and dal out of a three-compartment metal thali, complaining to my mother (under my breath, of course) that this was boring and that I would rather have some biryani. I now wish I could smack little me on the head, because today, this dal represents everything I love about Indian home cooking.

This simple, hearty dal is made with both pink and yellow lentils—the former break down while the latter remain chunky—and features the use of tadka (see page 30) to flavor the whole lot. Dal is nutritious, filling, and keeps beautifully; serve it over freshly steamed basmati rice for the full effect.

DAL

1 cup masoor dal (split red lentils)

1 cup toor dal (split yellow lentils, aka pigeon peas)

1½ teaspoons kosher salt

¼ cup diced red onion (about ½ medium onion)

¼ cup diced Roma tomatoes (1 to 2 tomatoes)

1 tablespoon powdered jaggery (see page 20) or dark brown sugar (optional)

TADKA

¼ cup neutral oil, such as grapeseed

2 teaspoons mustard seed

2 teaspoons cumin seed

1 teaspoon ground turmeric

¼ teaspoon hing (optional)

4 whole dried red chillies, such as Kashmiri (see page 18)

1 tablespoon peeled and finely minced fresh ginger (about a 1-inch knob)

1 tablespoon minced garlic (2 to 3 cloves)

¼ cup diced Roma tomatoes (1 to 2 tomatoes)

Hot water, as needed

Combine both dals in a bowl and fill the bowl with water; agitate with your fingers to rinse and pour the rinse water off the top. You don't have to use a strainer or colander, but three or four rinses this way should get rid of most of the starch and dust in the dal.

Once they're rinsed, cover the dals with water and soak for a minimum of 10 minutes and up to 30 minutes. Soaking the dal helps it cook faster—the 10 minutes you invest up front will save you 20 minutes of cooking time later on, so it's definitely worth it.

In a large heavy-bottomed pot, combine the dals with 8 cups of water and the salt; bring to a boil over medium-high heat. Once the water reaches a boil, add the onions, tomatoes, and jaggery (if using), then reduce the heat to a simmer. Cover partially with a lid, leaving just a small crack for steam to escape. Cook, stirring occasionally, until the dal is soft enough to mash between your fingers, 25 to 30 minutes. You'll notice a little scum or foam forming on top; scoop this off with a large spoon or ladle. The dal should thicken slightly as it cooks.

To make the tadka, heat the oil in a small sauté pan over medium-high heat until shimmering. Add the mustard seeds; when they start to wiggle and pop, turn the heat down to medium to avoid burning. (Make sure the oil is hot enough that the mustard seeds actually start to pop; otherwise they're not flavoring the oil!)

As soon as the mustard seeds pop, turn the heat to low and add the cumin seeds, turmeric, hing (if using), and chillies. Almost immediately add the ginger and garlic. Allow those to sizzle for 1 to 2 minutes. Add the tomatoes and stir until they break down and the moisture evaporates, 4 to 5 minutes.

Pour the tadka into the pot with the dal and stir well to incorporate. Swish the tadka pot with ½ cup or so of hot water to get all the bits loose, and pour this into the dal. Stir well and cook, stirring occasionally, over medium heat for 2 to 3 more minutes to fully incorporate the flavors.

Serve with Perfect Basmati Rice (page 276) and/or a spicy curry, such as the Shrimp Patia on page 197. Leftover dal keeps, tightly covered in the refrigerator, for up to 5 days.

APPLE SABJI

Serves 4

Sabji means "vegetables," but it also describes a dish of the same name. You can say you're going to "buy sabji" or "make sabji," and depending on what the vegetable is, you'd double down, calling it, for example green bean sabji, or eggplant sabji, or mushroom sabji. It's sort of like saying "queso cheese."

I was inspired to make this dish for a PBS shoot, where the producers wanted me to use an autumnal North Carolina ingredient. I chose apples. The sweetness of the apple is tempered by the masala it's cooked in, making it very savory, with lovely hints of sweet and tart flavors. This style of dry-roasted sabji is typically served with puris, a fried Indian flatbread, though you can also use chapati or any other flatbread of your choice.

2 tablespoons coconut oil
1 teaspoon yellow mustard seed
6 to 8 dried curry leaves
6 whole black peppercorns
1½ cups diced red onion (about 1 large onion)
1 Thai chilli or 2 serrano chillies (depending on your heat tolerance), finely chopped
1 teaspoon kosher salt, plus more to taste
½ teaspoon turmeric powder
½ teaspoon cumin powder
½ teaspoon coriander powder
2 sweet, crisp apples (such as Honeycrisp or Pink Lady), peeled, cored, and cut into large bite-size pieces (about 4 cups)
¾ cup finely grated fresh coconut, thawed if previously frozen and squeezed to remove any extra liquid
½ cup full-fat coconut milk

Perfect Basmati Rice (page 276) and/or warm bread, such as store-bought naan or chapati (see page 212)
Cilantro leaves, for garnish
Pinch of Garam Masala (optional; page 277)

In a large heavy saucepan over high heat, heat the coconut oil until it shimmers.

Add the mustard seeds; when they start to wiggle and pop, turn the heat down to medium to avoid burning. (Make sure the oil is hot enough that the mustard seeds actually pop, otherwise they're not flavoring the oil!) Turn the heat back up to high and add the curry leaves and peppercorns. Cook for 1 minute, stirring constantly.

Stir in the onion, chilli, and salt. Turn the heat to medium-high and cook, stirring often, until the onions are brown and soft and almost caramelized, 5 to 7 minutes. Turn the heat down to medium and add the turmeric, cumin, and coriander; stir constantly, until they start to smell incredible, about 30 seconds. You may need to add a splash of water to prevent scorching.

Stir in the apple and coconut and cook for 1 to 2 minutes, stirring often to make sure nothing sticks to the pan.

Add the coconut milk and ½ cup of water, stir well, and bring to a boil. Turn the heat to low, cover, and simmer, stirring occasionally, until the apples are tender but not falling apart, 8 to 10 minutes. Check for seasoning and add more salt if necessary.

To serve the sabji, spoon it over rice and garnish with cilantro and garam masala (if using). Serve bread alongside, if you like. Sabji keeps for a day or two in the refrigerator but is best eaten the day it's made.

BUTTERNUT SQUASH & GREEN BEAN COCONUT CURRY

Serves 4

I came up with this dish during the pandemic lockdown as a one-pot meal that gets better as it sits in the fridge. It truly captures how I like to cook at home—making foods that are familiar and comfortable where I currently live, cooked through the lens of where I come from. In the case of this recipe, that means the Indian truck stops of my youth, where meals tended to be hearty, simple one-pot creations not suffocated by the rich fats and spices of fancier locales. My American wife and daughter say this is possibly their favorite dish in this book.

This delicious all-purpose curry base is perfect for cooking pretty much any variety of vegetable that can stand up to being simmered in a sauce—cauliflower florets, carrots, corn, beans, potatoes, dark leafy greens, mushrooms, bell peppers, and so on (this is why I like keeping a variety of frozen veggies in my freezer). If you're the meat-eating type, it also works wonderfully with any mild, flaky fish, or with shrimp or shreds of leftover rotisserie chicken.

It's worth noting here that sauces made without butter or cream freeze particularly well. This is one of the few "curries" in this book where you can make a big batch of the sauce and, before adding vegetables or protein, stick it in the freezer for a rainy day. You can add in the ingredients of choice when you're ready to eat.

3 tablespoons neutral oil, such as grapeseed

1 teaspoon brown mustard seed

3 or 4 fresh or dried curry leaves (optional)

½ teaspoon hing (optional)

1 (2-inch) knob of fresh ginger, peeled and finely chopped

1½ tablespoons Ginger-Garlic Paste (page 276)

2 cups diced red onion (about 2 large onions)

Kosher salt

1 teaspoon turmeric powder

2 cups canned crushed tomatoes, or 2 large Roma tomatoes, chopped

1 (13.5-ounce) can full-fat coconut milk

1 cup chicken or vegetable stock

3 cups peeled, cubed butternut squash (from a 2- to 2½-pound squash)

2 cups green beans, ends trimmed, cut in half

Cilantro, for garnish (optional)

Perfect Basmati Rice (page 276), for serving

In a large heavy-bottomed pot, heat the oil over medium-high heat until it shimmers. Add the mustard seeds; when they start to wiggle and pop, turn the heat down to medium to avoid burning. (Make sure the oil is hot enough that the mustard seeds actually start to pop, otherwise they're not flavoring the oil!)

Add the curry leaves and hing (if using). Bring the heat back up to medium-high, add the ginger, and cook, stirring often, until aromatic, about 1 minute. Add the ginger-garlic paste and fry until the paste is starting to brown, another minute or so. Lower the heat to medium and stir in the onions and ½ teaspoon salt.

Cooking the onions in a certain way really matters. This step takes time and patience, and it may require finessing the heat level. Stir the onions into the oil frequently but not constantly, keeping them in an even layer. Make sure they're sizzling but not scorching, melting into each other and not frying. As the water cooks out of the onions, they will eventually start to resemble a marmalade with a rich bourbon color. This is good! The goal is to get the onions so jammy and reduced that they almost become one with the sauce (as opposed to being an ingredient in the sauce). Keep an eye on the heat; if the onions are starting to crisp on the edges, turn the heat down and add a teaspoon or two of water to stop the frying. Once the onions have hit the state described above, about 10 minutes, add the turmeric and tomatoes and cook, stirring frequently, until the tomatoes are glossy and the oil starts to separate at the edges, about 10 minutes.

Add the coconut milk and stock and stir. Taste for seasoning and adjust the salt if necessary. (If you're planning on freezing the curry sauce for later use, now is the time to do that.)

Add the squash and simmer until tender, 7 to 10 minutes, then add the green beans and simmer until tender, stirring occasionally, 3 to 5 minutes. The finished curry should be the consistency of a bisque. Taste and adjust the seasoning, garnish with cilantro if you like, and serve hot with rice.

Leftover curry keeps, tightly covered in the refrigerator, for up to 5 days.

BHINDI MASALA

Serves 4 to 6

India probably consumes more okra per capita than anywhere else in the world, and I say this while living in the American South. Okra was brought to India from Africa and, probably better than any other culture in the world, Indians have figured out how to counter the sliminess of the vegetable, using a myriad of genius hacks, such as par-frying rings of okra in a little oil, evaporating much of the water and eliminating almost all of the sliminess. A masala base, a touch of sugar, and low-and-slow cooking take care of the rest in this recipe. This is one auntie hack I developed on my own—an uncle hack, if you will.

This is a "dry" sabji (meaning there's no sauce—see Apple Sabji on page 203 for another example), and it's very Maharashtrian in that sense. It's the kind of dish that a farmer might have in their packed lunch, along with a couple of rotis and a few slices of raw onion. My favorite part of making this dish at the restaurant (and convincing someone to order it) is the inevitable "Whoa—why is this so good?!" exclamation that follows. Leftovers also make a great stuffing for parathas (see page 215).

1 cup canola oil

2 pounds okra, trimmed and sliced into ¼-inch rounds

1 teaspoon cumin seed

1 finely chopped fresh Thai or serrano chilli (depending on your heat tolerance)

2 tablespoons Ginger-Garlic Paste (page 276)

1 large red onion, diced

Kosher salt

1 cup coarsely chopped cilantro leaves

1 teaspoon ground red chilli, such as Kashmiri (see page 18)

1 teaspoon turmeric powder

1 teaspoon cumin powder

½ teaspoon coriander powder (optional)

¼ cup water

1 (14.5-ounce) can crushed tomatoes, or 3 medium Roma tomatoes, coarsely diced

1 teaspoon sugar

Perfect Basmati Rice (page 276), warm Chapati (page 212), or toasted crusty bread, for serving

In a large heavy-bottomed pot or Dutch oven, heat the oil over medium-high heat until it's shimmering. Working in batches to avoid overcrowding, fry the okra until its edges are brown, 3 to 4 minutes. Transfer with a slotted spoon to a paper towel–lined plate and set aside. This pre-frying step helps the okra stay crisp and gets rid of its characteristic sliminess.

Reserve ¼ cup of the okra frying oil and rinse out the pot. Return the reserved oil to the pot and heat over medium-high heat until it's shimmering. Add the cumin seeds, which should start sizzling within about 30 seconds. Quickly add the green chilli, ginger-garlic paste, onions, and 2 teaspoons salt, bringing the temperature of the oil down and preventing the cumin from burning.

Cooking the onions in a certain way really matters. This step takes time and patience, and it may require finessing the heat level. Stir the onions into the oil frequently but not constantly, keeping them in an even layer. Make sure they're sizzling but not scorching, melting into each other and not frying. As the water cooks out of the onions, they will eventually start to resemble a marmalade with a rich bourbon color. This is good! The goal is to get the onions so jammy and reduced that they almost become one with the sauce (as opposed to being an ingredient in the sauce). Keep an eye on the heat; if the onions are starting to crisp on the edges, turn the heat down and add a teaspoon or two of water to stop the frying.

When the onions hit the state described above (it will take about 10 minutes), add half of the cilantro, the ground red chilli, turmeric, cumin, coriander (if using), and water, stirring and scraping to get all the fond (read: good stuff) off the bottom of the pan. Do this for 2 to 3 minutes, until the water is sizzling and starting to evaporate.

Add the tomatoes and cook, stirring frequently, until they're glossy and the oil starts to separate from the edges, about 10 minutes.

Add the reserved fried okra, mixing gently so it doesn't break down, cover, and cook over low heat for another 10 to 15 minutes, stirring occasionally, until the okra darkens and starts breaking down a bit. The longer you can cook this dish low and slow, the more unctuous and rich it will become. When it hits a texture you like, stir in the sugar and remove from the heat.

Taste and adjust for salt, and serve, garnished with the rest of the cilantro, alongside freshly steamed rice, warm chapati, or toasted crusty bread.

Leftover bhindi masala keeps, tightly covered in the refrigerator, for up to 5 days.

RICE VERSUS ROTI

Rice and bread: These two ubiquitous Indian carbohydrates are both starchy vehicles with which to enjoy the goodness of sauces, gravies, curries, stir fries, and more. I love them both—but which to choose?

Both have historical importance. Rice cultivation became A Thing in South India and Sri Lanka back in the Iron Age (1200 to 500 BCE)—not coincidentally, also a time of major population growth in that neck of the woods. Wheat cultivation appears to go back even further: Archaeological records show it was first cultivated in the Fertile Crescent all the way back in 10,000 BCE. Many historians believe that wheat-based flatbreads made their way to India around 2500 BCE via the Aryans, a group of Indo-Iranian pastoralists (herders).

Broadly speaking, the breads—your naans, rotis, chapatis, parathas, and so on—are more common in the northern states of India, while rice is predominantly a southern staple.

Bread is (obviously) common in many parts of India, but rice is revered nationwide. My maternal grandparents were rice farmers in the north, growing basmati in the fertile foothills of the Himalayas, but we only got little tastes of their precious harvest on special occasions. There are just so many things you can do with rice: from Andhra Pradesh to Kerala, the grain is steamed, battered, boiled, mashed, pasted, and creped; if you ask for a roti or chapati in southern India, you will be looked at like you have three heads.

I grew up in Maharashtra, the giant central state that runs from the west coast to the Deccan Plateau, with Mumbai as its great, big beating heart. Mumbai draws people from around the country, who bring their own cuisines, ingredients, and dietary commandments. One of the unique ways that shows up on the Mumbai plate is in the prevalence of both rice and roti.

I was lucky to grow up in a household where often, both rice and roti (or its close cousin, chapati; for more information see page 212) were on the table at the same time. I still prefer to have both when possible—they are a true yin and yang in Indian cuisine—and I see no problem with doubling up on carbs. While I am leaving the rich bhaturas of Punjab and sweet saffron-scented sheermal of Hyderabad to the experts, we have included recipes for basic chapati on page 212 and perfect basmati rice on page 276, freeing you, dear reader, from having to choose a team. Go on, it's okay—you can have it all.

CHAPATI

Makes 8 chapati

Before there was bread, there was flatbread. Before there were ovens—clay or otherwise—humans were mixing unleavened flour with water, patting or rolling it out, and cooking it on a hot surface. In India, chapati and roti are the simplest forms of flatbreads; whether you're making chapati or roti, the rule of thumb is about two parts flour to one part water. The main difference is that chapati contain a bit of oil in the dough. This little bit of fat makes for a softer, more pliable flatbread that is more effective than roti for mopping up curries, sabjis, vegetables, and more.

This ancient recipe is still the daily bread of choice for hundreds of millions of Indians today. Most Indian moms and aunties are in the habit of making fresh chapati at home every day; after a few practice rounds, you'll be right there with them.

- 2 teaspoons kosher salt
- ¾ cup warm water, plus more for kneading
- 2 cups atta (whole wheat flour; see Note, page 213), plus more as needed
- 1 tablespoon neutral oil, such as grapeseed
- 2 tablespoons melted ghee or butter, for basting

In a small bowl, dissolve the salt in the warm water (the salt doesn't get as evenly distributed in the dough if it's added directly to flour).

Place the flour in a large bowl and make a small well in the center. Pour in the oil and half of the salted water and stir to combine. As the water gets absorbed, continue pouring more in in a slow stream, mixing and kneading until a dough starts to form. The ideal texture is a bit of a Goldilocks moment—it should be soft, not crumbly (not enough water), nor sticky and shaggy (too much water). Add a touch more flour or water as necessary if the dough feels too wet or too dry.

Once you have a dough ball that's neither crumbly nor sticky, wet your hands and run them over the surface of the dough, then cover the bowl with a cloth or with plastic wrap and let rest for 30 minutes (but no more than an hour) at room temperature.

When you're ready to make chapati, knead the dough on clean lightly floured surface with damp hands until it's soft and pliable, 1 to 2 minutes. Don't overknead, or it'll make the chapati hard; as soon as the dough feels soft and easy to divide, stop kneading. If the dough feels hard or dry, wet your hands and knead again. Don't splash water on the dough directly—at this stage this may add too much water!

Divide the dough into 8 evenly sized balls, set on the same surface you kneaded them on, and cover with a damp cloth. Let the balls rest for about 10 minutes.

While the dough rests, heat a tawa (carbon-steel griddle), seasoned cast-iron pan, or nonstick skillet over medium heat and brush lightly with ghee or butter.

Working with one ball at a time, dust the dough lightly with flour and shake off any excess. (Too much flour will make the chapatis dry out.) On a clean work surface, press the ball gently into a flat disc and use a rolling pin to roll out the disc into a circle, using as little force as possible. (Too much pressure with the rolling pin will either make the chapati too hard or cause it to stick to the rolling pin.) If the dough starts to stick, dust with a tiny amount of flour and start again. To make the disc into a circle, roll two or three times, then move the dough clockwise a quarter turn and roll again.

Once you have a chapati about 8 inches in diameter, transfer it gently to the hot pan. When a few bubbles start to form—about 1 minute in—flip the chapati and brush the top with a little bit of ghee or butter. After a minute or two, flip it back over and brush with ghee again.

If you notice burnt spots or the chapati feels hard, lower the heat. If it's taking more than a minute or so for bubbles to form in the chapati, turn the heat up a tad. Regulating heat while making chapati is part of the process, and you'll get the hang of it quickly once you make a couple.

Press the chapati down with the spatula (being careful not to puncture it), and you'll notice it starting to puff up wherever you press it. Do this a few times around the top surface, then flip over after a minute and press with a spatula on the other side.

After giving it one last swipe of ghee, remove the chapati and wrap it in a towel or cloth napkin to stay warm and soft while you make the rest.

Do note that the ghee on the hot griddle will make a little bit of smoke; that's normal. Wipe the griddle with a slightly damp paper towel in between baking the chapati to remove any ghee or flour.

Serve warm. Chapati are really meant to be eaten fresh, but they will keep, tightly covered in the refrigerator, for a day or two. To bring them back to life, drape them with a damp paper towel and nuke them in the microwave for a few seconds.

Note: ***Indian whole wheat flour is known as atta. It's milled from a wheat variety that has a higher protein content than either Western whole wheat flour or all-purpose flour. Atta is also stone milled (look for "chakki atta" on the label), which allows it to absorb more water, making softer, more pliable parathas and rotis.***

AUNTIE HACK

Ideally you're rolling out a new chapati or paratha as the prior one is cooking. That way, you don't have raw-dough discs taking up counter space, since you can't stack them raw.

It wasn't uncommon for my mom or aunties to stay in the kitchen making new parathas while the guests ate, and any attempt to get them to join us would be rebuffed with the retort, "And who's going to make sure the parathas are hot and fresh if I sit down?!"

BIG TICKET

While even a maharaja will slum it on the streets incognito every once in a while, a king still wants to eat like a king. This chapter has the baller dishes—the bangers of Indian haute cuisine invented years before the French even knew what cake was. Some of these recipes have histories stretching back thousands of years.

Yes, biryani and butter chicken and leg of lamb will take some time and prep, and use a few more ingredients, but they are all very doable—especially my recipes, since I bring a street food–inspired sensibility of using what you have and hacking what you don't to make these come together in a satisfying way (that's jugaad, baby!).

Why a Big Ticket chapter in a book about street food? Well, in order for street food to exist, you need to put it into the context of what's at the other extreme. Believe it or not, the spectrum in India between high cuisine and street food has a lot of overlap: Both styles utilize many of the same ingredients and techniques, just cranked up to different volumes, if you will.

Plus, I want people to experience this book like a party, and every party needs a centerpiece. If you make a bunch of chaats and some dhaba-style snacks and some Indian sandwiches, then round them out for a crowd with a show-stopping entrée; I guarantee it will be the best night of their lives.

CHICKEN BIRYANI

Serves 6 to 8

An Indian feast isn't complete without a biryani—the ultimate, decadent, time-consuming, over-the-top, one-pot dish that takes a lifetime to master. I make biryani two or three times a year and have been doing so for decades, yet I still cross my fingers every time. There are a billion restaurant hacks and techniques to make faux biryani, the most popular being to cook the rice and meat separately, then combine them in a small pot and throw it in the oven for a few minutes to make it seem like you're having a one-pot dish. This is bullshit. Biryani must be built from scratch.

This dish is probably Persian in origin, as the earliest references to rice cooked with meats, spices, and exotic dried fruits and nuts appear in early Mughal literature. Not to say that other cultures haven't invented what is essentially a rice casserole at various points in their culinary development, but there's something distinctive about a Mughal-style biryani, with its decadent layers of ghee, saffron, fried onions, dried apricots, cashews, mutton, and, often, silver leaf.

I'm presenting a slightly more approachable biryani, made with chicken and lacking in edible silver. I use boneless chicken for ease of prep, though a biryani in India would traditionally be made with bone-in meat. This is not a back-pocket pantry recipe—you will have to do your shopping with intention and set aside a couple of hours to get the dish right. Whether it comes out perfect (by which I mean each grain of rice is fragrant, fluffy, and separate) or a little bit soft (due to the infinite possible variations of water and heat), I promise you it will be deliciously worth the time you put in.

1 cup coarsely chopped cilantro
1 cup coarsely chopped mint
3 cups basmati rice

CHICKEN

1½ pounds boneless, skinless chicken thighs, cut into 2-inch pieces
1 teaspoon turmeric powder
2½ teaspoons kosher salt
1 teaspoon caraway seed
1½ cups fried onions (see Notes, page 223)
1 teaspoon whole black peppercorns
2 tablespoons fried onion oil (see Notes, page 223) or a neutral oil such as grapeseed
4 tablespoons ghee, warmed
2 tablespoons fresh green chilli paste (see Notes, page 223)
2 teaspoons Garam Masala (page 277, or use store-bought), plus extra for seasoning
1 tablespoon Ginger-Garlic Paste (page 276)
1 tablespoon freshly squeezed lime juice
10 to 12 green cardamom pods, broken open (see Notes, page 223)
1 teaspoon ground red chilli, such as Kashmiri (see page 18)
2 or 3 fresh Thai or serrano chillies (depending on your heat tolerance), cut lengthwise
1 tablespoon khoya (full-fat milk solids; see page 223), optional
1½ cups plain full-fat yogurt

RICE

1 tablespoon neutral oil, such as grapeseed, or ghee
1 tablespoon whole black peppercorns
2 bay leaves
1 tablespoon green cardamom pods, broken open (see Notes, page 223)
2 cinnamon sticks, broken into smaller pieces
1 teaspoon cloves
1 tablespoon caraway seed
2 tablespoons kosher salt

½ cup warm whole milk infused with a pinch of saffron
Kachumber (page 115) for serving (optional)

Mix the cilantro and mint together in a bowl and set aside. Wash the basmati rice, then soak in water to cover for 2 hours.

In a large, deep, heavy-bottomed pot with a tight-fitting lid (a Dutch oven is perfect), combine the chicken with the turmeric, salt, caraway seeds, ½ cup of the fried onions, black peppercorns, fried onion oil, 2 tablespoons of the warm ghee, green chilli paste, garam masala, ginger-garlic paste, lime juice, crushed cardamom pods, ground red chilli, green chillies, khoya (if using), and ½ cup of the cilantro-mint mixture.

With your hands, massage the spices and other ingredients into the chicken, making sure everything is well coated. (I recommend wearing vinyl kitchen gloves for this step and the next.)

Continued

CHICKEN BIRYANI

Continued

Add the yogurt and mix well with your hands, ensuring that the masala is completely mixed in with the yogurt and is coating the chicken completely. Spread the chicken evenly around the bottom of the pot.

To make the rice, fill a second large pot with 4 quarts of water and bring to a boil. (We'll be boiling the rice like pasta so make sure there's plenty of water.) Add ½ cup of the cilantro-mint mixture, the oil or ghee, black peppercorns, bay leaves, crushed cardamom pods, cinnamon, cloves, caraway, and salt. Stir well and boil for 2 to 3 minutes until the water is aromatic. Taste a (cooled) teaspoon of the water for salt—you should be able to taste a bit of salinity, as this will flavor the rice. If the water does not have a discernible salt flavor, add more: It should taste seasoned, like a good broth, but not salty.

Drain the soaked rice and add it to the pot. Stir gently and cook, uncovered. Once the rice has been boiling for 5 to 7 minutes, check the texture by fishing out a few grains. Our goal is to get rice that's around 75 percent cooked. It should be semi-hard, but you should be able to break/smush it between your fingers into a grainy paste.

While the rice is cooking, spread another ¼ cup of the cilantro-mint mixture and ¼ cup of fried onions in layers over the top of the marinated chicken—do not stir them into the chicken! Sprinkle a pinch of garam masala over the top.

As soon as the rice has hit the desired texture, cut the heat completely and move the chicken pot next to the rice pot. Do not discard the rice cooking water; instead, with a large slotted spoon, transfer about half of the rice over the chicken, in an even layer. Don't worry about straining all the water out of the rice; you want the rice somewhat wet so that it can continue steaming as the dish cooks. Smooth the rice gently across the surface of the chicken, then sprinkle another ½ cup of the fried onions and ¼ cup of the cilantro-mint mixture over the top.

Sprinkle the remaining half of the rice on top and smooth it out. In a small bowl, combine ½ cup of the rice cooking water and the saffron-infused milk and pour it over the top of the biryani, spreading it evenly as best as you can. Sprinkle the remaining 2 tablespoons of warm ghee over the top and then sprinkle over the rest of the fried onions and the rest of the cilantro-mint mixture.

Place the biryani over medium-high heat and cook for 10 minutes—don't touch or stir! After 10 minutes, turn the heat down to medium-low and cover the pot with a cloth (a kitchen towel is perfect) to absorb excess moisture, and then seal the pot as tightly as you can by pressing and tamping the lid down tightly over the cloth, then wrapping any longer parts of the towel up over the top of the lid to ensure they don't dangle near your burner. If you have masking tape or painter's tape, use that to seal the edges of the lid to the pot. (Traditionally the biryani pot is sealed with a rope of dough around the lip of the pot, which must be broken off when serving the finished dish.)

Continue cooking for another 25 minutes. Turn the heat off and let the dish rest for another 10 minutes.

Remove the lid and check the doneness of the rice. Going in from the side with a long fork to keep the rest of the rice layers intact, pry out a piece of chicken to see if it's cooked through. (If in doubt, check with a meat thermometer for an internal temperature of 165°F.)

To serve, push a flat ladle down the side of the pot to the bottom and scoop up a layer of chicken and rice. Serve with kachumber, if you like.

Leftover biryani keeps, tightly covered in the refrigerator, for up to 4 days.

Notes: *I get that frying onions is an extra step, and if you want to save time, grocery stores sell pre-fried onions. If you go this route, look for a brand with no salt or additives—that means no batter-coated French's fried onions. Many Asian grocers sell coating-free fried shallots, which work well here. However, frying your own onions is an excellent idea and it'll give you the best results. I prefer red onions, thinly sliced and fried to a golden brown in a neutral oil such as grapeseed. Don't salt them. These are deep-fried: Use about 8 cups of oil to fry about 2 cups of onions at a time, working in batches to avoid overcrowding. You'll need about 6 cups of sliced onions to get 2 cups of fried onions. The fried onion oil (which keeps for about a week in the fridge) is amazing: Use it as the oil in this dish; to cook the pakoras on page 50, the okra fries on page 64, or the fennel-crusted eggplant fritters on page 67; or even in a salad dressing or on your scrambled eggs.*

Green chilli paste can be made by pounding two or three fresh green chillies (Thai or serrano, depending on your heat tolerance) in a mortar and pestle with ¼ cup of water, or buzzing them in a mini food processor or Magic Bullet with ¼ cup of water.

To break open cardamom pods, you can crush them lightly in a mortar and pestle, or place on a cutting board and hit them with a skillet to pop them.

UNCLE HACK

Khoya (also known as mawa) is the name for dried full-fat milk solids. When Indian cooks make it themselves (by slowly cooking milk down), it takes on a fudge-like texture that can be crumbled into desserts, where it adds body without adding liquid. But for convenience's sake, store-bought "instant" versions of khoya abound, usually packed into a brick shape. It's readily available at South Asian markets and online, but if you can't find it, you can use powdered milk—just try to find a version that's full-fat and sugar-free.

My experience with milk solids has been almost entirely in desserts—it's a key ingredient in the carrot halwa on page 248—so it seemed weird to add it to biryani. But the more I thought about it, I realized that, since we don't fry the chicken in oil or ghee before we start cooking the biryani, the additional fat from the milk solids will help keep the chicken juicy and moist, and it also contributes to an incredible mouthfeel and taste. This is an uncle hack that I first gleaned from a professional biryani-walla and it hasn't failed me since.

शक्ति

CHUTNEY FISH IN BANANA LEAF

Serves 4

I've only had this dish, called patra ni macchi in Gujarati, at Parsi special events like a wedding or Navjote ceremony (a religious ceremony initiating young people into the Zoroastrian faith, similar to a bar mitzvah). As Parsis have spent most of their many centuries in India living in coastal communities, fish is almost always on the menu for these and other celebrations. And you may not be surprised to learn that a Parsi special occasion is usually more about the food than about the official reason for the gathering—it's almost like we rush through rites and rituals to get to the meal.

There's something very fun, and almost ceremonial, about unwrapping this little gift at the table, revealing its delicious contents inside. While patra ni macchi is traditionally made with whole pomfret, thick-sliced kingfish, or mackerel steaks, you can use almost any meaty fish successfully. The brilliance of this dish is that the masala, while keeping the fish moist, transforms into a delicious gravy as it cooks. You can eat the finished product straight off the leaf, scooping rice into the vessel, or you can slide the fish off the leaf onto the rice separately. (If you're discarding the leaf, be sure to scrape the good bits off onto the rice first.)

MASALA

- 1 (2-inch) chunk dried tamarind or 2 tablespoons tamarind paste (see page 19)
- 2 tablespoons shredded dried unsweetened coconut
- 4 fresh Thai or serrano chillies (depending on your heat tolerance)
- 4 garlic cloves
- ¼ cup coarsely chopped cilantro leaves
- 5 or 6 coarsely chopped mint leaves
- ½ teaspoon kosher salt
- 1 tablespoon powdered jaggery (see page 20) or dark brown sugar
- 1 teaspoon roasted cumin powder (see page 32)

FISH

- 1½ pounds firm-fleshed fish, such as grouper, sea bass, or salmon, cut into 4 fillets
- ½ lemon
- Kosher salt
- Neutral oil, such as grapeseed
- 1 banana leaf, central rib removed, cut into 4 pieces (see Note)

Perfect Basmati Rice (page 276), for serving

To make the masala, soak the tamarind chunk (if using) in ¼ cup of hot water for about 5 minutes to soften. Combine the coconut, chillies, garlic, cilantro, mint, salt, jaggery, tamarind, and roasted cumin in a mini food processor or Magic Bullet and buzz into a coarse paste. Alternatively, you can use a mortar and pestle to mash everything into a paste. (If you do so, and you're using the tamarind chunk, reserve the tamarind soaking water and, if the paste is too thick, use some of the soaking water to thin.)

Preheat the oven to 375°F.

Pat the fish pieces dry with paper towels—the less moisture on the fish, the more readily it absorbs other flavors. Squeeze the half lemon over the fish and sprinkle salt lightly on both sides of each piece. (Don't oversalt, as there's salt in the masala.)

Liberally apply the masala all over the fish (if you are using skin-on fish, do not apply masala to the skin side). Drizzle a bit of oil over the masala.

Place each piece of fish on a piece of banana leaf and wrap so it's completely enclosed, and tie with kitchen twine to secure. Don't overwrap the fish—a single layer of leaf is fine.

Place the fish parcels on a sheet pan and roast until cooked through, 18 to 20 minutes.

Serve the still-wrapped parcels at the table, with rice, so guests can open them.

This dish is best made and eaten on the same day, but leftovers will keep, tightly covered in the refrigerator, for a day or two.

Note: *Fresh banana leaves are available in many Asian grocery stores, as well as Latin American grocers. (We get ours from a Sav-Mor in a Latino strip mall.) Look for leaves that are vibrant green in color. As they age, banana leaves get darker—these are also okay, but make sure you wipe them well with a wet cloth to get any weird spots off. You probably only need one banana leaf, center rib removed and cut into pieces, to wrap all of the fillets, but get two just in case. Frozen will work in a pinch (defrosted, of course). If you can't find banana leaves, parchment paper is a decent substitute.*

BUTTER CHICKEN

Serves 4 or 5

Butter chicken is to Indian food as the drum solo from "In the Air Tonight" is to a certain era of pop music. It's so iconic and beloved by so many people that Indians have gotten into lawsuits over who invented it. Mohti Mahal in Delhi claims it, but that's ferociously disputed by a number of other parties.

So how do you make a dish with butter in the name not *incredibly heavy and over the top? As hard as it is to believe, my version of butter chicken is actually delicate, relatively speaking. I replace the traditional cashew paste and poppy seed paste (which I find excessively cloying) with charred bell peppers that give the sauce body and smokiness without heaviness. Yes, there is butter; yes, there is heavy cream. But when you find yourself going back for more, you won't pay by feeling awful the next day.*

I'm giving you an option to "smoke" the sauce via the Auntie Hack on page 229.

Note: *Kasuri methi are dried leaves of fenugreek, a savory-aromatic-sweet herb that is somehow reminiscent of maple syrup (butter chicken will still taste good without it, but it does help give the dish its signature taste).*

CHICKEN MARINADE

2 whole boneless, skin-on chicken breasts (about 1½ pounds total), cut into ½-inch pieces

½ teaspoon Ginger-Garlic Paste (page 276)

½ teaspoon turmeric powder

½ teaspoon ground red chilli, such as Kashmiri (see page 18)

½ teaspoon kosher salt

1 teaspoon neutral oil, such as grapeseed

SAUCE

¼ cup neutral oil, such as grapeseed

½ teaspoon cumin seed

3 cups finely diced yellow onions (about 2 large onions)

1 fresh green Thai or serrano chilli (depending on your heat tolerance), finely chopped

Kosher salt

1 small green bell pepper, finely chopped (about 1 cup)

2½ teaspoons Ginger-Garlic Paste (page 276)

¾ teaspoon turmeric powder

½ to 1¼ teaspoons ground red chilli (such as Kashmiri, see page 18), depending on your heat tolerance

1 tablespoon coriander powder

1½ teaspoons cumin powder

1¼ cups canned crushed tomatoes

2 cups hot water

3 tablespoons powdered jaggery (see page 20) or dark brown sugar

½ teaspoon Garam Masala (page 277, or use store-bought)

¾ teaspoon kasuri methi (optional; see Note)

1 cup heavy cream

6 tablespoons unsalted butter, cut into small pieces

1 tablespoon neutral oil, such as grapeseed, to cook the chicken

Perfect Basmati Rice (page 276) and/or Chapati (page 212) or store-bought naan, for serving

Cilantro, for garnish (optional)

To marinate the chicken, combine the chicken, ginger-garlic paste, turmeric, ground chilli, salt, and oil in a large bowl. Mix together well to fully coat the chicken. Cover and store in the refrigerator for a minimum of 30 minutes or up to overnight.

To make the sauce, heat the oil in a large heavy-bottomed pot over high heat until very hot, almost smoking. Turn the temperature down to medium-low and add the cumin seeds. Let them sputter until they darken a bit in color, 10 seconds. (You can check the temperature of the oil by dropping in one seed. If it doesn't wiggle and start darkening in color, the oil isn't hot enough.) Quickly add the onions, the green chilli, and a pinch of salt and increase the heat to medium.

Cooking the onions in a certain way really matters. This step takes time and patience, and it may require finessing the heat level. Stir the onions into the oil frequently but not constantly, keeping them in an even layer. Make sure they're sizzling but not scorching, melting into each other, and not frying. As the water cooks out of the onions, they will eventually start to resemble a marmalade with a rich bourbon color. This is good! The goal is to get the onions so jammy and reduced that they almost become one with the sauce (as opposed to being an ingredient in the sauce). Keep an eye on the heat; if the onions are starting to crisp on the edges, turn the heat down and add a teaspoon or two of water to stop the frying.

Once the onions have hit the state described above—after about

Continued

BUTTER CHICKEN

Continued

10 minutes—add the bell pepper and continue cooking, stirring often, until the peppers are starting to brown, another 4 to 6 minutes. Add the ginger-garlic paste and turmeric, stir in well, and cook for about 1 minute, until fragrant.

Reduce the heat to medium and add the ground red chilli, coriander, and cumin powder. Stir and cook for about another minute.

Stir in the crushed tomatoes, hot water, and 1 teaspoon of salt. Cover and cook over medium-low heat, stirring occasionally, for about 30 minutes. The crushed tomato has a tendency to bubble up like molten lava as it cooks and thickens, so be careful not to burn yourself. You want the mixture at a simmer, not bubbling hard; be careful because the natural sugars in the onion and tomato can cause it to scorch.

Remove the pot from the heat and, with an immersion blender, carefully blend the sauce until it's completely smooth. No immersion blender? Let the sauce cool a bit, puree it in a standard blender, and pour it back into the pot.

Stir in the jaggery, garam masala, kasuri methi (if using), heavy cream, and butter. Put the pot back over medium heat, cover, and let it simmer until thickened, about 5 minutes, stirring occasionally. If you're employing the auntie hack to add more smoky flavor, now is the time to do so (see right).

When your sauce is ready, keep it at a low simmer while you cook the chicken. In a large nonstick skillet over high heat, heat the oil until it shimmers. Working in batches to avoid overcrowding, cook the chicken pieces through, about 5 minutes, then add the chicken to the sauce. Stir to combine, taste for salt and sweetness, and adjust to your liking.

Serve piping hot with basmati rice and/or chapati or naan, and garnish with cilantro if you like.

AUNTIE HACK

To give your butter chicken sauce an extra dose of smoky flavor without actually smoking the chicken, check out the Dunghar technique below. (This also works for the lentils in the dal makhani on page 133 and for the eggplant in the baingan bharta on page 134.) To "smoke" the sauce (or lentils or eggplant) via Dunghar auntie hack, you'll need:

1 cinnamon stick
A few black cardamom pods
A few green cardamom pods
A few whole black peppercorns
1 charcoal briquette
1 tablespoon ghee

Rest a small metal bowl with the cinnamon stick, black and green cardamom, and black peppercorns on top of the sauce (or whatever you're smoking). If the sauce is the right consistency, the bowl will float! Using tongs, heat a single piece of charcoal over your gas stove until it's glowing hot all over. Place the charcoal in the small bowl with the spices, then pour the ghee directly onto the charcoal. The heat will instantly vaporize the ghee, causing a blast of smokiness. Immediately cover the pot and the bowl with an airtight lid. Let everything sit for 10 to 15 minutes. When you remove the lid, the charcoal should have stopped glowing, and the sauce (or the lentils, or the eggplant) in the pot below will be infused with a smoky flavor that's so soft and buttery it's almost impossible to describe. (Run cold water over the charcoal to make sure it's completely out before dumping.)

PORK (OR CHICKEN OR LAMB) VINDALOO

Serves 4 to 6

Vindaloo is probably the most misunderstood of all Goan dishes—even by Indians. Most people assume that the "aloo" stands for potato, and I can't tell you how many vindaloo dishes I've had with potato. However, the term is derived from vinha d'alhos*—Portuguese for "vinegar and garlic." As those crazy seafaring explorers set sail searching for trade routes to India, they brought salt- or vinegar-cured pork with them. When they converted the Indians they encountered to Christianity, they introduced them to the cured pork, and eventually it was transformed into a fiery hot, spicy curry. (The Portuguese also brought the chilli peppers that were responsible for the fiery heat to begin with.)*

Interestingly, of the big five Indian dishes that most Americans are familiar with (chicken tikka masala, butter chicken, saag paneer, naan, and vindaloo), this is the only southern Indian entry, and it's localized to one tiny little province at that. The OG vindaloo is a vinegary, red-hot pork curry that's on the thick side and is sweetened with palm sugar. The version popularized in Indian restaurants around the world, however, is a thin, one-note, chilli pepper–hot curry, often with chicken or lamb. My version is somewhere in between the two, and on the drier side—something you can use a little bit of to add a lot of flavor, so you can enjoy it as a more mellow main dish that still clings to its roots. Pork is the traditional meat of choice—the fattier the better, which is why we call for shoulder—but it's equally delicious with lamb or chicken. You do you.

2 pounds boneless pork shoulder, leg of lamb, or boneless, skinless chicken thighs, cut into large cubes

Pinch each of kosher salt, turmeric, and Kashmiri red chilli powder (see page 18; optional)

5 to 10 whole dried red chillies, such as Kashmiri (see page 18), depending on your spice tolerance

2 cinnamon sticks, each broken into 2 or 3 pieces

1 tablespoon whole black peppercorns

1 teaspoon cumin seed

4 cloves

½ cup rice wine vinegar

1 (2-inch) piece peeled fresh ginger, roughly chopped

6 garlic cloves

¼ cup vegetable oil, plus more as needed

2 cups finely diced white onions (about 2 large onions)

2 teaspoons kosher salt, plus more to taste

3 cups hot water

2 tablespoons distilled white vinegar

1 tablespoon powdered jaggery (see page 20) or dark brown sugar (optional)

Coarsely chopped cilantro, for serving

Perfect Basmati Rice (page 276) and/or pav (sweet dinner rolls), for serving

Rub the meat with the salt, turmeric, and ground chilli mixture and set aside. You can do this ahead of time and let the meat dry-marinate for up to 6 hours in the refrigerator. (This step is not required, but it is a very traditional way in India of making sure that the meat is seasoned well—and that any surface bacteria is killed off by the salt and turmeric.)

In a small skillet over high heat, toast the whole chillies, cinnamon, peppercorns, cumin, and cloves until fragrant, 2 to 3 minutes. Place the toasted spices in a bowl, add the rice wine vinegar, and soak for 15 minutes.

In a mini food processor or blender, combine the vinegar and spice mixture, ginger, and garlic and blitz into a thick, coarse paste. Add a few tablespoons of water if necessary to get the right texture.

Heat the oil in a large heavy-bottomed pot or Dutch oven over medium-high heat until shimmering, then add the onions and salt. Next, add the seasoned meat and cook, turning every few minutes, until it's evenly browned on all sides, about 10 minutes total. Add an extra splash of oil if necessary to prevent the meat from sticking. Remove the meat from the pot and set aside. Lower the heat to medium.

Continue cooking the onions in the same pot. This step takes time and patience, and it may require finessing the heat level. Stir the onions into the oil frequently but not constantly, keeping them in an even layer. Make sure they're sizzling but not scorching, melting into each other and not frying. As the water cooks out of the onions, they will eventually start to resemble a marmalade with a rich bourbon color. This is good! The goal is to get the onions so jammy and

Continued

PORK (OR CHICKEN OR LAMB) VINDALOO

Continued

reduced that they almost become one with the sauce (as opposed to being an ingredient in the sauce). Keep an eye on the heat; if the onions are starting to crisp on the edges, turn the heat down and add a teaspoon or two of water to stop the frying.

Once the onions are nice and jammy, add the meat back to the pot along with the vinegar-spice masala and stir to combine. Let everything sizzle and meld for 1 to 2 minutes, then add the hot water and distilled white vinegar. Bring to a boil over high heat, then turn the heat to low. Cover and simmer, stirring occasionally, until the meat is fork-tender, anywhere from 30 to 60 minutes depending on the type of meat used (pork will take longer to tenderize than lamb, and lamb longer than chicken). Start testing the larger pieces of meat for tenderness at the 30-minute mark, testing two or three pieces in different parts of the pot.

Taste for salt and add as needed. The dish should be spicy, with a prominent and pungent tang of vinegar, and aromatic with the cinnamon and clove. Some vindaloo specialists will swear that there needs to be a sweet component, too. If you like the dish slightly sweeter, add the optional jaggery or brown sugar at this point and stir it in well.

Garnish with chopped cilantro and enjoy with rice or sweet dinner rolls (pav, another Portuguese import).

Leftover vindaloo keeps, tightly covered in the refrigerator, for up to 4 days.

CHETTINAD SPICE–CRUSTED DUCK BREAST WITH COCONUT "PAN SAUCE" CURRY

Serves 4

The spice blend used here goes by different names in different parts of South India, and usually appears in the form of a coarsely ground paste used in fish or crab frys. But the Chettinad region of Tamil Nadu gained notoriety when a spicy, gravy-covered dish known as "Chettinad chicken" started appearing on restaurant menus in other parts of India as an "exotic" South Indian specialty.

What makes the Chettinad spice blend flavor profile interesting is the interplay of aromatic spices like cardamom, star anise, cinnamon, and cloves alongside sharp black peppercorns and ajwain seeds. Unlike garam masala, which tends to lean toward the aromatics, this blend is truly peppery, with just a hint of the warming spices.

I don't love the chicken version, but I do think the fattiness and gaminess of duck holds up to this bold spice blend beautifully, hence my golden-crispy take—a bastardized version of an already bastardized regional specialty. The pan sauce, in the same spirit, is a nontraditional way of making your life easy instead of having to create a curry from scratch.

This is a heady, spicy dish with a lot going on and a restaurant-style presentation. Save it for date night or anytime you're looking to impress company.

CHETTINAD SPICE BLEND

6 dried red chillies, such as Kashmiri (see page 18)

2 or 3 green cardamom pods

1 star anise

1½ cinnamon sticks, broken into 2 to 3 pieces

2 whole cloves

2 tablespoons coriander seed

1 tablespoon cumin seed

1 teaspoon fennel seed

½ teaspoon poppy seed

10 whole black peppercorns

¼ teaspoon ajwain or caraway seed (optional)

¼ teaspoon fenugreek seed (optional)

¼ teaspoon mace powder (optional)

2 (10- to 12-ounce) skin-on duck breasts

Kosher salt

Melted coconut oil

PAN SAUCE

1 tablespoon peeled and minced fresh ginger (about a 1-inch knob)

¼ teaspoon turmeric powder

¼ teaspoon ground red chilli, such as Kashmiri (see page 18)

1 cup chicken or vegetable stock

1 cup full-fat coconut milk

Juice of 1 lime

Perfect Basmati Rice (page 276), for serving

Coarsely chopped cilantro, for garnish

To make the spice blend, place a medium skillet over medium-low heat and toast all the ingredients (from chillies to mace), stirring often, until it's fragrant and the cumin starts to slightly darken, 60 to 90 seconds. Do not overcook! You just want the spices heated up until they are quite warm to the touch but not so hot that you can't handle them. Transfer them to a bowl to cool and, once cooled, grind them coarsely in a spice or coffee grinder reserved for this purpose. (You may have to split it into two batches so it all fits.)

Pat the duck breasts dry with paper towels. With the skin side facing up, run a sharp knife diagonally about halfway down through the fat, scoring the skin every half inch, then scoring it the other way, again every half inch, making a crisscross or lattice-style pattern. Don't make the cuts so deep that you hit the flesh—you want to just lightly cut through the skin so that the fat between the skin and the meat will render out.

Season both sides generously with salt (as the fat renders off in the pan, the salt will sluice off with it, so don't be shy).

Add a few drops of coconut oil to the spice blend and mix until you have a somewhat oily but still crumbly paste. Apply the spice paste liberally to both sides of the breast, working it into

Continued

CHETTINAD SPICE–CRUSTED DUCK BREAST WITH COCONUT "PAN SAUCE" CURRY

Continued

the places where you've scored the skin. (Any leftover spice paste can be refrigerated in a glass jar and will keep well for several months.)

Heat a large heavy-bottomed pan or cast-iron skillet over medium-low heat. Place the breasts in the pan skin side down. You should hear the lightest of sizzles when the duck hits the pan; keep the temperature at low to medium-low, maintaining a very light sizzle as the fat heats up and starts to render out. If the fat is bubbling or popping, the pan is too hot.

In about 15 minutes, there should be a lot of liquid duck fat in the pan and the skin should start to look golden and crispy. Turn the heat up to medium for another couple of minutes to ensure the skin turns golden brown. Then gently flip the breast over; I use the two-cooking-spoons technique, one on either side, to lift and turn the meat in a way that doesn't splatter. Cook over medium heat for 2 to 3 minutes, until the internal temperature hits 130°F on a meat thermometer.

The duck will be a perfect medium rare at this point, so pull the breasts out of the pan and rest them on a wire rack set over a plate (or just on a plate if you don't have a rack). After 5 to 7 minutes—enough time to make the pan sauce—the duck will be rested and ready to slice.

To make the pan sauce, strain the warm duck fat through a strainer into a jar and reserve for future cooking (crispy oven-roasted potatoes!). Keep a tiny bit of the fat and the pan bits (fond) in the pan—if any bits of fond are in the strainer, tap them back into the pan.

Turn the heat to medium-high and, once the duck fat is sizzling, add the ginger, turmeric, and ground red chilli, and stir for 30 seconds. Add the chicken or vegetable stock and as it heats, use it to deglaze the pan, scraping the fond off the bottom and into the liquid.

Once the liquid is simmering and has reduced by half, 3 to 4 minutes, add the coconut milk and bring to a simmer, then turn the heat down to medium-low. Cook until the sauce looks silken and starts to slightly thicken, 5 to 7 minutes. Taste for salt and adjust (there will probably be plenty left over from the duck), and finish with the juice of the lime.

To serve, with a sharp (not serrated) knife, slice the rested duck on the bias into ¼-inch-thick slices. Serve over basmati rice with the pan sauce drizzled on top. Garnish with cilantro.

Leftover duck keeps, tightly covered in the refrigerator, for up to 3 days.

MAHARAJA LAMB SHANKS

Serves 4

I didn't really discover slow-cooked braised meats until I arrived in the US. I'm talking about your classic pot roast, osso buco, braised oxtail, etc. These things were all new to me, and I delighted in learning about the joys of low-and-slow cooking. However, in my frequent travels back to India, during which I explore and discover subsets of my home country's cuisine that are new to me, I met a stewed meat dish called nihari that's popular in North India and Pakistan, and I couldn't get it out of my mind.

Nihari is a rich, slow-cooked stew typically made with a shank cut of mutton or goat; it's flavored deeply with an abundance of spices, including long pepper, a cousin of black peppercorns. It was likely invented by royal chefs in Awadh under the Mughal Empire in the eighteenth century—hence my nickname for it.

I started running a stew inspired by nihari as a special at Chai Pani, with a more streamlined technique than the traditional recipe, and it's to this day one of my most-requested dishes. Lamb shank is traditional here, but use shoulder or stew meat if you can't find shanks.

MARINADE

- ¼ cup Ginger-Garlic Paste (page 276)
- 1 tablespoon neutral oil, such as grapeseed
- 1 teaspoon turmeric powder
- 1 teaspoon ground red chilli powder, such as Kashmiri (see page 18)
- 1 teaspoon kosher salt

LAMB

- 4 (1-pound) lamb shanks, or 2½ pounds lamb shoulder or stew meat
- ¼ cup neutral oil, such as grapeseed
- 1 tablespoon cumin seed
- 1 teaspoon whole black peppercorns
- 4 small whole dried red chillies, such as Kashmiri (see page 18)
- 4 green cardamom pods
- 4 cloves
- 2 cinnamon sticks, broken into a few pieces
- 1 black cardamom pod (optional)
- 1 tablespoon minced garlic (2 or 3 cloves)
- 1 tablespoon peeled and minced fresh ginger (about a 1-inch knob)
- 1 tablespoon finely chopped fresh Thai or serrano chilli (depending on your heat tolerance)
- ½ cup coarsely chopped, tightly packed cilantro leaves and stems
- 3 cups diced yellow onion (about 3 medium onions)
- 2 teaspoons kosher salt
- 3 tablespoons tomato paste
- 4 cups low-sodium chicken or beef stock (beef stock has more depth of flavor)
- 1 teaspoon Garam Masala (page 277, or use store-bought)
- 2 medium carrots, peeled and cut into 2-inch pieces
- 10 to 12 small fingerling potatoes
- Perfect Basmati Rice (page 276) and/or naan or pav (Hawaiian sweet rolls), for serving

To make the marinade, in a large bowl, combine the ginger-garlic paste, oil, turmeric, ground red chilli, and salt until they form a paste. Rub the paste all over the shanks, coating them thoroughly. Let rest for 30 minutes.

Preheat the oven to 325°F.

In a large heavy-bottomed ovenproof pot with a lid (a large Dutch oven is perfect), heat the oil over medium heat; the oil should cover the bottom of the pot completely in a thick layer. The pot should also be large enough for all the shanks to fit side by side in a single layer before you place it in the oven. If your pot isn't big enough, sear the shanks in it, then transfer them to a baking dish that can accommodate them before placing into the oven.

When the oil is shimmering, add the seasoned shanks, working in batches if necessary, and brown on all sides, being careful to avoid any burnt spots on the bottom of the pot. Stand the shanks up to get their "heads" nice and brown, too.

The lamb shanks should have a bit of a crust but won't be cooked through; take them out of the pan and set them aside. The pan should have some brown bits of the marinade either in the oil or stuck to the bottom; these are a good thing, as long as they aren't burnt black.

With the oil still in the pot, turn the heat to medium-high and heat until the oil is shimmering again, then add the cumin seeds. After 30 seconds of the seeds sizzling, add the peppercorns, dried red chillies, green cardamom, cloves, cinnamon, and black cardamom (if using) and stir for a minute.

Continued

MAHARAJA LAMB SHANKS

Continued

Stir in the garlic, ginger, green chillies, cilantro, and onions plus 1 teaspoon of the salt. Scrape the bottom of the pan to deglaze the browned bits and cook on medium heat until the onions start to brown on the edges; this should take 5 to 7 minutes.

Mix in the tomato paste and stir until it's melted into the other ingredients. Add the stock, garam masala, carrots, and potatoes, and bring to a simmer over medium-high heat. Taste for salt and add the remaining teaspoon now if necessary.

Add the lamb shanks, cover the pot, and transfer to the oven on the middle rack. The shanks should be mostly submerged in the liquid; if a little bit sticks out, that's okay. If there isn't enough liquid, add some water. (If you're using a baking dish, transfer the liquid to the dish and then add the shanks, and cover the dish with a double layer of foil.)

Cook for 2 to 2½ hours. At the 2-hour mark, check the meat with a fork to see if it's tender and pulls easily off the bone. If not, continue cooking for another 30 minutes, or until it does. It's hard to overcook lamb shanks as long as there's enough liquid in there with them. At this point, when the lamb is very tender, the braising liquid should be reduced to a thick sauce, and the carrots and potatoes should be tender.

Serve with rice, naan, or pav to mop up the gravy!

Leftover lamb keeps, tightly covered in the refrigerator, for up to 3 days.

MASALA POT ROAST CHICKEN

Serves 4 to 6

Before the advent of ovens, the traditional way to roast a chicken was on the stove in a pot with a tight-fitting lid, a technique that's part braise, part roast, and all flavor. I still think cooking a chicken this way is the best—it makes for an exceptionally juicy, fall-off-the-bone bird with way more appeal than one cooked in a hot, dry oven.

When I was growing up in India, we didn't have many occasions to roast a chicken, but when we did, this was how we did it. It's a sort of Parsi pot roast, enlivened with fresh lemongrass and served with all of its glorious juices over Mom's Quick 'n' Easy Potatoes (page 207) or freshly steamed basmati rice (see page 276).

- 1 tablespoon Ginger-Garlic Paste (page 276)
- 1 tablespoon freshly squeezed lemon juice
- 1 tablespoon finely chopped lemongrass (optional)
- 2 teaspoons cumin powder, toasted in a dry skillet until aromatic
- 1 tablespoon kosher salt
- 1 teaspoon coarsely ground black pepper
- 1 whole chicken (about 5 pounds)
- 2 tablespoons neutral oil, such as grapeseed
- ½ teaspoon ground red chilli, such as Kashmiri (see page 18)
- 3 garlic cloves
- ½ cup water
- Mom's Quick 'n' Easy Potatoes (page 207), for serving (optional)
- Perfect Basmati Rice (page 276), for serving (optional)
- Cilantro sprigs, for garnish
- Thinly sliced red onion, for garnish

In a small bowl, mix together the ginger-garlic paste, lemon juice, half of the lemongrass (if using), the toasted cumin, salt, and pepper.

Rub the spice mixture all over the chicken, inside and out (as my mother would say, "very nicely"). Set the chicken aside in the refrigerator to marinate for at least 1 hour and up to 3 hours.

In a large, lidded, heavy-bottomed pot tall enough to hold an entire chicken (such as a 5- or 6-quart Dutch oven), heat the oil over medium-high heat until shimmering, otherwise the chicken will stick to the pot when you put it in.

Add the remaining lemongrass and the ground red chilli and garlic to the pot and stir for 45 to 60 seconds, until sizzling.

Carefully lower the chicken into the hot oil. Brown the chicken all over, turning it until it's evenly browned, 2 to 4 minutes per side. If the heat is too high, turn it down a notch or two—the chicken should brown without burning.

Once the chicken is brown on all sides, add ½ cup of water. Lower the heat to maintain a simmer, cover the pot, and cook until the meat is cooked through and falling-off-the-bone tender, 45 to 60 minutes. Start checking for doneness at the 35-minute mark. The drumsticks and wings should move freely in their sockets, and it should feel as if you could easily pop them off with your hands sans knife.

Serve with potatoes and/or rice to soak up all of the delicious juices, and garnish with cilantro and onion.

Leftover chicken keeps, tightly covered in the refrigerator, for up to 3 days.

'आझाद', 'जयहिंद' संघ प्रथम
उंबरे गावामध्ये दिवसा घरफोडी
'अंबालिका'वर गुरुवारी नोकर भरती
प्राथमिक आरोग्य केंद्रात वृक्षारोपण

DESSERTS & SWEET MEATS

Sweets (mithai) in India are intricate and made by specialists, and some of the most prominent ones have been doing it for generations. They aren't really street food, but much like the only way to get chaat is to go to the chaat walla, the only way to get mithai is to go to the mithai walla, who likely has his treats stacked up high at street level in eye-catching displays. Although sweets aren't bought and eaten on the spot like chaat, they have some of the same spirit—hawkers selling their wares to the crowds on the streets, enticing passersby with all kinds of over-the-top displays. In my mind, it's all part of the tapestry of street food in India.

Many sweets in India feature expensive ingredients like saffron, silver or gold leaf, cashews, raisins, or other exotic fruits or nuts. They're often given as gifts in beautiful packaging, and are not necessarily something a home cook would bust out.

So instead, I'm picking a few of my favorite homestyle Indian desserts—mostly of the one-pot, simple cooking variety—to end your Indian street food feast on a sweet note. These are the kinds of desserts you can actually make at home with minimal equipment and fuss, though they still deliver big in terms of both flavor and fun.

KHEER (RICE PUDDING)

Serves 4 to 6

To even compare glorious kheer to workaday rice pudding is an insult, but for the purposes of giving you some context, and those purposes alone, I'll allow the comparison just this once. Because kheer is so much more than rice cooked in a rich dairy base. It has a lovely caramelized flavor with hints of saffron, cardamom, and rose water, and it's topped with golden raisins and cashews fried in pure ghee for extra credit. Behold!

½ cup short-grain white rice
2 quarts whole milk
¼ cup sugar
Pinch of salt
2 (14-ounce) cans sweetened condensed milk
2 green cardamom pods, split
3 to 4 strands of saffron (optional)
¼ teaspoon rose water
3 tablespoons ghee
2 tablespoons cashews, whole or halved, plus more for garnish (optional)
2 tablespoons golden raisins, plus more for garnish (optional)

Place the rice in a small bowl and cover with water; stir with your fingers to rinse, then drain the rice in a strainer. Repeat at least two more times, until the water runs clear. After the final rinse, return the rice to the bowl and add enough water to cover the rice; set aside.

In a large pot over medium-high heat, heat the whole milk. Stir frequently, making sure to scrape the bottom of the pot to prevent scorching. Once the milk just starts to come to a simmer, lower the heat to medium. (Keep a close eye on it—the simmer happens suddenly and the milk can boil over if you're not paying attention.)

Simmer the milk, stirring frequently, until it's reduced to two-thirds of its original volume, about 30 minutes. As the milk reduces, adjust the heat as needed to keep it simmering but not boiling.

Once the milk has reduced, drain the water from the rice and add the soaked rice to the milk. Cook the rice over medium heat, stirring frequently, until very soft, about 15 minutes. Add the sugar, salt, and sweetened condensed milk, stirring well to fully incorporate the additions and to dissolve the sugar. Bring the kheer back to a simmer and cook, stirring often, for another 5 to 6 minutes. Turn off the heat and stir in the cardamom, saffron (if using), and rose water.

In a small sauté pan over medium heat, heat the ghee until melted. Add the cashews and cook, stirring, until they're lightly golden along the edges. Add the raisins and sauté until they puff up. Scrape the contents of the pan into the kheer and stir to combine.

Ladle the kheer into serving bowls and serve warm or chilled. Garnish with extra cashews and raisins if you're entertaining. Leftovers keep, tightly covered in the refrigerator, for up to a week.

CARROT HALWA

Serves 8 to 10

Many people associate halwa with the Middle Eastern sesame dessert halva. Halva was indeed introduced to India from the Middle East, but Indian dessert culture didn't take to the original sesame- or flour-based versions—instead, we made a softer, creamier version, typically with semolina flour and lots of butter (or ghee) and sugar, and with root veggies like carrots and beets. As we changed the original halva to suit our tastes, we also tweaked the name to "halwa."

Unlike a traditional loaf-shaped halva, Indian halwa is typically soft and thick, almost like a pudding, and is usually served warm and garnished with nuts. It's a very rich, sweet dessert, so we recommend serving it in small portions—plan on doling out about 4 to 6 ounces (½ to ¾ cup) per person.

2½ pounds carrots, coarsely grated in a food processor
⅓ cup plus ¼ cup ghee
4 cups whole milk
1 cup sugar
⅓ cup crumbled khoya (see Uncle Hack, page 223)
¼ cup halved cashews
¼ cup golden raisins
Kosher salt (optional)

In a large sauté pan over medium-high heat, combine the carrots, ⅓ cup of the ghee, and 1 cup of water. Cook until the carrots are very soft and most of the water has evaporated, about 10 minutes.

Stir in the milk and turn the heat down to medium. Cook, stirring occasionally, until the milk has evaporated, about 30 minutes.

Add the sugar and khoya. Turn the heat up to medium-high and cook, stirring often, until the sugar and khoya dissolve into a liquid, about 5 minutes. Continue cooking, stirring often, until the mixture begins to thicken, another 5 minutes or so.

Slowly, a tablespoon at a time, add 3 tablespoons of the remaining ¼ cup of ghee (reserve one tablespoon to toast the cashews in later). Continue stirring as the carrot mixture thickens.

Once all the liquid has cooked out of the carrot mixture, lower the heat slightly and continue to cook for 15 to 20 minutes, until it has a soft, fudge-like consistency. Remove from the heat.

In a small sauté pan over medium-high heat, heat the remaining tablespoon of ghee until it's shimmering. Add the cashews and cook, stirring occasionally, until the edges are lightly golden and toasted, 2 to 3 minutes. Add the raisins and cook, stirring often, until they're puffy and aromatic, 1 to 2 minutes.

Stir the cashews and raisins into the halwa and mix well. Taste and add a pinch of salt for balance if you deem it necessary.

Serve warm or at room temperature, scooped out into individual bowls. Leftovers keep, tightly covered in the refrigerator, for up to 5 days.

SOOJI HALWA

Serves 6 to 8

Sooji halwa is a semolina-based dessert that falls, texturally, somewhere between pudding and polenta, with the most deliciously buttery, sweet, creamy flavor carrying it along. It's dead simple to make and can be dressed up with all kinds of spices and nuts, or even fruits as you see fit (my mom sometimes mashed a banana in there—why not?). This recipe is on the straightforward side, with the raisins adding a welcome tart hit to the sweet flavor, and cashews and ghee there for richness.

Sooji *means "semolina"; when shopping, skip the yellow-hued Italian durum and look instead for what's commonly called farina or cream of wheat in the US—the whitish stuff with little flecks of brown. Indian brands are super easy to find, and will give you the option of fine or coarsely ground. I prefer fine, which creates a creamier halwa, though the coarse stuff works too—it's really a matter of personal preference.*

3 or 4 saffron strands (optional)
¼ cup warmed whole milk (if using saffron)
1 pound salted butter
4 cups fine sooji (semolina flour)
2 cups sugar
½ cup golden raisins, plus more for garnish
2 teaspoons cardamom powder
Ghee
A handful of cashews, for garnish

Break up the saffron strands (if using) and sprinkle them in a small bowl with the warm milk.

While the saffron soaks, bring 6 cups of water to a boil in a medium pot.

While the water boils, melt the butter in a large heavy-bottomed saucepan over medium-low heat. Add the sooji and stir constantly, until it's toasted to a pale golden brown. Sooji will burn if you're not standing there stirring it, so take your time and don't rush this step, which can take 9 minutes or so.

Add the sugar, raisins, and cardamom to the sooji, stirring well for about 1 minute to incorporate. (This step allows the cardamom to heat up and infuse the sooji with its aroma.)

Carefully pour the boiling water, followed by the saffron-infused milk, into the pan with the sooji, stirring while you add the liquid. The sooji will quickly start to thicken, but just keep stirring until all of the liquid has been absorbed, about 1 minute.

Cover the pan with a tightly fitting lid and turn the heat off. Let the sooji sit for 10 minutes. Just let it sit. Really. No touching, no stirring, no peeking. This resting period is what allows the sooji to become ultra soft and fluffy.

While the sooji rests, heat a few spoonfuls of ghee in a small sauté pan over medium heat. Toss in a handful of golden raisins and cashews and heat until they're warm and toasted, about 2 minutes.

You may now—finally—uncover the sooji. Serve warm, garnished with the raisins and cashews and drizzled with any remaining ghee.

Leftovers keep, tightly covered in the refrigerator, for up to a week. You may need to sprinkle a little water over the sooji before reheating to get it to loosen up a bit in the microwave or on the stovetop. (As a heads-up, leftover halwa is delightful with yogurt for breakfast.)

DRINKS

Beverages in India are very specific to regions and seasons (lassi, for example, originates in North India, land of yogurt). Accordingly, the handful of drinks in this short chapter are closely tied to my personal memories of a time and place—everything here is nostalgic for me in different ways. These recipes also play well with the food featured in this book.

NIMBU PANI

Serves 2

As ubiquitous on street corners as it is in homes, nimbu pani (literally "lime water") is a refreshing, cooling drink that makes the Indian summer bearable. A fresh nimbu pani can cool the body down, aid in digestion, balance pH levels, and even cure a hangover—I swear!

I can still hear, clear as a bell, my grandmother calling out at 6 p.m. each night for nimbu pani to be served to the guests at the bed-and-breakfast my family ran. Since moving to America, I've met many of those former guests, who fondly recount their memories of staying at Viloo Villa. Unfailingly, at some point in their trip down memory lane, they will imitate my grandmother's high-pitched voice calling for this drink.

Nimbu pani is on the menu at Chai Pani, and even when a case of limes quadruples in price in the wintertime, it stays put, a permanent and refreshing homage to that part of my childhood.

You can swap soda water or seltzer for regular water to take this to the next level of refreshment. And feel free to adjust the amount of sugar to your liking.

¼ cup sugar, or to taste

¼ cup freshly squeezed lime juice (from about 2 limes)

½ teaspoon kosher salt

2½ cups cold tap water, soda water, or seltzer

2 lime wheels, for garnish

¼ teaspoon toasted and crushed cumin seed, for garnish (optional)

Bring a small pot with ¼ cup of water to a boil. Add the sugar and stir to dissolve and make a simple syrup, about 2 minutes.

In a pitcher, combine the simple syrup, lime juice, and salt. Stir vigorously until the salt is completely dissolved.

Add the cold water and stir to incorporate. Serve over ice with a lime wheel and a sprinkle of cumin seeds over the top if you like.

MANGO LASSI

Makes 8 to 10

It's hard not to fall in love with lassi, the OG smoothie of India. With origins in Punjab, lassis are now ubiquitous across the nation, and with good reason. The combination of refreshing yogurt, milk, and fruity flavorings is not only delicious, it's also cooling with a spicy meal. And the enzymes in the yogurt act as a digestive, too.

Like ice cream, lassi is also a standalone treat. In Rajasthan and Punjab in the north of India, there are lassi stalls on almost every street corner in the summer. Classic lassi is either salted or sweet—the former being the original digestive aid, the latter being more of a treat. The most popular sweet lassi flavors are mango, rose, pistachio, and saffron, and mango is the king of them all. Chai Pani serves what I am convinced is one of the best mango lassis out there—because I obsessed over getting it right.

This recipe makes a large quantity because I'm particular about the type of canned mango pulp I use. I highly recommend the Deep brand of kesar mango pulp, which is sold in 30-ounce cans. If you'd like to cut this recipe in half, you certainly can; just save half of the pulp in the freezer for future lassis.

3¾ cups canned kesar mango pulp, preferably Deep brand (one 30-ounce can)
2¼ cups plain full-fat yogurt
3 cups whole milk
¼ cup half-and-half
2 teaspoons cardamom powder
3 tablespoons sugar

Combine the mango, yogurt, milk, half-and-half, cardamom, and sugar in a blender, working in batches if necessary, and blend until smooth, 2 to 3 minutes. Serve chilled.

LIME RICKEY

Serves 1

I have no idea why this drink, which I've only ever seen served at Irani cafes or canteens, is called a lime rickey. The one I remember from my childhood featured a teeth-shatteringly sweet raspberry syrup, with that classic artificial taste you'd expect out of a bottled product.

When I decided to put this on the menu at Chai Pani, we spent a long time developing a recipe for a fresh raspberry syrup to get the best of both worlds—the nostalgia of the classic lime rickey, with the refreshing flavor and taste of real raspberries and lime. It's a fun party drink, and pretty, too, especially when garnished with fresh mint and/or a handful of fresh raspberries. If you're up for it, gin or white rum work particularly well as alcoholic additions.

RASPBERRY PUREE

1½ cups fresh or frozen raspberries
½ cup water
3 tablespoons sugar

2 tablespoons simple syrup
1½ tablespoons freshly squeezed lime juice
Soda water

To make the raspberry puree, combine the raspberries, ½ cup of water, and sugar in a small pot and bring to a boil over medium-high heat. Turn the heat down to a steady simmer and cook until the mixture resembles a thick syrup with the consistency of hot fudge, 10 to 15 minutes. Allow to cool to room temperature. Strain the puree through a fine-mesh sieve into a clean container to remove any seeds.

If using a cocktail shaker, combine 2 tablespoons of the raspberry puree with the simple syrup and lime juice in the shaker. Fill with ice, shake, strain, and pour into a Collins or other tall glass. Fill to the top with soda water and stir before serving.

If you don't have a cocktail shaker, simply combine all the ingredients in a tall glass, stir well, and add ice.

Note: *The raspberry puree will make more than you need for one drink—¾ to 1 cup, which is enough for many rounds of lime rickeys. It keeps, tightly covered in the fridge, for up to a week.*

WHAT MAKES CHAI CHAI

There's a great story of the history of chai called Tea War: A History of Capitalism in China and India. *Written by Andrew B. Liu, it's a marvelous book and should be required reading in all Indian classrooms. I shall now attempt to summarize part of it in order to explain how chai became the national drink of India—but really, go read the book.*

We'll begin at the beginning: China invented tea as we know it thousands of years ago (the Chinese word for "tea" is cha, *hence chai). For many hundreds of years, trade from China to Europe was limited—and tea exports were also tightly controlled by the Chinese government. By the early 1700s, the British East India Company had begun importing tea directly from China, at great expense and with a heavy markup, so that only the wealthiest Brits could afford this luxury good. The act of drinking tea—out of a fancy tea set with separate containers for milk and sugar (additions the Chinese, who kept the best-quality stuff for themselves, would never dream of using)—was associated with British aristocracy.*

By the mid-1800s, the British Parliament had cut tea taxes significantly, and the East India Company monopoly ended, making tea much more widely available to the masses. By the time of the Industrial Revolution, Brits of all social levels were loony for tea. Factory workers demanded tea breaks for a boost of energy; by the early nineteenth century, tea was cheaper than beer. Tea was one of England's most important imports, but the country had a massive trade deficit with China, which required payment in silver.

The Brits were running out of silver, so the British East India Company—aka the forebears of English colonization of India—turned, naturally, to growing opium in Bengal to sell to the Chinese illegally, in order to get some silver back and continue buying tea. I will now summarize a complex geopolitical issue thusly: Opium was being smuggled into China fairly openly, and the Chinese government was not happy about it, so an overly zealous governor of Hong Kong burned down a bunch of warehouses and shops with British opium in them. This led to the infamous "Opium Wars" between Britain and China (1839–1842 and 1856–1860)—and, among other things, the annexation of Hong Kong as a British territory.

At this point, Britain realized that having such a massive dependence on China for so much of their import economy was a tenuous situation at best. So in one of the most brazen acts of corporate espionage in history, they sent spies to China to learn how to grow tea, then looked to one of their largest colonies—India—to actually grow it in.

Eventually, India did start growing tea commercially, primarily in Assam, which became ground zero for tea production from roughly 1850 onwards. But in a classic example of "too much too late," a few decades later, as the Indian tea industry was hitting its stride, global demand for tea was dropping. World War I and the Depression didn't help matters. By the time the British left India in the 1940s, India's tea plantations were producing far more of the crop than anyone could drink, so the British-backed Tea Cess Committee (later renamed the Indian Tea Market Expansion Board) turned to what they hoped would be their single largest market: Indians themselves.

The problem was that not only did Indians have absolutely no taste for good tea, they also considered it unpatriotic to drink the stuff. Many Indians were in the midst of a fervent Swadeshi (nationalist) movement (thank you, Gandhi), so tea, with its British baggage, was a hard sell. On top of that, in order to drink tea the way Brits did, you had to own an entire tea set, and the average Indian family wasn't about to go around boiling water, steeping tea, keeping hot milk and sugar separately, and then putting it all together—that involved way more vessels than most owned, and way too much work.

Out of desperation, the tea council launched a huge propaganda campaign, advertising like crazy with the message that to drink tea was in fact very Indian. It dispensed mobile "tea vans" across cities and small towns to give away free cups and individual packets of tea. Of course, they were giving away the poorest-quality tea—what's known as CTC, or cut, torn, and curled. This tea is crap. It's cheap, overly roasted, powdery—the instant coffee of tea leaves, if you will. And, as it happens, it is absolutely essential to making chai: In a nation-altering, wholly unforeseen side effect, tea stalls started popping up as Indian entrepreneurs started trying to make a buck off what was essentially a free ingredient.

To hell with heating and cooking all the ingredients separately—out of sheer necessity, the tea wallas threw tea, milk, and sugar into a single pot together. In keeping with the Indian palate for sweet dairy things, the milk-to-water-to-sugar ratio evolved to be heavy on the milk and sugar. Invariably, Indians started adding more flavors to make the chai interesting—spices like cardamom, clove, black pepper, and cinnamon, which today we think of as masala chai, but also roots and herbs such as ginger, mint, and lemongrass. (See page 266 for recipes riffing on these variations.) Over the course of a few decades, Indians successfully transformed a potent signifier of British colonialism into a beloved drink uniquely their own.

For a long time, due to its origins, chai was considered a street drink. But as is usually the case when street culture becomes commercialized and "elevated," street chai is now served in the fanciest hotels throughout India, at prices that would make a train station chai walla's head explode. This, dear readers, is the intriguing paradox of India. A cup of chai can cost 10, 100, or 1,000 rupees, depending on who made it and where you're drinking it. But any way you sip it, it's all the same chai: a symbol of national pride in making something great out of whatever is available; jugaad writ large.

CHAI AND ITS VARIATIONS

The milky sweet tea concoction referred to as chai in India is a very specific drink. Just as a cappuccino and a latte would never be confused in Italy, Indian chai is never confused with American variations on it, nor with the British tea with milk and sugar. Though the specific masala varies from household to household and street vendor to street vendor, chai itself is a mixing of specific time-tested and time-honored ingredients with a specific technique.

The first and most essential ingredient is the tea itself, which should be CTC tea, or cut, torn, and curled. I go full-on history nerd about this on page 262, but the TL;DR of why this matters is because chai as we know it would not have originated if tea factories, with their rapidly shrinking local market, didn't need to offload their cheapest, poorest quality, most overly roasted "tea powder" to a country full of people who had absolutely no taste for classic Chinese or British-style teas. Paradoxically, the higher quality tea leaf you try to use to make chai, the further you're getting from what it's supposed to taste like.

True chai involves copious amounts of CTC tea, boiled rapidly in varying ratios of whole milk and water, until the milk is slightly reduced (and thus creamier), sweetened to the point of tasting like a dessert, flavored with spices or herbs and roots, and served in small shots not much larger than a double espresso. It's hot, sweet, milky, and strong, meant to give you a boost of energy in the middle of your workday. It's not shaken. It doesn't come out of a bottle or a pump. It's not meant to be sipped slowly out of a grande cup over several hours. Anything other than what I have described is chai-adjacent and has its place, but it is not chai.

Some of the most revered chai spots in the larger cities in India pride themselves on still using water buffalo milk, which is pretty much the only milk I grew up drinking. It took me a long time to get used to the taste of cow's milk as opposed to the fresher, tangier, more grassy buffalo milk. If you can find some, use it.

CHAI PANI CLASSIC CHAI

Makes about 3 cups

The foundation of chai is black tea leaves, milk, water, and sugar. The ratio of milk to water to tea and sugar changes, serving to differentiate among different communities, cultures, and seasons. This is the chai we make at Chai Pani, modeled after the version you'll find on the streets of Mumbai.

More than anything else, I like ingredients that match the season. In the cooler months, I want adrak chai, aka ginger chai, with spice and heat; in the summer I want chai with the floral flavors of cardamom, mint, and lemongrass. At Chai Pani we found a happy compromise with a hint of ginger and cardamom. We also cut the milk ratio to half of the water, to make it less milky and more appealing to the American palate. This is not to say that I'm trying to appease the American palate—this is to say that, after thirty years in America, I prefer it this way, too.

You can make this chai exclusively with ginger, or cardamom, or even exclusively with mint, depending on your taste and the time of year. Play around to find your favorite combination of flavors, and if you want to go crazy and mix all three, go forth and get your chai on.

2 cups water

1 (2-inch) knob fresh ginger, peeled and pounded in a mortar and pestle

4 green cardamom pods, pounded in a mortar and pestle

1 cup whole milk

4 teaspoons Indian CTC loose-leaf black tea (such a Wagh Bakri)

3 teaspoons sugar

In a small pot over medium-high heat, bring the water to a boil. Once boiling, add the ginger and cardamom and boil together for 2 to 3 minutes. It's important to boil the ginger well to neutralize its acidity, otherwise it will curdle the milk when you add it. (We've done this countless times at Chai Pani, and learned the hard way there's no such thing as boiling the ginger for too long.)

Add the milk and carefully bring to a boil—just until the milk starts to rise—stirring occasionally, so the milk doesn't scorch on the bottom of the pan. Lower the heat until the milk is simmering but not rising, then add the tea. Stir occasionally, keeping the milk at a low simmer and regulating the heat so it doesn't boil over. Once the milk has turned a walnut-brown color, after 3 to 5 minutes, turn the heat up to maximum to make the milk rise again, then take it off the heat before it spills over. My mom calls this the double boil method, aka the good luck second boil. Boiling the milk twice evaporates more water and concentrates the flavor of the chai. (Some Parsi aunties swear by the three-boil technique, but at this point we're splitting boils.)

I like stirring in the sugar during the last phase of the boiling, but if you prefer sweetening to taste, add the sugar after pouring out the chai. Strain the liquid into clean cups using a fine-mesh strainer and serve piping hot.

MASALA CHAI

Makes 4 cups

This is the flavor profile that I think most Americans associate with chai—cardamom, cinnamon, clove, black pepper, and so on. It's not my favorite variation—I prefer herbs and roots in my chai (see Irani Chai) to whole or powdered spices, but the people want what the people want. You'll find similar masala chais at upscale hotels in India, but not on the streets. In my recipe, I try to not overdo the spices so much that they give a potpourri effect.

- 2 cups water
- 4 green cardamom pods, pounded in a mortar and pestle
- 4 whole black peppercorns
- ¼ teaspoon fennel seed
- ½-inch piece cinnamon stick
- 1 clove, roughly broken in a mortar and pestle
- 2 cups whole milk
- 4 teaspoons Indian CTC loose-leaf black tea (such a Wagh Bakri)
- 3 teaspoons sugar

In a small pot over medium-high, bring 2 cups of water to a boil. Once boiling, add the cardamom pods, peppercorns, fennel seeds, cinnamon, and clove, and boil for about a minute. From this point, follow the directions for the Chai Pani Classic Chai (page 265).

IRANI CHAI

Makes about 3 cups

This is the chai I grew up drinking, and the technique is different from the other chais in this chapter. While in Hyderabad "Irani chai" denotes milky tea with lots of masala (cinnamon, cardamom, cloves, etc.), the true preferred chai for Parsis at home is brewed with the more floral, Brit-baiting flavors of lemongrass and/or mint. Have it with Britannia digestive biscuits or tea rusks for the full experience.

- 1½ cups water
- 2 tablespoons finely chopped fresh lemongrass (optional)
- 4 teaspoons Indian CTC loose-leaf black tea (such a Wagh Bakri)
- 1½ cups whole milk
- 1 tablespoon sugar
- 8 leaves fresh mint

In a small pot over medium-high heat, bring 1½ cups water and the lemongrass (if using) to a boil. Add the tea and reduce the heat to medium. Let the tea simmer for 30 to 45 seconds, then add the milk, sugar, and mint leaves. Bring back to a boil, then reduce the heat and simmer until the chai is nutmeg-brown in color, 3 to 5 minutes.

Strain the chai into clean cups using a tea or fine-mesh strainer and serve piping hot. If you prefer a stronger, darker chai, continue to simmer the tea for another 2 to 3 minutes. Having said that, Parsis prefer their chai more on the milky side.

Pantry

These are the little recipes that have a huge payoff in terms of adding flavor and texture to your Indian home cooking—including the sauces, the chutneys, the pastes, and the masalas that will help separate you from the rest. Most of these things are very easy to whip up and keep well, so I recommend keeping your refrigerator and pantry stocked at all times.

A few of these recipes are for ingredients that you might think of buying at the store (i.e., paneer or garam masala) and, truly, if that's what's going to make it easier for you to cook more Indian food at home, I'm all for it. But if you'd like to try your hand at creating some of the building blocks of the cuisine in your home kitchen, use these recipes as your guide.

RAITA

Makes about 2 cups

As I have pontificated extensively, yogurt plays a huge part in Indian cuisine, and one of our favorite ways to add yogurt to a meal is by making a raita. A raita is simply yogurt whisked with some salt and sugar to accentuate its natural sweetness and to balance the acidity, then flavored with seasonings based on region, style of cuisine, or ethnicity.

Raita adds a cooling factor to spicy dishes, so it's often served alongside curries, kebabs, sabjis, and the like. I like this version because it requires very few steps to make, but regional variations abound—feel free to stir in finely diced green apples, grated daikon radish, tomatoes, or cooked rice (the last of which is such a delicious concoction that you can and should eat it as its own dish).

- 2 cups plain full-fat yogurt
- ¼ cup water
- 1 tablespoon sugar, plus more to taste
- 1½ teaspoons kosher salt, plus more to taste
- ½ teaspoon roasted cumin powder (see page 32)
- ¼ teaspoon freshly ground black pepper
- ¼ cup finely chopped cilantro leaves
- ¼ cup finely diced red onion (about ½ small onion)
- 1 tablespoon finely chopped mint leaves

In a medium bowl, whisk the yogurt, water, sugar, salt, roasted cumin, and black pepper together until smooth. Taste for salt and sugar and adjust if necessary—it's easier to do it now than after the vegetables have been added.

Add the cilantro, onion, and mint and stir to combine. Serve cold or at room temperature; it will keep, tightly covered in the refrigerator, for up to a week.

EASY-PEASY PANEER

Makes about 3 cups

While Europeans mastered the art of cheesemaking, Indians were more focused on using dairy in sweet rather than savory applications—meaning we don't do aged cheeses at all. The two cheeses that were ubiquitous when I was growing up were paneer and Amul, the Indian Velveeta.

The popularity of paneer as the everyday cheese of a billion Indians is due to the fact that, much like yogurt, it can be made quickly and easily at home, with minimal time, equipment, or skill. The closest equivalent to this kind of cheesemaking in Europe is probably ricotta, in which milk is combined with some form of acid (for us, traditionally, the acid comes from yogurt) to cause it to curdle. The result is a fresh, light, creamy, crumbly cheese that's not meant to be eaten on its own but, much like tofu, used as a key ingredient in countless dishes, from saag paneer to pakoras.

Yes, you can buy paneer in many stores, but this recipe is ridiculously simple, involving stuff that I'm 99 percent sure you already have in the fridge. If you're really strapped for time and can't find paneer at the grocery, halloumi will do in a pinch (note that it is saltier and firmer than paneer). But I really do encourage you to try making your own at least once. It's so versatile and it keeps well for weeks—what do you have to lose?

- 1 gallon whole milk
- 2 cups heavy cream
- 1 teaspoon kosher salt
- ¼ cup distilled white vinegar, plus more as needed

In a large heavy-bottomed pot over medium-high heat, bring the milk and heavy cream to a boil, stirring frequently to prevent scorching and watching closely so the milk doesn't boil over. It can be useful to keep a digital thermometer nearby—212°F is boiling, so once you hit 200°F, start stirring constantly and, the moment it starts to shimmy on top, reduce the heat to low and let carryover cooking bring it to a boil. Regardless, watch carefully—the milk will go from simmering to boiling over in a second.

As soon as the milk comes to a boil, turn the heat down to low (if you haven't already), add the salt and the white vinegar, and stir gently until the curds start to separate, about 30 seconds. The curds will clump together and a greenish-clear liquid (the whey) will be left behind. If the curds don't separate, you can add more vinegar, a teaspoon or so at a time, and continue stirring gently until the separation starts.

Continued

CHAOKOH
COCONUT MILK
Maggi
TOMATO CHILI SAUCE
MDH
CHAT MASALA
Ghar se
KEWRA WATER
ASHOKA
Mango Pickle Hot
Net Wt. 500 g
Dabur
Keora Water
SPICEWALLA
CUMIN SEED
deep
CHUTNEY
DRY GARLIC
SPICEWALLA
MADRAS CURRY POWDER
SPICEWALLA
GARAM MASALA
SPICEWALLA
CLOVES

EASY-PEASY PANEER

Continued

Strain the curds through two layers of cheesecloth or a very fine-mesh strainer set over a bowl, until the liquid is just an occasional drip. Press or squeeze gently to remove most of the rest of the whey. Discard the whey, or keep it for another use (e.g., as a poultry brine, to soak dried beans or grains before cooking, to cook oatmeal in, to add to soups and stocks, to feed your dog, and so on).

Once strained, transfer the paneer into a shallow container, cover with a damp cloth, and let cool to room temperature. The paneer will take the shape of the container and will firm up as it cools, though it will still be softer and creamier than many store-bought versions, which are pressed of all liquid. Keep, covered in the refrigerator, for up to 2 weeks, slicing off pieces as necessary.

GINGER-GARLIC PASTE

Makes about ½ cup

If there is one recipe from this entire book that you seek to master, let it be this. GGP is the savior of flavor, the mortar between the bricks of Indian cuisine, the most cherished combination of ingredients in a country with one billion highly opinionated cooks.

This stuff is pureed gold, and you'll see it called for in dozens and dozens of recipes in this book, lending its flavor to various recipes in unexpected and delicious ways. Here is just a partial list of how we use GGP: to marinate; to tenderize; to sauté with; to fry into a delicious fond that you can scrape off the bottom of the pan and add to a sauce; to stir into curries and chutneys; to smear across toast; and so on. Good luck doing all that with sliced garlic.

Although store-bought versions are available at many South Asian grocers, GGP takes all of two minutes to make at home, lasts for weeks in the refrigerator, and is pretty much always worth having on hand. I'm giving amounts of each ingredient below because my co-author says I have to, but the real recipe is just this: Equal parts peeled garlic and peeled ginger, both preferably freshly peeled, blitzed together with a few tablespoons of oil until it forms a coarse paste.

A mini food processor or blender will make your life easier, but you can also hand-mince it in a pinch. Either way, store the finished product in a glass container, not plastic, otherwise you'll never get the smell out.

¼ cup peeled and coarsely chopped fresh ginger (a knob about 3 inches long)

¼ cup garlic cloves (about 1 head)

1 to 2 tablespoons neutral oil, such as grapeseed

Combine the ginger, garlic, and 1 tablespoon of oil in a blender or mini food processor and blend until smooth, scraping the sides of the bowl with a rubber spatula as needed. Add more oil if necessary to get an even paste.

Store GGP in a glass container in the refrigerator for up to 1 week. GGP will keep for longer, though after a week I recommend mixing in a teaspoon or so of distilled white vinegar to keep the flavor and color fresh.

PERFECT BASMATI RICE

Makes about 6 cups

My mother, Amrit, is from the town of Dehradun, in the foothills of the Himalayas, which is considered the basmati capital of India. She knows her rice so well that she makes it entirely by feel, though when she's forced to measure, she does so by checking the space between the top of the rice and the top of the water based on the knuckle lines in her index finger (the water line should be halfway between the first and second knuckles). I do not yet possess her level of skill, so I use this recipe instead.

Don't skimp on rice quality. Buy good long-grain basmati rice, such as India Gate or Nirav brands. Basmati is usually aged for at least a year before being sold, and aged rice will yield much longer grains. It should say on the bag how long your rice was aged; don't buy a brand that doesn't include this info. And though the addition of butter is optional, I highly recommend it—the fat coats each grain, making it fluffier and keeping the grains from sticking together. And also: It's butter. It's delicious.

2 cups long-grain basmati rice

3 cups water

1 teaspoon kosher salt

½ tablespoon salted or unsalted butter (optional)

Place the rice in a large heavy-bottomed pot. Wash with cold water to remove excess starch: stir the rice lightly with your hand while rinsing, then drain the water completely. Repeat two or three times; the water on the last rinse should be almost clear. Drain the water completely after washing.

Pour 3 cups of clean water over the rice in the pot, add the salt and butter (if using), and cover the pot. Bring to a boil over high heat and boil until about 80 percent of the water is absorbed—there should be no water on the top, and the surface layer of the rice will start to form small craters or holes.

Once you see the craters, very gently bring the rice from the bottom of the pot toward the top so that everything cooks evenly. To do so, slide a spatula between the side of the pot and the rice and gently fold the grains from the bottom up to the top. Do this 3 or 4 times—no more. Cover the pot again, turn the heat down to low, and let the rice cook for another 7 to 8 minutes.

Turn off the heat. Do not remove the lid—the rice needs to absorb the remaining steam in the pot. Wait 10 minutes, then remove the lid and fluff the rice with a fork. This ensures that no grains will break from excessive mixing. Serve hot.

Leftover rice keeps, tightly covered in the refrigerator, for 2 to 3 days, but nothing compares to freshly made.

AMRIT'S GARAM MASALA

Makes about ¼ cup

Ah, garam masala. The Indian spice most misunderstood by American cooks. Listen up: Garam masala is not—I repeat, NOT—the taste of Indian food. I can't tell you how many home cooks I've met who tell me they love cooking with garam masala. That's how I know they're full of it.

Garam masala, as you can tell from the following ingredient list, is a highly aromatic, non-spicy finishing spice blend, traditionally used to give certain North Indian dairy-based dishes a pop of aromatics at the end of cooking. This blend is rarely used in everyday home cooking (though savory variations used in other parts of India are also called garam masala, confusing the issue). Garam masala recipes vary widely by region—Parsi and Maharashtrian styles often include cumin and coriander seeds to make it earthier, while in South India, garam masalas might include more black peppercorns. Sometimes other aromatic spices like fennel and mace show up just to confuse matters further.

The garam masala recipe I'm including for this book's purposes is the North Indian aromatic version—the one that my mom scribbled down on a piece of paper when we were still learning how to cook before Chai Pani opened.

1 tablespoon green cardamom pods

4 black cardamom pods

2 tablespoons whole black peppercorns

6 star anise

4 cinnamon sticks

1 nutmeg pod, broken up with a mortar and pestle (or whacked with a flat pan)

1 tablespoon cloves

1 tablespoon dagad phool (optional; see Note)

Place a large dry skillet over low heat. Add the green and black cardamom, peppercorns, star anise, cinnamon, nutmeg, cloves, and dagad phool (if using) and toast, stirring often, until the spices are lightly toasted and aromatic, 2 to 3 minutes. The minute the spices are toasted, transfer them to a cool plate or bowl to keep them from scorching.

Once the spices are cooled to room temperature, grind in a spice grinder (or coffee grinder exclusively used for that purpose) and store in an airtight container for up to 4 months.

Note: ***Dagad phool, better known in the US as black stone flower, is a small lichen that grows wild on rocks and trees, both here in the Smoky Mountains and in Indian hill stations. It has an earthy, musky smell and a dry, light texture, and it may or may not have some medicinal value. It's used as an additive to spice blends in India, or, as an old geezer in the Appalachians once told me, as a thickener for soups and stews. I'm not entirely sure why my mom adds it to her garam masala, but my best guess is that it reflects her tendency to use traditional Maharashtrian ingredients while still satisfying her North Indian leanings toward more aromatic spices. It's totally optional, but if you can find it, give it a shot!***

ACKNOWLEDGMENTS

Writing this book was like setting off for a rumored land with only the vaguest idea of how to get there. And without the merry band of travelers that joined me on this journey, I'd probably still be going around in circles.

So here's heartfelt thanks to:

Jamie Feldmar, wielder of the Staff of Infinite Patience, and the best co-writer, co-pilot, co-navigator, and taskmaster that any wanderer and serial procrastinator could ever ask for.

Mikey Files, book designer, creative genius, art guru, and my brother in misadventures with street food.

David Black, the Jedi Master of book agents, who I'm convinced used the Force to get me to agree to write a cookbook.

Kelly Snowden, my book editor, whose trust in our vision for this book is a breathtaking gift for which I'm eternally grateful.

Matt Rodbard, who gave me the courage to believe the world needed a cookbook by me.

Poras Chaudhary for capturing Mumbai in all its tropical, mysterious, moody monsoon magic.

Tim Robison, whose photography turned the recipes into lush desire leaping off the pages.

Stacey Ballis, Erin Hawley, and James Grogan for making sure the recipes work as intended, look amazing, and taste the way they're supposed to.

Kelsey Burrow, media relations savant and best afternoon Lambrusco buddy. If you're reading this book, chances are Kelsey had a hand in making you aware of it.

Isaac Clay for being the first to believe and give his all to Chai Pani, and Daniel Peach, my culinary *bhai,* whose knowledge of and dedication to Indian cuisine is part of the DNA of these recipes.

To Allison, the person who keeps me pointed in the right direction at all times with grace and tenacity. Her ability to take care of the details, and insistence on me fulfilling my commitments, is a huge part of how this book ever got written.

Charlotte Stack, the restaurant group's leader extraordinaire, who manifests grace and wisdom every day and whose steady hand at the wheel allowed me to take the time to set off on this journey.

My mom, who is the greatest, most intuitive cook I've ever known. Her food and the way she cooks set the bar that I'll forever attempt to clear.

My dad, who is my number one champion and cheerleader. His unshakable belief in the power of faith sets my moral compass.

My mother-in-law, Roz Taubman, the first and only chef I ever worked for, who taught a fresh-off-the-boat me how to properly order a steak at a restaurant and along the way made me fall in love with éclairs, cookbooks, and the art of fine dining.

My brilliant daughter, Aria, for whom the sun and the moon rise and set for me. Wherever she finds a place to stand, she will move the world.

My wife, Molly, the love of my life, my partner, my heartbeat, the person whose force of magnetism always tugs on my mind and heart every time she comes into my field of vision. We hold hands tightly together every time we leap, and wherever we land is better because of her.

And, finally, to Meher Baba, and to love—the universal force that suffuses everything with the power to want us all to be our better selves.

INDEX

TEN SPEED PRESS
An imprint of the Crown Publishing Group
A division of Penguin Random House LLC
1745 Broadway
New York, NY 10019
tenspeed.com
penguinrandomhouse.com

Typefaces: Martype Company's Behover, Device's Hounslow, Vanarchiv's Lab Sans, TypeType's TT Rationalist, Hanoded's Silent Echo, Jonny Pinhorn's Shrikhand, and Bhel Puri Stand Narrow

Library of Congress Cataloging-in-Publication Data
Names: Irani, Meherwan author | Feldmar, Jamie author
Title: No. 1 best Indian cookbook in the world : at-home recipes from the streets, truck stops, villages, and palaces of India / by Meherwan Irani with Jamie Feldmar.
Other titles: Number one best Indian cookbook in the world
Identifiers: LCCN 2025031415 (print) | LCCN 2025031416 (ebook) | ISBN 9780593836132 hardcover | ISBN 9780593836149 ebook
Subjects: LCSH: Cooking, Indic | LCGFT: Cookbooks
Classification: LCC TX724.5.I4 I576 2026 (print) | LCC TX724.5.I4 (ebook) | DDC 641.5954—dc23/eng/20251118
LC record available at https://lccn.loc.gov/2025031415
LC ebook record available at https://lccn.loc.gov/2

Hardcover ISBN 978-0-593-83613-2
Ebook ISBN 978-0-593-83614-9

Editor: Kelly Snowden
Production editor: Terry Deal
Editorial assistant: Gabriela Ureña Matos
Designer: Emma Campion and Mikey Files
Production designers: Mari Gill, Faith Hague, and Claudia Sanchez
Production and prepress color manager: Jane Chinn
Food coordinator/chef on site: James Grogan
Stylists: Erin Hawley and Mikey Files
Stylist assistants: Ben Goodrum and Allison Dotson
Recipe tester: Stacy Ballis
Copy editor: Clancy Drake | Proofreaders: Rachel Markowitz, Rachel Holzman | Indexer: Elizabeth T. Parson
Publicist: Jana Branson | Marketer: Brianne Sperber
Cover design: Mikey Files

Manufactured in Malaysia

10 9 8 7 6 5 4 3 2 1

First Edition

"When Meherwan Irani takes on a project, you know a sensory feast awaits. In his first book, *No. 1 Best Indian Cookbook in the World*, he delivers exactly that. Meherwan has long championed Indian cuisine once dismissed as 'too ethnic,' bringing it into the mainstream through his amazing restaurants and addictive spices. This deeply personal book is filled with stunning photographs, heartfelt stories, Meherwan's signature wit, and unforgettable recipes. Once you pick it up, it's nearly impossible to put down."

—**Maneet Chauhan,** chef and television personality

"At last! Meherwan Irani brings the incandescent magic of his restaurants Chai Pani and Botiwalla into our home kitchens. Irani's voice is warm, generous, and encouraging, divulging all the 'auntie holdbacks'—those critical steps that family cooks rarely share—and his shopping notes and spice guide alone are well worth the cover price! *No. 1 Best Indian Cookbook in the World* is a bold claim for sure, but we're 1,000% certain this volume is the best guide we've found yet to bringing the joy of Indian food into your home!"

—**Matt Lee and Ted Lee,** authors of *The Lee Bros. Charleston Kitchen*

"The only thing more exuberant and outrageous than the flavors in this book is the writing itself. Not only was *No. 1 Best Indian Cookbook in the World* an adventure for my kitchen, but I can't say that I've ever learned more from a cookbook. It's not just recipes—it's a window into the history and culture of one of the world's oldest and most fascinating places and the food of its everyday life."

—**Andy Pforzheimer,** chef and founder of Barcelona Wine Bar and Bartaco